A hierarchy of streets with jacaranda groves in the center and major buildings on the periphery.

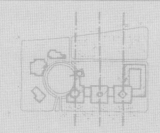

The new Civic Center fronts on Perris Boulevard, a major connector road in the area.

Along D Street future buildings must leave view corridors to the Civic Center roof element with the most important cultural building placed close to the circle.

Parking is concentrated under the shade of the jacarandas. Visitors park around the circle and along Perris Boulevard for convenient access to the complex.

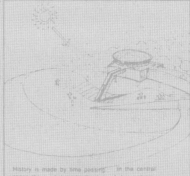

"History is made by time passing" in the central space the sundial marks the time of day and time of year. The gnomon of the sundial is the stairs to the roof.

The circle responds to the geometry of existing structures. The center of the new civic center influences the pattern of the surrounding landscape.

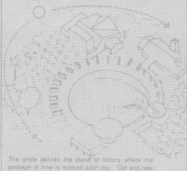

The circle defines the place of history where the passage of time is marked each day. Old and new landscapes merge, and new buildings are linked to the old.

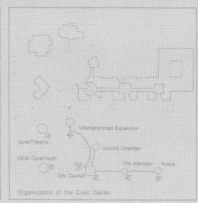

Organization of the Civic Center.

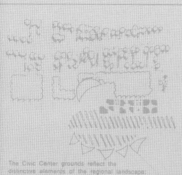

The Civic Center grounds reflect the distinctive elements of the regional landscape: the city garden grove; the orchard; the crop-fields; and the mountains.

The Garden Grove is divided into plots by stone walls and defines the passive recreation domain of the Civic Center. A sweeping, curved wall announces the complex from D Street.

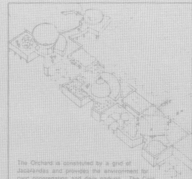

The Orchard is constituted by a grid of jacarandas and provides the environment for civic congregation and daily parking. The Civic Center roof is a learning arboretum.

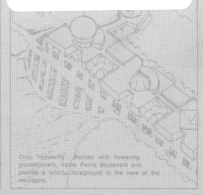

Crop frequency planted with flowering groundcovers, frame Perris Boulevard and provide a colorful foreground to the view of the mountains.

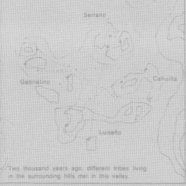

Two thousand years ago, different tribes living in the surrounding hills met in this valley.

This process continues on a far larger scale as various modern cultural and economic influences come together.

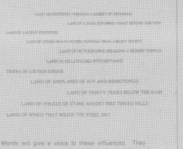

Words will give a voice to these influences. They will form a pattern that connects the activities of the present with the past, the future, the environment.

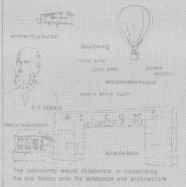

The community would collaborate in transcribing the oral history onto the landscape and architecture.

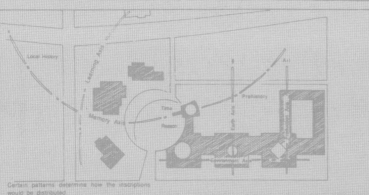

Certain patterns determine how the inscriptions would be distributed.

A series of blocks and inlays cut from the local granite are arranged in arcs radiating from the circle.

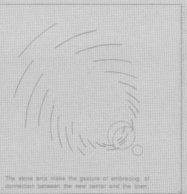

The stone arcs make the gesture of embracing, of connection between the new center and the town.

Adèle Naudé
A Form of Practice

Adèle Naudé
A Form of Practice

ORO Editions
Publishers of Architecture, Art, and Design
Gordon Goff: Publisher

www.oroeditions.com
info@oroeditions.com

Published by ORO Editions

Editor: Julia van den Hout, Original Copy
Author: Adèle Naudé
Book Design: Chris Grimley, Signals.
Project Manager: Jake Anderson

10 9 8 7 6 5 4 3 2 1 First Edition

ISBN: 978-1-957183-43-5

Color Separations and Printing: ORO Group Inc.
Printed in China

ORO Editions makes a continuous effort to minimize the overall carbon footprint of its publications. As part of this goal, ORO, in association with Global ReLeaf, arranges to plant trees to replace those used in the manufacturing of the paper produced for its books. Global ReLeaf is an international campaign run by American Forests, one of the world's oldest nonprofit conservation organizations. Global ReLeaf is American Forests' education and action program that helps individuals, organizations, agencies, and corporations improve the local and global environment by planting and caring for trees.

Introduction

This monograph covers approximately forty years of practice and teaching across many locations globally. Early in my career I made a personal commitment to combining teaching, practice, and research where possible. I saw these activities as synergetic. Teaching could engage different forms of research, and practice could teach students in pragmatic ways. Teaching became a research project, a questioning process, translating word ideas into conceptual diagrams that could evolve into architectural thinking. The selected research projects to study always contained more agendas than simply finding design solutions. I developed a teaching concept which I named a "workshop," namely an unsolved problem which included a sociopolitical issue in a real context, needing solutions at multiple scales. From local projects in Cape Town these workshops evolved to visiting global contexts by invitation, working with local communities to solutions of importance. These workshops mostly focused on concepts for better housing provision, socially and economically.

In my first practice in Cape Town in 1968, I worked with my husband and partner Antonio de Souza Santos on housing projects, both affordable and luxury. This was an intense and creative collaboration over three and a half years where our roles were so entwined that we had difficulty differentiating them. I had intense interest in building landscape dialogues and he was more involved in the tectonics of building, but these areas overlapped. Housing was becoming an area of specialization for both of us. At this time I was awarded the Wheelwright Traveling Fellowship from Harvard University to study mass housing in Latin America, India, and Hong Kong. We traveled to these locations together. Tony was the photographer. In our professional office the team was kept small, mostly employing student assistants. We never chose to publicize the work as was the norm. I was particularly interested in doing competitions that kept my urban design training in focus, such as the successful entry to the Santiago Redevelopment Competition in Chile. For the planning and urban design of Ormonde, a new 1,600-acre town in Johannesburg for 42,000 people, we participated individually as members of a three-firm consortium, Urban Design Consultants. We were responsible for the design and development of the first residential sector—a good use of our planning and urban design backgrounds.

Although I enjoyed a part-time commitment to academia I had not deliberately sought out the positions of leadership that I later assumed. I felt strongly that architectural education had not evolved much since my early education, and it was methodologically wasteful of time for both faculty and students. However, my early education and teaching career at important institutions led to offers for increasingly important leadership positions including Architecture Chair at the University of Pennsylvania and the deanships at the University of California San Diego (UCSD) and later at MIT. My practice followed these academic positions to new locations around the world. Although this might have been a risky proposition, it came with new opportunities for practice, new collaborations, and different networks of contacts to develop internationally, including Swaziland, India, Japan, Colombia, Brazil, Guatemala, Taiwan, and China.

The presentation of my career in this joint form of practice and teaching follows time and place for clarity in the following four chapters.

Personal Background

I grew up in Cape Town, South Africa, one of the most beautiful natural settings in the world. Framed by the Table Mountain range with the rock face bathed in rosy light each morning, with spectacular indigenous flowers and extensive botanical gardens on the mountain slopes, its nature left most of us in awe. The careful consideration of building in this exceptional landscape, as I was to do, was an important entry point to architecture. The interaction between building and nature was to become one of the most passionate themes throughout my career.

My father was an architect; my mother a poet and writer. My uncle ran an organization called The Cape Flats Distress Association. This was located in the flatlands, which were prone to flooding and were a common site for squatters living in marginal conditions, often needing temporary shelter and food. My uncle's organization included a kitchen that supplied them soup year-round and second-hand clothing. My father contributed pro bono work, designing low cost housing to be built as a village.

The house I grew up in, designed by my talented father, was elegant and modern. My mother had a passion for gardening and the property was a showcase of lush flowering plants. This background was an incentive to a career in architecture. I had every intention to go to architecture school, but I was surprised that my parents showed some hesitancy. Architecture was still considered a male profession in South Africa with very few exceptions. At seventeen, I was fearless and, as my parents predicted, I enrolled. When I entered the third year, I was the only woman among fifty students. I graduated top of the class. My father wisely suggested moving to the Architectural Association (AA) in London, which was a superior institution and could give me the best contemporary education. The entry exam was known to be brutal, but if I could pass the exam he would support me, he said.

The AA was a perfect setting for me and very challenging. In contrast to my former academic context where students and faculty were hesitant to debate any issues of substance, members of the AA were in continual debate mode. The students were international and multiracial, and there were more women than men. Team 10, a group of international architects and urbanists, was frequently visiting and several members were a part of the AA's faculty, like Peter Smithson. I was invited to several Team 10 events and found their work and thinking to be very compelling.

At the AA, I was introduced to complex issues in urbanism, namely social change and ramifications for living at higher densities. The issues raised by Team 10 members and published later in the Team 10 Primer were central to my education. I was invited to attend their annual meeting in Royaumont, France, in 1962. Importantly, at the AA I was taught how to create meaningful diagrams that could express design concepts. This was to evolve into a working process that continues today.

Shadrach Woods, member of Team 10 and principal of the firm Candilis-Josic-Woods, invited me to join his team in Paris where they were about to do a big housing competition for Caen in Normandy. There were no official office hours, which was refreshing. Each lunchtime I explored

Paris to understand the unique form of the city, and we worked late at night. This alone was a perfect educational experience; being part of a collaboration that included all of us. We were shortlisted but did not win this new housing concept which integrated Woods's concept of "activity spines" of nonresidential uses to form housing clusters.

After the AA, the next obvious step, advised by my academic faculty, was to broaden my education further with a recently established Urban Design degree at the Graduate School of Design (GSD) at Harvard. My employers and supporters wrote strong letters of recommendation, and I was accepted into the graduate program in 1963.

One year at the GSD was intense, exciting, and productive. The students were international and from diverse backgrounds. Shadrach Woods taught in the architecture program and other Team 10 members, including Aldo Van Eyck, participated in studio reviews. Fumihiko Maki taught a housing workshop which I attended. This work, including my designs, were published later in *Kenchiku Bunka*. Maki's creative thoughts, published in 1964 as *Investigations in Collective Form*, were very influential in our studio discussions. The studio critiques were very much like the lively debates that I observed at Team 10 meetings.

The GSD was a crossroad in the world of architecture and urban design in 1963. Annual conferences with international speakers—a regular participant was Serge Chermayeff—occurred each year with different themes. For us fortunate students, there were also regular lectures to attend. This amounted

to an intellectual overload! After graduation most of my class attempted to return annually to these seminal urban design conferences.

After graduating from Harvard, Jerry Miller from Montreal and I got job offers from Daniel van Ginkel, the planner working with the Exhibition Corporation for the Canadian World Exhibition in Montreal. We were invited to join the team being formed to plan and design the concept for the 1967 World's Fair. The challenges were great, the schedule was rapid, and the politics were intense. I was to be one of the design architects. For a young graduate this was an exceptional opportunity and I was intensely committed to the fast track, political process we went through. Many of our early design ideas were considered too radical but were sufficiently interesting to be kept in the archives of the World's Fair '67 in Montreal. After two years the design work and my role in this process was completed.

I departed Montreal to return to my family in Cape Town on what I thought was a temporary visit. I intended to repay my father for his financial support and to help the family plan for their next house. This was to be my first personal commission, which I looked forward to. I had spent many years of intense work as an urban designer, which was a diversion from architecture, and I realized that I wished to return to designing again as an architect.

Shadrach Woods and Alison Smithson attend a Team 10 meeting. That's me in the background.

Article in the Montreal *Gazette*, July 13, 1964.

1

The Cape Town Years

1965-67 House Naudé with Hugo Naudé and Adèle Marie Naudé
1969-72 A P de Sousa Santos and Adèle Naudé Santos

All of the work in this period was framed by the design of housing—luxury and low-cost—from the smallest scale to the role of housing in creating urban form. I was attracted to the subject as an architect because I knew that access to decent housing was an essential component for a productive life. As an urban designer housing was the largest land use and a key to community building and, ultimately, city form. Almost every spatial construct in the urban environment is composed of spaces that are aligned along a relative axis of public to private space. The house is a sanctuary, a place of retreat from the public domain. Most of the houses shown here are relatively closed with strategically placed windows and a layered processional entry sequence. The houses open to gardens and interact spatially with landscapes and views. The household, whatever its size, is a small building block in a complex social network that coalesces into communities.

House Naudé
Cape Town, South Africa
1965

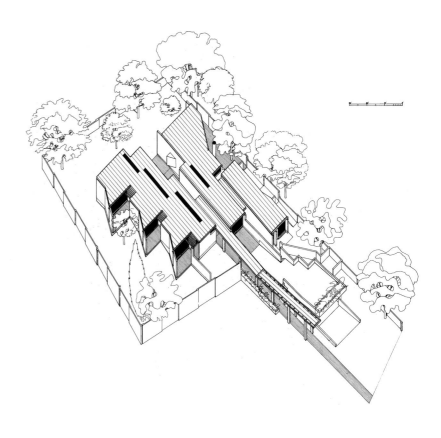

My professional experiences until this moment had been large-scale urban design challenges such as the work for Expo '67 in Montreal. The commision to design House Naudé initially brought with it the conceptual challenge of meeting the scale of thinking required for a single residence. It was the first moment that I had to consider material selection, detailing, construction documentation, and site supervision. I also wanted to place the design process in the context of my larger spatial concerns. Not surprisingly, I turned to issues of creating hierarchies of public and private spaces in the city, of which the single family house as a private retreat is a significant typology.

The site in Newlands Cape Town was a pan-handled property with a narrow space from the street to an interior square plot. It was a very private place visually and aurally. There was little vegetation, it had no special views, and compared to my parents' previous land this site felt cramped. The land rose slowly to the southeast giving the possibility for good solar access. Neighbors had built landscaped

private boundaries. The first request from my parents—the clients—was that I find strategies to expand the sense of space. The other was that the bedrooms feel very private and isolated from the rest of the house. The program was basic, with four bedroom suites, including one for service. There should be a generous living room space with a separate but connected dining area with garden access to both. The path to the front door should be generous and separated from that of the back door. In this era, it was common in Cape Town for service persons to live in the houses. The clients needed two covered parking spaces with covered access to the house. In the garage, there would be storage space and work space for landscape projects.

My agenda for the house was more ambitious. Having recently graduated in urban design and participated in discussions on city form, I was interested in concepts that saw the house as part of a continuum of public to private places in the city. One of my critics from Harvard, Aldo van Eyck, made an explicit diagram comparing the structure

of the leaf to that of the tree as reflective of the relationship of the house to the city. He stated in an article "Is Architecture Going to Reconcile Basic Values," for CIAM '59, "A house must be like a small city if it's to be a real house; a city like a large house if it's to be a real city." In São Paulo at much the same period, the famous architect and teacher João Batista Vilanova Artigas introduced a similar concept, saying that characteristics of a house were similar to that of the structure of a city where each household was part of a complex social network that coalesced into a community or a neighborhood. The idea that the house could represent a microcosm of the city seemed very potent and correct to me!

Reflecting on this idea for House Naudé seemed straightforward. The bedrooms could easily be read as "houses" within the house as a "city." I had started to think of circulation as street-like, paved in blue brick and ramped. These "streets" could join paved paths in the garden. The slope of the site was similar to a good pitch for the roof, which would allow the bedrooms to be more

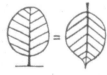

The House is a microcosm of the city, Aldo van Eyck.

House Naudé

autonomous, separated by level. The roof pitch allowed the use of corrugated metal sheets. A split in level between dining and living was a good idea as well. The most important concept was to partially sink the garage near the street. Building an artificial hill above this would remove the street from public view. I was familiar with the concept of "borrowed landscapes" from Japanese landscape designs. We could borrow the view of the neighbors' trees, which would vastly increase the apparent size of the property.

The bedrooms are offset in plan and in level. Served by ramps with landings rising every thirty inches, the bedrooms have a focus on full-height windows with garden views. From here, recessed doors open to skylit dressing areas and bathrooms. Beds are placed to face the window and covered porches. The splayed walls enhance the width of the unique views. Along the ramp, sky lit alcoves are designed as a display gallery for artworks. Detailing the house became obsessive. I counted all the brick courses since these were expressed on the exterior. White bagged brick was typical in the neighborhood. Where walls join brick floors the blue brick skirting is recessed. The juncture of ceilings to walls also received a recess. Overall, I wanted to create simple, clean finishes.

The house was awarded a bronze medal from the local Institute of Architects. My father, Hugo Naudé, was recorded as the architect of record and I, Adèle Marie Naudé, as the designer. Sadly, after this award, which we were both proud of, my father became ill. Fortunately, he was able to move around the whole house using the ramps in his wheelchair and enjoyed the house we had created together.

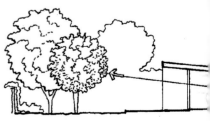

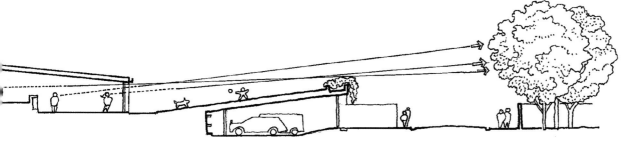

Left The dimensions of the site are enlarged by adopting views of the neighbors' trees. Sinking the garage to form a landscaped hill above dissolves the view of the entry road.

House Naudé

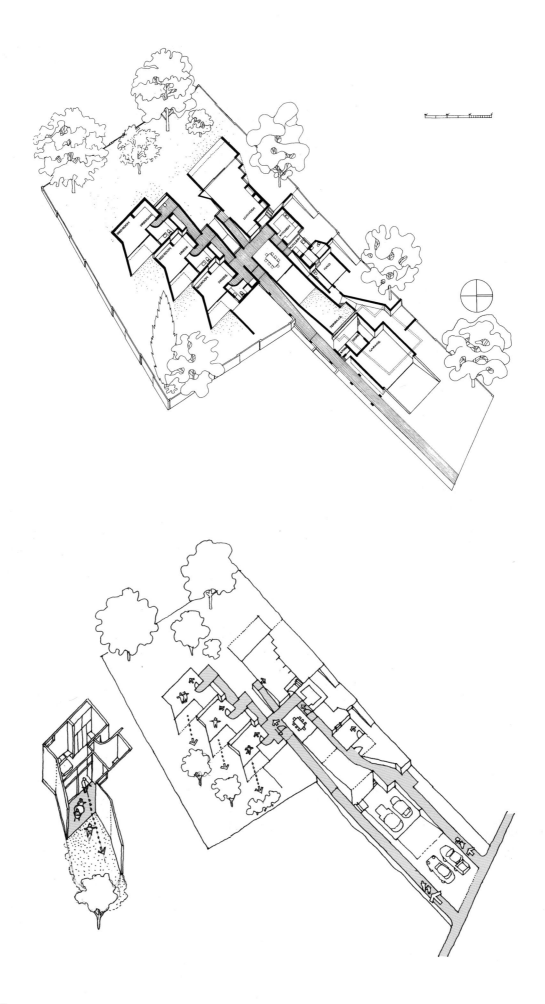

Opposite The bedrooms are designed as autonomous "houses within the house," and circulation is designed as brick paved ramped streets. A long ramp from the street makes a transition from public to private space.

Cape Town practice
with A P de Souza Santos
1968-72

During the design and construction of House Naudé, I gave lectures at the Architecture Department at the University of Cape Town. On one occasion I was asked a stimulating question by a senior student and followed up afterwards with a long conversation. This was Antonio (Tony) de Souza Santos, and we became serious friends.

After one and a half years I returned to the United States to teach for a year at Columbia University. I felt that my education was not yet complete despite moving from architecture to urban design. I wished to understand more fully the design complexity and planning principles for urban development. I decided to get a master of city planning at the University of Pennsylvania, under the well-known urban designer David Crane. I also worked in his office part-time. Meanwhile, I had married Tony, who was also studying urban design there. In 1968, after graduating with masters degrees in city planning and architecture, Tony and I were ready to start a practice together. Where this would take place was the dilemma. We had no intention of returning to South Africa where the apartheid era was still flourishing. My desire to develop a practice with teaching and research was important.

In 1968, Tony and I were approached by two firms in South Africa to join in a competition to design a "Town in Town" for 40,000 people in Johannesburg. This came as an enormous surprise. Luckily, both of these firms became finalists. By this time both my family and Tony's needed emotional support, so we knew that a return to South Africa was inevitable. The Cape Town team fortunately won the contract with Roelof Uytenbogaardt, a friend, leading the team. We formed a three-firm consortium named Urban Design Consultants. This two-year contract was an important financial asset to all of us and a boost to a viable practice.

We quickly set up office space that the consortium could share in the center of Cape Town. We all had other smaller scale commissions pending as architects and planners. The University of Cape Town also wanted us to teach. We were incredibly fortunate to have this unusual opportunity to start a practice. The earlier commissions were needing attention as we set up the structure for the team to study the new town.

University of Cape Town School of Architecture Studio Master/Critic 1968-72

Tony and I were both hired for part-time positions in the Department of Architecture at the University of Cape Town. Tony had graduated from the school with a Bachelor in Architecture in 1966, and I spent my first three years of study there. The undergraduate students were very well-read in the housing literature of the time. The squatter settlements surrounding parts of the city became the focus of most of my upper-level studios. This inevitably engaged the staff in the Divisional Council of the Cape, a low-cost housing agency, with whom we also advised. We jointly studied an area called Elsies River, which had a large squatter settlement that was due for clearance. We demonstrated that it was possible to upgrade this area through the construction of adequate infrastructure and by inserting new housing typologies to increase the density.

We conceived of several pro-bono, modest affordable housing projects during this period. Some of this continued later working with Ze Forjaz, an architect in Swaziland. Two villages are worth noting. For the first, Workers Housing in Kromvlei (1974), built by the apple farm workers, we had a $5,000 budget for a free-standing three-bedroom unit. The second was Matsapa Housing (1975) for staff and teachers of the National High School Swaziland, built with an $8,000–$10,000 budget for an attached three-bedroom unit.

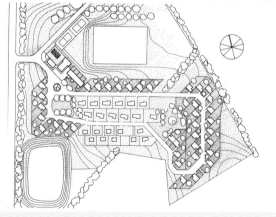

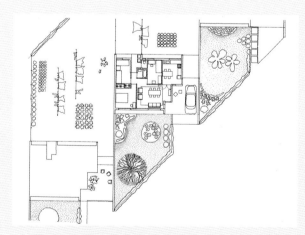

Left Plots are placed diagonal to the street, forming a street edge but allowing a gap in the demising wall between houses. This creates an urban feeling but still makes single-family houses.

Right Closest to the street are porches with front doors and entry into the kitchen. The living room features a picture window display. The bedrooms are located farther from the street to allow more privacy.

Rowan Lane Houses
Cape Town, South Africa
1967

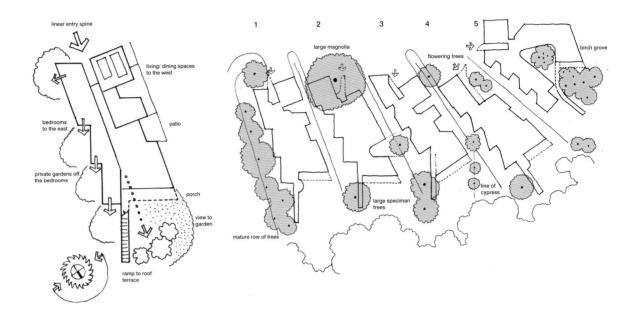

The client for Rowan Lane Houses lived close to House Naudé and appreciated its concept. The same conceptual approach was continued in this new project, with view-oriented bedrooms, generous living spaces, and a strong dialogue between the building and the mature existing landscape.

The site was located in an exclusive residential area, part of a large estate with a well-developed garden with specimen trees. These were all to be preserved. The land sloped gently to the north with views of the mountains from the north and west. The owner lived up-slope on an adjacent property that overlooked this land. Mature oak trees lined the southern boundary which logically was the best place for access. We were to give her entry from this new lane and build five new houses, one for each of her children.

The overall concept was to create a small community where neighbors could interact. To establish aesthetic uniformity, similar design principles were used to interrelate the houses. Climatic response to light zoned the bedrooms to receive early morning sun while living rooms enjoyed mid-day to late after-noon light. Saving the existing trees modified the basic plan typology making each house site specific. Further thematic variations were created to differentiate house entries. Living rooms and dining spaces were planned to be unique, either separated, off-set, or spatially continuous. Each house has outdoor dining space and was configured to respond to specific landscapes and views.

The most important concept was to consider the buildings and landscapes as one inter-related spatial construct. The client could view the planted roof of the buildings as a landscape. The gardens are continuous and multi-leveled. Inhabitants can enjoy gardens at grade, while stepped ramps lead to the

Opposite Typical house plan concept with a circulation spine from the front door to the garden.

Right The splayed lots widen to the north. Each property is unique, varying in proportion by saving existing trees. The common access road is flanked by mature trees. Houses have very private entries opening to the gardens downslope. Each house has a ramped stair leading to gardens on the roof.

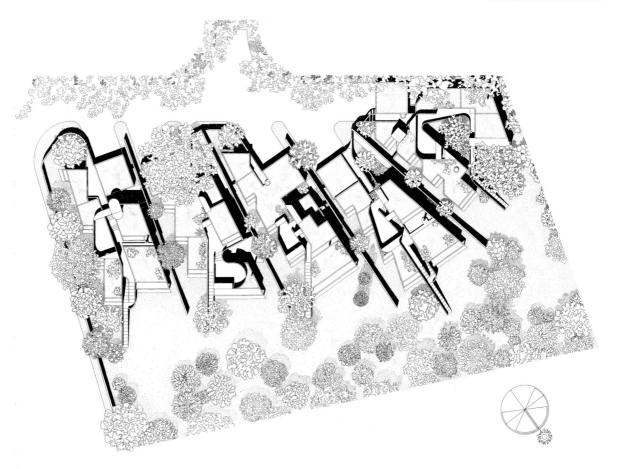

Rowan Lane Houses

upper terraces and solaria, with exceptional mountain views. Some of the houses physically incorporate trees or the geometry of the trees influenced the shape of interior walls.

Given the landscape theme and anticipating serious planting on the roofs, we decided to use concrete-framed construction. This also allowed us to develop a more fluid geometry, expressive curves, and display a different aesthetic to House Naudé.

The five properties are narrower at the street and widen in depth. From the street, the houses were designed to be private. Paired garages with white -washed brick garden walls are joined to solid gates to service areas. House entries all feature naturally lit front doors. Circulation is a central spine that steps down gradually from entry towards the north. Bedrooms have access from small lobbies that run parallel to this. Like House Naudé, these rooms have individual porches and gardens with long views. Except for House 5, the primary bedroom suite is on the second level with spacious terraces adjacent to a solarium completely private from neighbors. The circulation spine culminates in the large living room facing the main garden with generous full height windows shaded by porch roofs.

22

Rowan Lane Houses

24

Rowan Lane Houses

Rowan Lane Houses

Rowan Lane Houses

House Stekhoven
Cape Town, South Africa
1972

The Newlands site for House Stekhoven was another panhandled property in a neighborhood characterized by small lots with big houses. The entry is from a small lane. To the rear the property has an unobstructed view of the Table Mountain range. A small stream defines one property edge with mature oak trees set in an undulating topography.

Conceptually the design presents blank and anonymous facades to the street and adjacent houses. This secures the privacy of both the client and their neighbors. A ramp leads up to the front door and down to parking. On the garden side the building opens to the mountain view framed by mature trees. Large glass walls enable expansive views and are protected by a continuous loggia providing shelter and

verandah space. At the stream edge the living room floor steps down to a large shaded terrace with river views. From here a spiral stair connects to the second floor terraces. The dining room at entry level has a protected patio over the garage and forms part of the service zone.

On the second floor children's rooms are accessed by a corridor with a window and a seat over the fireplace for a warm place in winter. The bedrooms are repetitive cells with built in desks and glass corner windows facing the view. An outside door to the loggia gives the children independent access to the garden via the spiral stair. A communal space shared with the parents separates the sleeping zones. The curvature of the loggia provides the parents with a private terrace. Their suite

includes a compartmented bathroom with a top-lit shower and a spacious bedroom.

The loggia is the defining element of the house and critical to its reading. Raised above the roof to let the breezes through, this shade element protects the house on the upper and lower levels. The undulating free form responds to landscape and interacts visibly with the profile of the mountain. Importantly, the width of this shade element is larger than the space below allowing for a tea terrace to be created near the kitchen.

The owner of this house was also the contractor that built this with enormous care on every detail. Over time he also bought land to extend the garden towards the mountain.

Opposite Houses in the neighborhood are typically placed close together. For privacy, this house has two faces—blank walls toward the neighbors, and open on the garden side. Views to the garden focus on the mountains beyond.

Right A shade canopy, lifted off the roof, allows air flow. Each bedroom has a skylight.

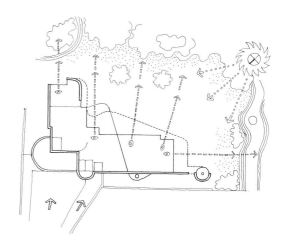

House Stekhoven

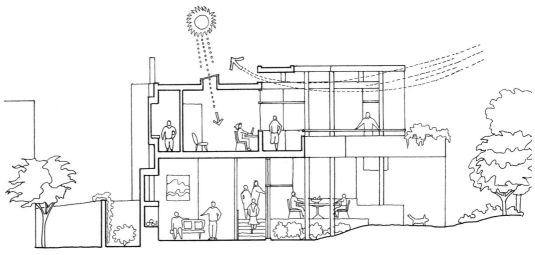

House Stekhoven

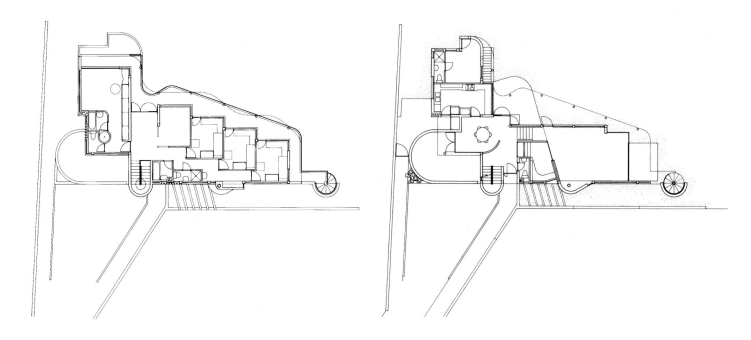

Above The children's rooms have doors to the terrace allowing them access to the garden below via a spiral stair.

The Cape Town Years

House Stekhoven

36

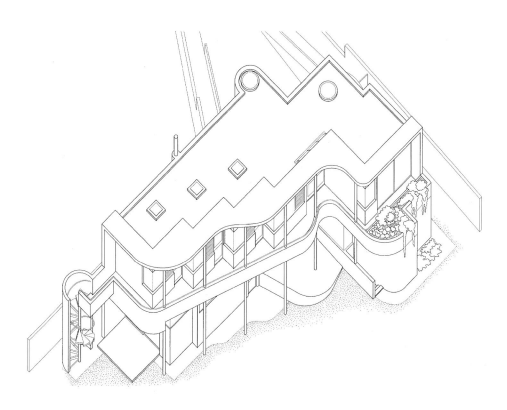

Left The profile of the shade canopy is in dialogue with the mountain and landscape.

House Stekhoven

House Stekhoven

House Shear
Cape Town, South Africa
1972

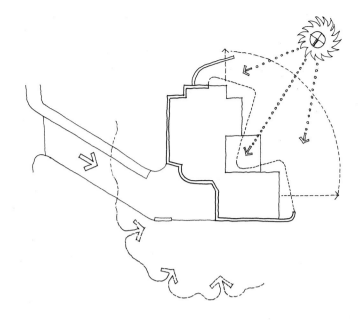

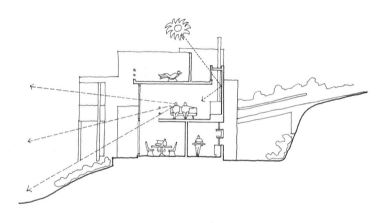

House Shear was built for a family living in another city, who used this home in Simonstown as a holiday retreat a few times in the year. The property was small and was located below the access street by one and a half levels. A bridge, sloping down to the house, was made for pedestrians and to park a car. The house was very private from the street. Entry on the second level with sheltered parking left only enough space for the living room, a large view terrace, and the primary suite. The focus was on the spectacular ocean views.

We created a double-height corner void vertically linking the living and dining spaces, facing the most spectacular view. A butt-jointed glass corner improved this view dramatically. On the ground level the dining space with the void above occupied the best land and opened to a patio shielded from the neighbors by a freestanding curved wall. Two children's bedrooms and bathroom were located on this level each open to small patios. The kitchen occupied the back wall of the house with high windows. A service suite, located adjacent to the kitchen, completed the program.

A spiral staircase linked the levels together and continued to the roof where the solarium was protected from the winds by curved walls. From this space the remarkable panorama of the bay could be enjoyed.

The owners retired and moved permanently to Cape Town. They built another house adjacent to this one and joined these together. The freestanding building, which could be viewed from all sides, was considered to have a very sculptural character, but this was lost in the process.

Opposite The house is shaped to be protected from the mountain winds, open to the sun and with views to the ocean.

Opposite Below The site sits one floor below the road, requiring a ramped bridge for pedestrian and car access.

House Shear

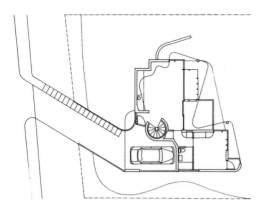
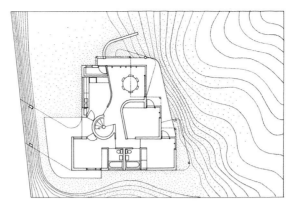

Above The entry level houses the primary suite, a large terrace, a living room, and parking for one car. The ground level includes a double-height dining room in a glazed corner with the best views. The solarium on the roof is protected from the winds.

42

The Cape Town Years

House Shear

44

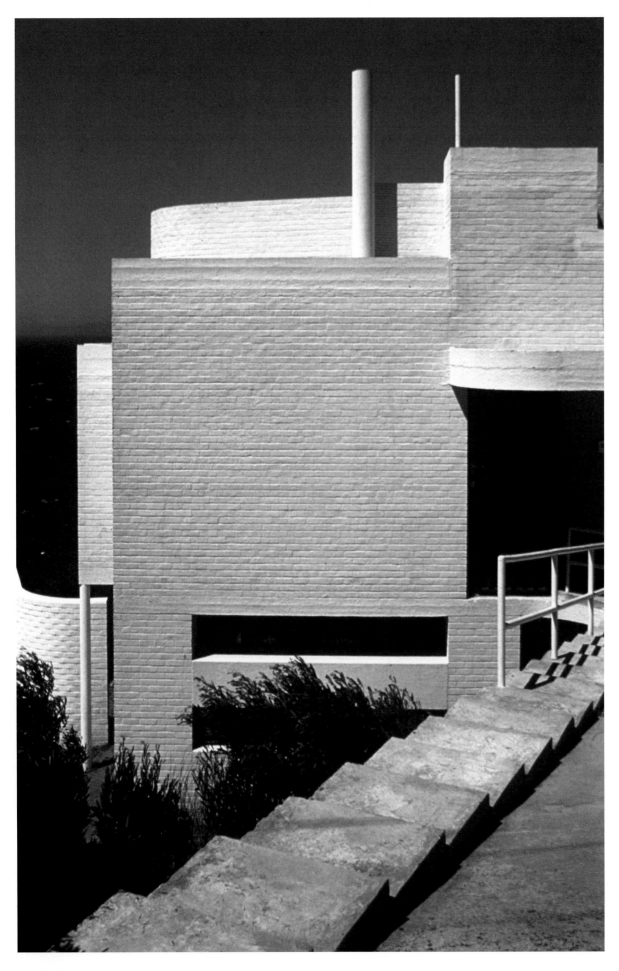

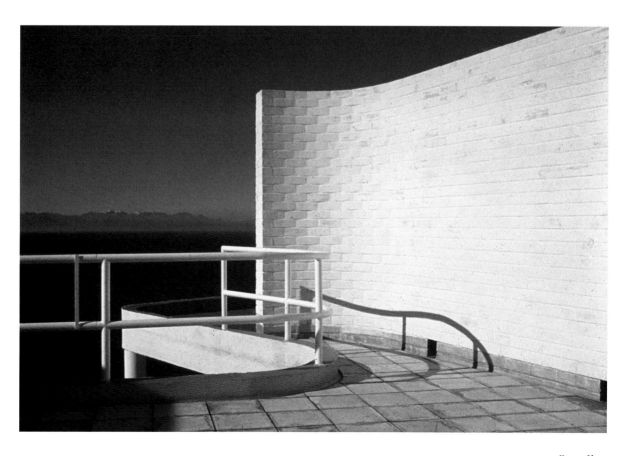

House Shear

The Cape Town Years

House Shear

Landscape Building Dialogue

Sites with strong natural features can be a source of inspiration by providing a set of conditions and opportunities. Where the natural character can remain we always attempt to create a dialogue between building and landscape. Typically we try to save mature trees, retain and use the topography, and exploit vistas and unique site features. Response to the micro-climate is part of this ethos. Many of the Cape Town houses had to be protected environmentally. House Shear, for example, needed protection from strong mountain winds, and House Stekhoven needed protection from the western sun. This was the origin of the loggia, which is high enough to allow breezes to pass through. Spatial strategies that wove indoor and outdoor spaces together required careful micro-climatic study to be effective.

Landscapes are potential sources of pleasure, adding beauty and vitality to most settings. The whimsical aspects inherent in nature provide contrast to the predictable permanence of buildings. Framed by windows or sculpted interiors, landscape spaces are often the antidote to structures. Outdoor space is a desirable component of habitation used to extend the dwelling. In designing these homes, we attempted to find the balance between built solids and framed voids, between gardens or courtyards and views, between a spatial matrix that saw the interior and exterior as a continuum. The buildings were not seen as isolated objects but compositionally and systematically part of the land.

Intentionally blurring the boundaries between buildings and landscapes started as a recurring theme in Cape Town, where exceptional landscapes were the norm. We used earth and plant material to cover structures, thereby creating artificial topographies. Buildings were sculpted and planted to become landscapes. At grade party lines were left ambiguous, increasing the dimensional experience of space. Capturing special vistas, orchestrating journeys through space was focused on unexpected views to enhance visual enjoyment.

Continuity between indoors and outdoors is a useful approach to increase the sense of spaciousness. Full-height windows, glass corner windows, pocket doors that vanish, and extending exterior paving indoors all help spatial merging. Ultimately, we attempted to see indoor and outdoor space compositionally as two sets of rooms. Planted roofs literally merge building and landscape as demonstrated in the Rowan Lane Houses. Double readings are possible depending on the eye levels of viewers.

Using light as a design tool is a well-established facet of architectural language to enhance space and illuminate formal qualities. Light and the time of day play a big role in these houses. Waking to the warmth of early morning light is valued as is returning in the late afternoon to the fading light. The houses are zoned for these experiences, and value is given to sunlight in living rooms most of the day. In the Rowan Lane Houses, the cross section through the stepped ramps brings surprising eastern light into living rooms with northern orientation. We also used natural light to enhance entrances giving front doors natural light through skylights or courtyards. Placing windows to frame special views or to wash walls with light occurs frequently in House Naudé. Garden views frame ramp landings and wash light on long walls. An "ear" window cants out to allow a long vista from my father's chair to a specimen tree in the garden.

Another aspect of building landscape dialogue I describe as "inflecting towards nature." This is graphic rather than spatial and is evident in House Stekhoven where the roof of the loggia curves and frames the profile of the mountain, and flirts with the form of the trees. The reflection of the trees on the butt-jointed glass of the children's rooms can be quite mesmerizing at times of the day. In House Shear, the roof curves to create a V shape, which gives focus to the best view of the ocean. The built-in bench in the living room reflects and joins the graphic lines of the canopy. In Rowan Lane, a line of birch trees is echoed by the geometry of interior walls.

Scott Road
Claremont Cape, South Africa
1969

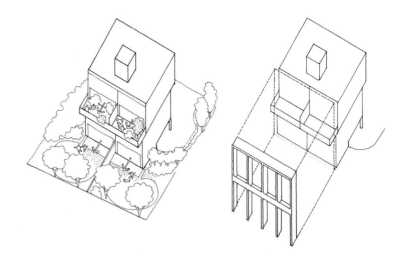

The property for this project is centrally located with one side on a busy road requiring a planted buffer. There is site access from a small road a half level above the property. It has a north view of Table Mountain range and upper level views of a botanical garden close by.

The conceptual challenge was to design a dwelling to be as close as possible to a "house in the sky" for a South African lifestyle. This concept included a suite for a live-in helper and a back door to the kitchen with separate access for deliveries. It has an elevator and public stair serving the living rooms and generous outdoor space including a dining patio, planting beds for flowers, and good landscapes with views. Two-level units are stacked with two at garden level and two units above, which have large terraces. Second floor

bedrooms—typical in local houses—required two stairs. The main stair is paired with a central elevator, and a second stair is needed for egress and service, interlocking above the main stair with landings facing the street. This allows complete separation of service access to kitchen doors. Parking at grade partially under the building was planned with entry to the lower units at garden level. The dining space in these units are raised above at the kitchen level. The service access from the street crosses to the back stair by a short bridge.

The north-facing gardens are at grade and placed on generous terraces on the third level. To provide shade to the living room and to the gardens above, a concrete framed loggia with planting boxes defines the facade to the north. This creates a dramatic hanging garden which is completely unique

in the city. The upper units have a patio for dining and the bedrooms have balconies which join this garden space. To enhance privacy, side windows are recessed into the building capturing diagonal views. Small trees have been grown on the upper planters which give privacy to the gardens used below. Over time this garden structure has become very verdant but still allows for the view to the mountains and ensures privacy for the owners.

Left Each unit has a garden—two at grade and two with patios on the third level. A planting wall serves as a sunscreen, defining the upper two level garden and shading the north-facing facade.

Right The scissor stair weaves together the service stair and main stair. Kitchens can be independently accessed from the street from a bridge, and the front doors are entered from the middle interior.

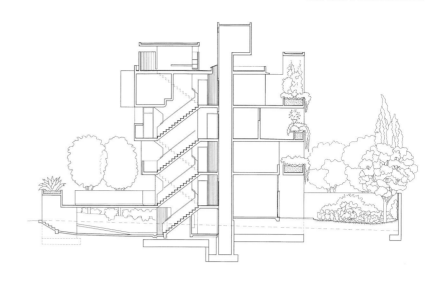

Scott Road

52

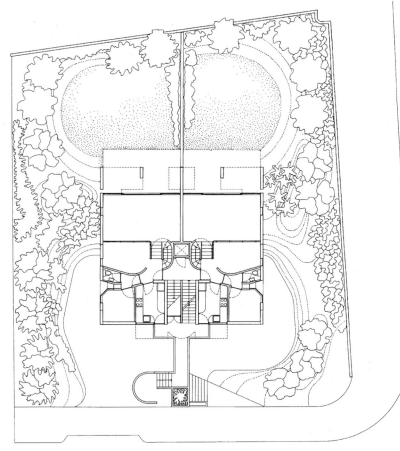

Scott Road

54

The Cape Town Years

IONA Rondebosh
Cape Town, South Africa
1968

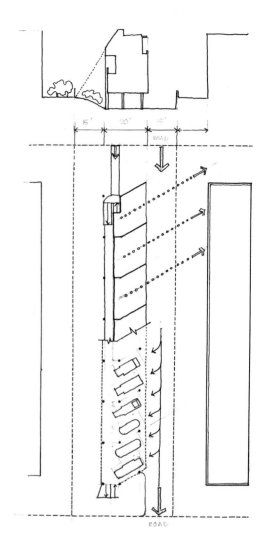

Given the proximity of this site to the University of Cape Town, the rental population was likely to be students. The owner planned to live in the triple-level unit with a private roof terrace. This was a low-budget project located in a densely packed neighborhood with minimal opportunity for open space.

Due to setback rules and the obvious need for a multi-level building, only one access open air corridor would be possible. The neighborhood building typology consisted of long slab buildings placed too tightly together, almost overshadowing each other. A lower-level, one-way driveway with angled parking would be needed.

The strategy we adopted was to place duplex units above the parking with entries off the single corridor on the middle level into their living rooms. Stairs serve the bedrooms and bathrooms below. The studio units also enter from the single corridor and have their stairs interlock with the duplex units to arrive at the top level where a wide window wall enhances the space. A sleeping alcove is placed on the back wall, and kitchens and bathrooms are tucked under the sloped roof of the vertical setback. The demising walls of the units are placed on the same diagonal as the parked cars below with walls the height of the windows providing ninety-degree corners. The rationale for this was a less frontal aspect to the neighboring building with a longer diagonal view to the property.

Given the tight space and minimal standards we opted to build in concrete where vertical walls required minimum dimensions. From the main street a ramp leads to the living room door of the three- level unit from which a stair meets the corridor with all other front doors. A back stair returns to the ground. This was a popular building much in demand with a socially active population using the minimal communal space—the corridor.

Opposite A very narrow site with severe setbacks from both sides left barely five meters for a building and needed one-way angled sunken parking. The structure follows the parking grid, with enlarged oblique views to the adjacent building.

IONA Rondebosh

The Cape Town Years

IONA Rondebosh

Opposite Units have only one access level. Studio stairs rise over duplex stairs which descend to the bedrooms. The angled roof setback contains the bathroom and kitchen.

The Cape Town Years

61

IONA Rondebosh

Santiago Redevelopment
Santiago, Chile
1972

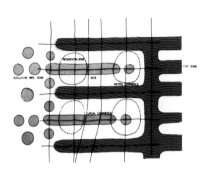 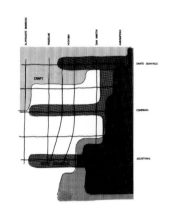 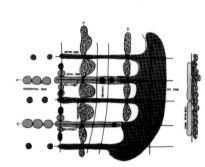

In 1972, the Metropolitan Redevelopment Agency in Santiago launched an international competition for a dense, mixed-use development. The site was a sixteen-block area, bisected by a highway at the edge of downtown, that formed the intersection between local and metropolitan systems.

We visited the site for a week before beginning our design work. We learned that these city blocks were much more complex than described in the brief. An interesting circulation pattern had evolved, alternating pedestrian streets, many arcaded, with vehicular traffic streets. Although the grid crossed over the highway, the character on the other side was very neighborhoody, with an exclusive zone of residences and a zone with craft production. Many existing buildings were to be preserved, some of them with a strong local character. From this visit we were determined to avoid building

high-rise structures in a park setting as was a current trend in urban planning. The existing fabric of the city allowed for much complexity and variety, and the human scale expressed livability and charm. It was important to our design to keep an ordered open space system similar to the present condition.

Our proposal kept the street grid because the scale of the blocks appeared comfortable, but we modified this to form four urban blocks (manzanas), bisected by pedestrian-oriented streets. The existing buildings further modified and differentiated these larger blocks. We understood the desire for variety in housing choices, good social mix, and integration of different lifestyles. This was to be a place for all to live and work in a comfortable, sustainable environment.

Housing provided a strong infrastructure to order these manzanas and was key to the

north-south pedestrian access system. We created two housing typologies to do this. "Interface Buildings" mixed several uses in the same structure depending on the context. Their base contained parking and there were upper level walkways crossing the east-west streets. Above the stepped level of parking, we placed courtyard housing. "Spines" contained housing with community buildings connected to pedestrian routes. Upper levels were for housing and the lower level and ground floor for activities such as child care and service functions. We designed a few elevators to serve the housing units, preferring low-rise, high-density housing on a substantial part of the land. Open space was still plentiful but controlled by numerous schools along the sites close to the highway and in proximity to housing precincts. We proposed high-income housing in the taller structures, many on the downtown side.

Opposite Sixteen blocks are divided into four manzanas defined by vehicular streets going east-west and pedestrian streets in the center. North-south pedestrian spines give access to existing schools and other public buildings.

Linear community buildings have social services on the lower two floors with apartments above.

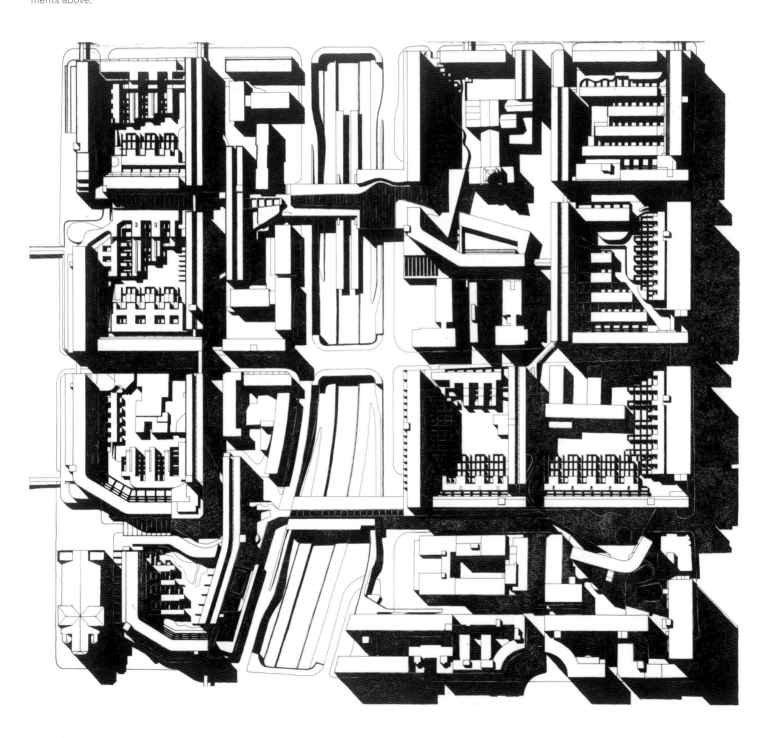

Santiago Redevelopment

The pedestrian streets were envisioned as vibrant places for retail, complemented by two existing marketplaces. Some repetition among the manzanas was inevitable, but these were modified by existing buildings and higher structures on the downtown edge. The presence of socially functional churches also enriched the planning concept, allowing history to be preserved in environments that could respond at an appropriate scale.

We were awarded third place in the competition and invited to talk to the competition sponsors. The winning entry was in fact a design that placed high-rise housing complexes in parks! None of the entries were built in the end, but this was considered an important moment in the evolving history of urbanism, and the competition is still frequently referenced in discussion. Even recently, there was a re-examination of the different approaches to this interesting competition by the shortlisted competitors. I was invited to discuss our proposal to highlight "Housing as Infrastructure," which was a new concept.

64

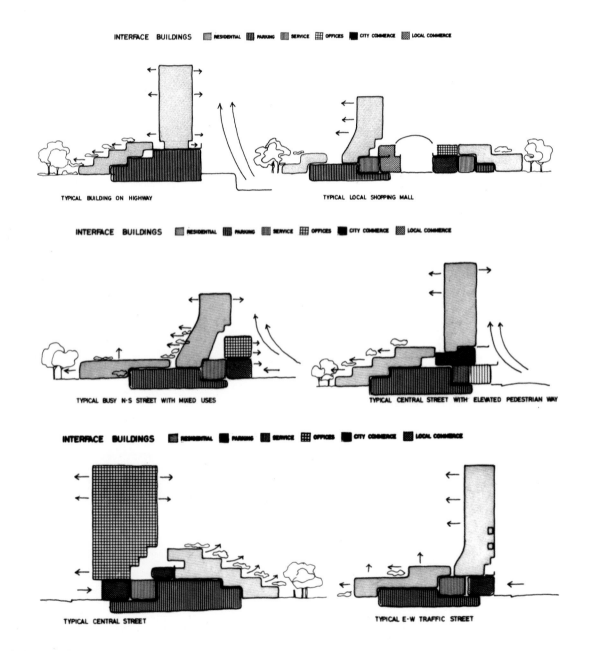

Left Diagrams of housing typologies in cross section. Interface buildings carry pedestrian routes with housing above. Mixed-use and parking levels are located below. Patio housing sits over parking decks as affordable units. The tall buildings shield highway traffic noise, while the covered, double-high pedestrian streets maintain an intimate scale.

Opposite Model with existing buildings to be retained articulated in a darker tone.

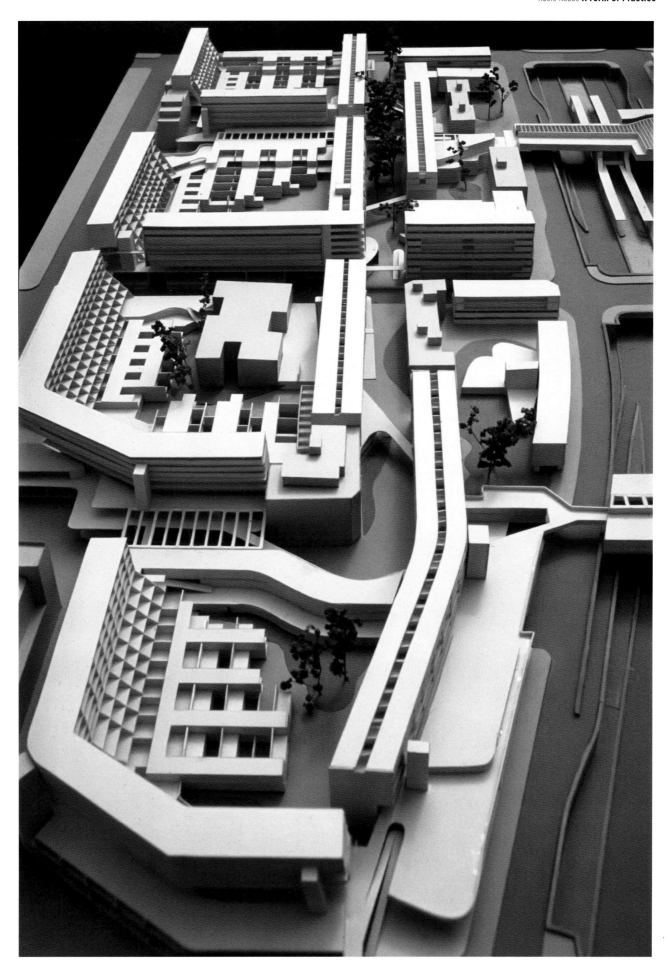

Santiago Redevelopment

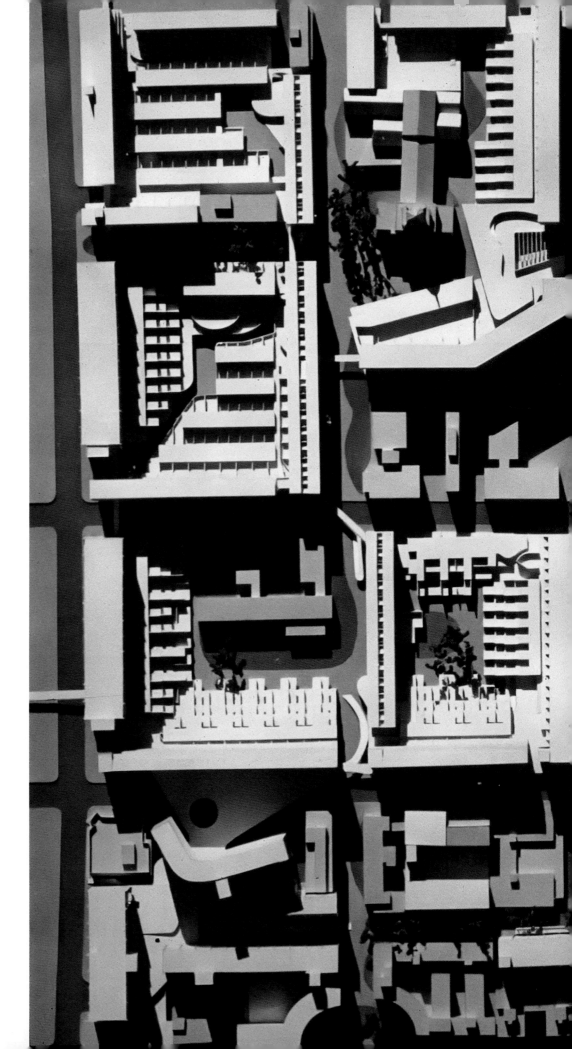

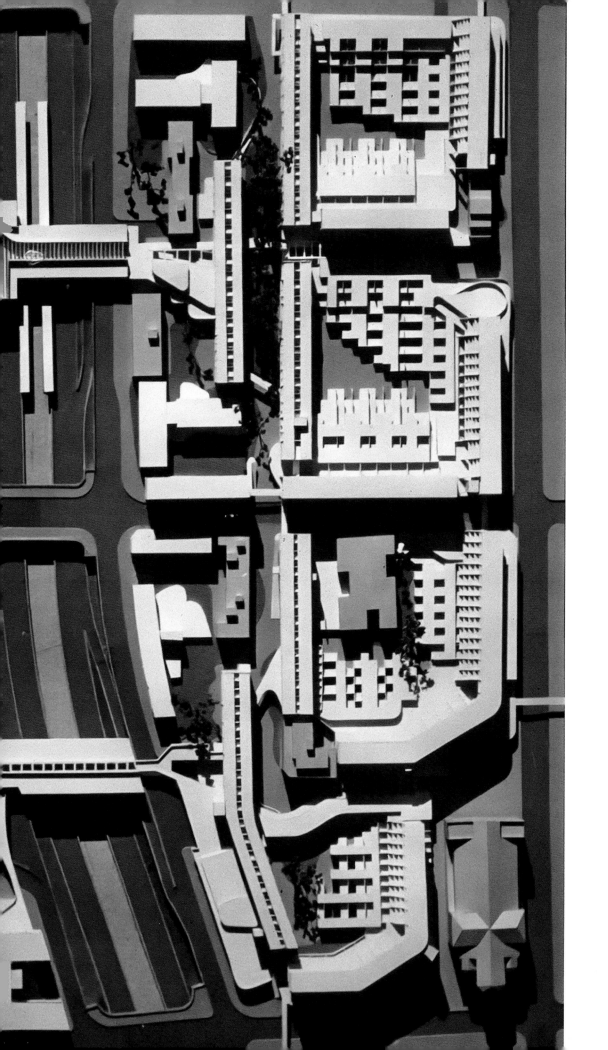

67

Santiago Redevelopment

Ormonde New Town
Ormonde, South Africa
1968-70

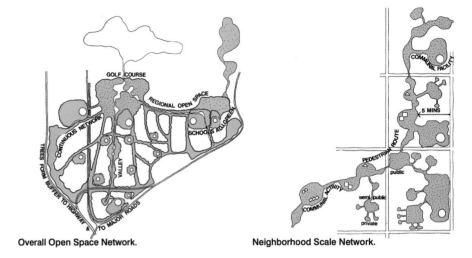

Overall Open Space Network.

Neighborhood Scale Network.

In 1968, we were commissioned to design a new town for 40,000 people in Johannesburg. The team consisted of me, Tony, and Roelof Uytenbogaardt, as well as L. Anthony Barac. We had two years to design and develop the first sector and submit this to the Township Board in sufficient detail for approval. This first sector was to contain offices, commerce, community buildings, and the full roster of what would be housing choices.

The large site was considered convenient to transportation, largely buildable with a good micro-climate. A mature and well-maintained golf course occupied the site and was to be preserved. A valley and water course bisected the area and together with the golf course created the basis for an amenable open space system. Some unbuildable areas, because of rock outcroppings, added size and character to the open space network. We selected the first residential area close to the golf course

because the landscape was already mature, and access to the existing regional transportation networks was easy.

Needless to say, this was to be a white suburban community where, as elsewhere in South Africa at the time, service staff lived in the household. In reality, the population was racially mixed. The competitive population was considered to be the typical buyer omnipresent in the sprawling suburbs of Johannesburg: middle to upper-middle income households, mostly with families. We did anticipate a community with diverse lifestyles, and we felt it was important to create choices of environments and building types. The suburban environments around the city were repetitive with cookie-cutter houses on repetitive streets. Ambitions for this town were to create new spatial alternatives, to create an exceptional level of amenity, and provide significant choices in

dwelling typologies and housing formations. The density of twenty to twenty-five dwellings per acre was considered a bit higher than the norm.

Our office was assigned to develop the residential fabric, which included creating a population profile. Simultaneously we were engaged in the overall concept planning, such as the location of sub-centers and major recreation areas. The site had distinctly different zones and topographical conditions which we welcomed as we developed clear environmental choices buyers might want. We were looking generally at housing typologies that could lead to fewer and shorter roadways, as well as typologies that could be spatially complimentary, such as shielding other structures from wind and defining semi-public spaces for collective use. By developing a range of typologies, we created a housing vocabulary that could help us test the viability of a series

Opposite Strong open space network combines the existing golf course and mature trees.

70

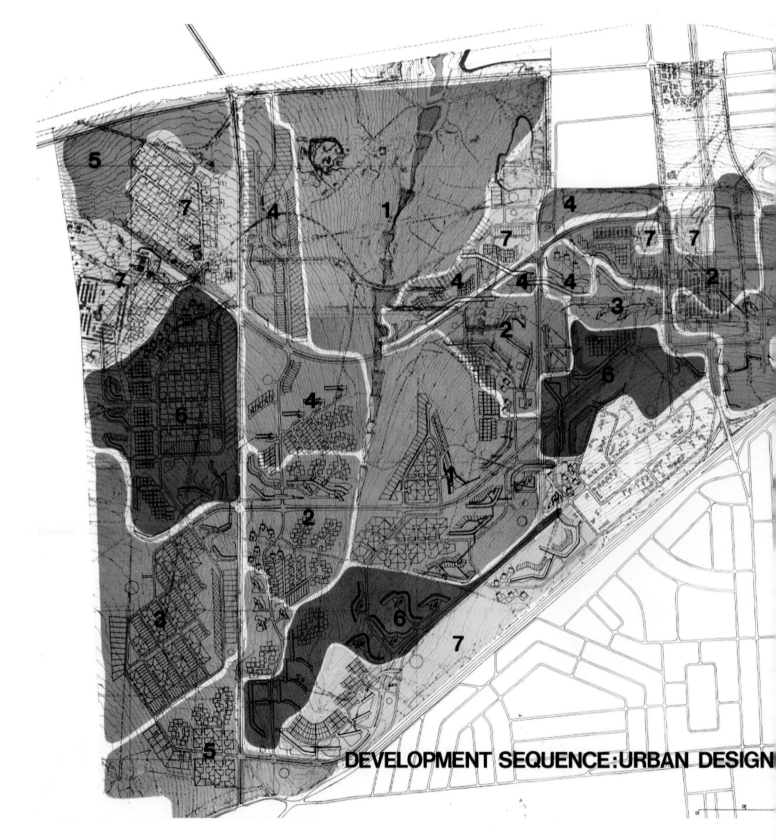

DEVELOPMENT SEQUENCE:URBAN DESIGN

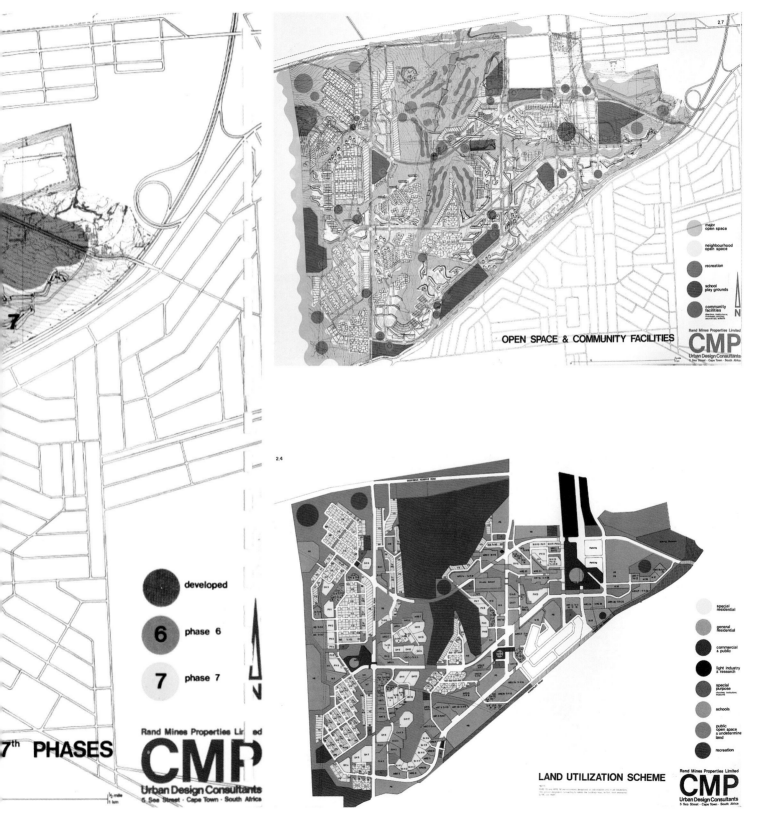

2.7

OPEN SPACE & COMMUNITY FACILITIES

major
open space

neighbourhood
open space

recreation

school
play grounds

community
facilities

N

Rand Mines Properties Limited

CMP
Urban Design Consultants
5 Sea Street · Cape Town · South Africa

developed

6 phase 6

7 phase 7

7ᵗʰ **PHASES**

N

Rand Mines Properties Limited

CMP
Urban Design Consultants
5 Sea Street · Cape Town · South Africa

2.4

LAND UTILIZATION SCHEME

special
residential

general
residential

commercial
& public

light industry
& research

special
purpose

schools

public
open space
& undetermined
land

recreation

Rand Mines Properties Limited

CMP
Urban Design Consultants
5 Sea Street · Cape Town · South Africa

Ormonde New Town

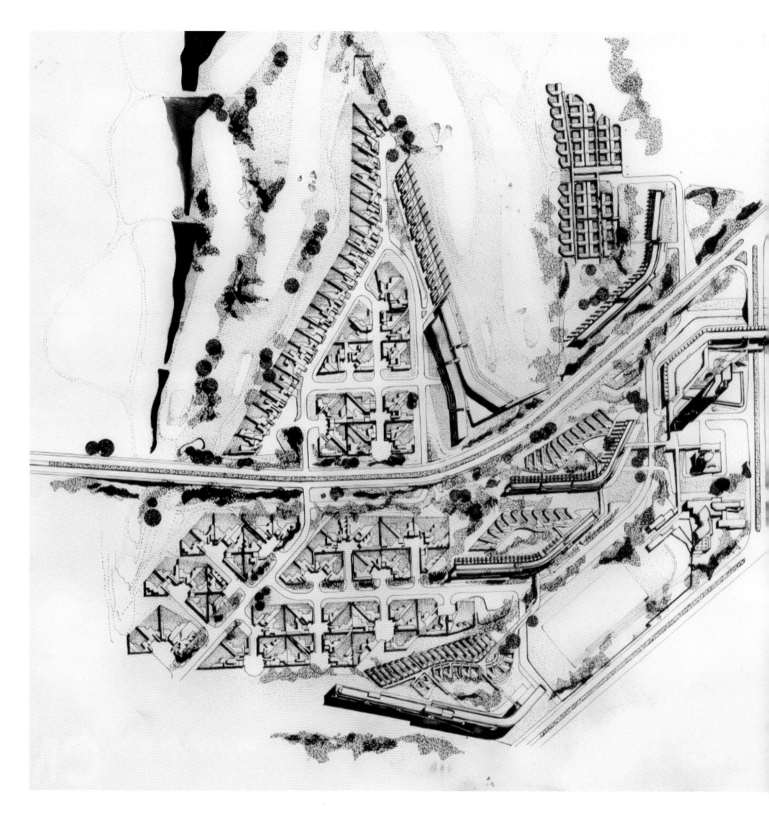

Above The plan of the first residential development around the existing golf course demonstrates a range of housing typologies that compliment the site and follow principles for landscape building integration.

The Cape Town Years

of principles. We were establishing necessary criteria to create a truly amenable residential environment. We were also anticipating that users would seek different kinds of locations dependent on household structure, age, and abilities. Desire for community life versus the need for privacy was one of the issues to be measured. Need for adjacency to retail, open space, and other services or amenities would be varied as well.

Maintenance of all of the public realm would be a key sociological factor. Preservation of the safety and cleanliness

of the neighborhood was an issue from the beginning. During this early phase we postulated at least thirty different housing conditions that represented real choices with dwellings to match. Feedback from prospective users, financial analysis, maintenance, and aesthetic choices all contributed to a refinement of these proposals. Only about twenty of these studies were included in the final housing vocabulary.

Over two years with many participants we filled three major reports, made architectural and planning guidelines, and drafted

architectural briefs for major sites. Making models was the preferred representative tool at that time, and we had teams doing this work constantly. In these few pages I can only convey the essence of what we were proposing and demonstrate that this would have been an attractive and desirable place to live. Ultimately, we had created a financially viable project, and Rand Mines decided to sell the land and urban plan to another corporation to develop. This was a total surprise and, after two years of intense work, a very disappointing outcome.

74

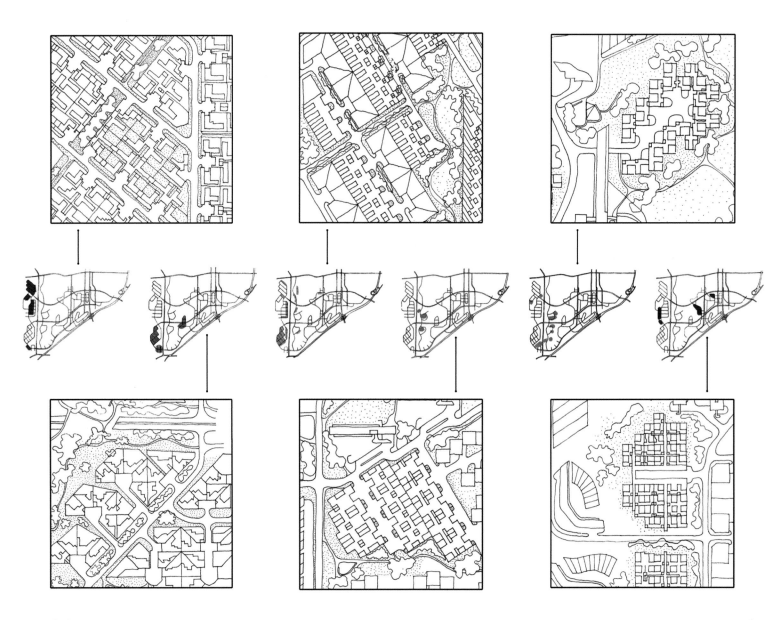

Taller buildings shield open space from the winter winds.

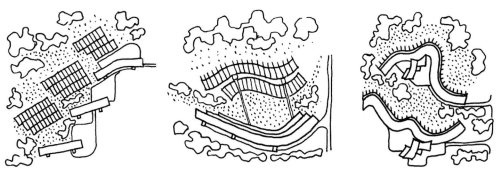

Complementary building types: low rise used to form common garden spaces.

Views emphasized by deployment of the topography.

Reflections
Landscape and Housing Form as Public Infrastructure

Our design for Ormonde was the first attempt to develop a robust series of housing and contextual typologies. The notion of creating distinct choices for users was a response to the paucity of these in most markets we had experienced internationally. South Africa was not the exception with the single-family house dominating the market with minimal side yards, questionable privacy, and very long access roads. Over the years, developing housing choices became one of my special interests.

In combination, the form of housing and the structured intention of landscape had become an important design tool for planning public infrastructure in our office; modulating the climate of spaces, protecting walkways, framing spaces. In the Ormonde and Santiago designs, we were viewing urbanism creatively in a different way. In later projects with topography—found or created— this interdisciplinary dialogue was able to be more sculptural, inventive, and formative.

Reflections
Leaving Cape Town

These three years in Cape Town were very intense and productive. It is hard to remember how all of these events were done in the timeframe available. Our small architectural office built seven single-family houses, two apartment buildings, one four-unit development for my mother and another with thirteen apartments for a client, my uncle. We designed low-cost farm workers' housing that they were able to build themselves. And as pro bono consultants to the Cape Town Public Housing Department, we proposed new housing typologies and plans to upgrade a squatter housing community.

I also engaged in my first real estate development, a hillside terrace of victorian cottages which I bought with friends and relatives. One of these became our home and office, radically reformulated, and set the pattern for combining living and working thereafter. A family member was widowed with four children and no assets so I created a design store based on Design Research, a well-respected venue for well-designed furniture and products in Cambridge, Massachusetts. "Design Media" imported famous furniture from Herman Miller, including those designed by Charles and Ray Eames, and by Alvar Aalto. To increase profitability I developed a line of clothing made from exotic fabrics and hired staff to create these. We renovated the space to feel like a museum, generating many visitors but not many buyers. As the first store of its kind in the region, this was a marginal financial concept and only survived two years.

Alongside our practice, Tony and I were both teaching three half days a week. We enjoyed teaching with the socially committed undergraduate students who cared about improving the living conditions of the urban poor.

Inevitably, offers to return to the United States were on the horizon, and the political context in South Africa had become extremely uncomfortable. Our family responsibilities were resolved, projects were built, and teaching at the graduate level was becoming very attractive. Finally, it was time to move on to new challenges.

The work of Adèle Naudé and her former partner Antonio de Souza Santos, built in Cape Town from 1968 to 1972, has inspired local architects and students alike, for more than fifty years. In a relatively short period of time, they executed some of the most recognized and noteworthy pieces of late modern architecture in South Africa. This early work was marked by an intensity of creative energy rarely seen in South Africa at that time; an energy that produced a prolific body of building design and urban planning work. In addition, they both made a considerable contribution to teaching at the School of Architecture, University of Cape Town (UCT); the school where they had both done their undergraduate studies. It is telling that Adèle, now "completing the circle," returned fifty years later to the School at UCT in August 2022, to do her last workshop there.

This early work was produced amidst a time of international discussions, competitions and projects that sought to revisit the ideas of CIAM and that of Team 10. In a way, it sought to reimagine architecture's purpose in relation to society, and to reinterpret the "project" of modern architecture. With such ideals Adèle (as well as others) brought a new energy to the UCT School of Architecture in the late 1960s, and with this vigor she recognized the importance and value of integrating good architecture with social ideas. It was, of course, also during the height of apartheid.

For Adèle, teaching as well as designing and making buildings in Cape Town was one and the same thing. This early work demonstrated inventive planning, an exceptional clarity of the "design concept/idea" and a consistent spatial richness. It responded to context in a manner that enriched the qualities of the individual sites on which they were built.

Unperturbed by the prejudices of apartheid practices of that time, Adèle and Tony offered me employment as a third-year student. Later they introduced me to their Mozambiquan friend José Forjaz, whom I also went to work with in Mbabane, Swaziland (now Eswatini). Upon graduation, they invited me to pursue a master in urban design at Rice University, Houston, where they had relocated to in the mid-1970s. And still later in the 1980s, I was able to join the staff at the School of Architecture, University of Pennsylvania as a visiting teacher. Over the years I have enjoyed a rich and long friendship with Adèle.

In Adèle's more recent design work in the USA and Asia—as presented at her public lecture at UCT in August 2022—the relevance of the ideas explored in her early work are pursued further. While these more recent buildings had more complex programs and are of a larger scale, the preoccupation of earlier design concerns have remained relevant.

This is not just a house. This was a radical proposition for the time it was built. This is a house that can't be divorced from its context, which here means apartheid South Africa. This is not architecture that looked to the past, that used styles to reinforce idea of nationhood. This was architecture that broke away from those values and offered a new proposition. Adèle has said at length that good architecture in social housing can give people a better quality of life. Space, light, air, sanitation are basics that people need to live humanely. To study modernist architecture in Africa is complex and interesting to unpack. This is a house that looked toward Europe and America, modern democracies. This house, in this context, was absolutely breaking the mold, moving away from traditional ideals.

When I came across House Naudé, it wasn't in a great state. To be honest, I wasn't really looking for a house at the time, and not in this area. I was more curious than anything, but as I walked inside, I saw I was walking into a gem, and before I knew it, I made an offer to buy the house. I certainly didn't know the journey I was about to embark on.

Not only was the house built by one of the foremost modernist architects in South Africa, but it was the first house she ever built and is seen to be the prototype for all the other houses and buildings she designed. Four years after buying the house, the architect would be walking up the long walkway, after decades, to see the house she designed and built for her father.

Sadly, Adèle's father, Hugo, passed away a few years after the house was completed. It was passed on to new owners, and the previous owner to me lived in it for twenty-five years. It had not been properly maintained. It's strange that out of all the buildings she designed in South Africa, this was the one that people had forgotten about; no one other than its owners had entered for over two decades.

Adèle built the house when she was in her late twenties, and it's a testament to how a brilliant mind can organize and design space. You can feel the human touch, as she drew everything free-hand; it's not designed by a computer. The house is built on a slope and rather than having steps, the house has ramps that lead you effortlessly through the incline of the property. The house is split into three parts: the sleeping area, the living area, and the service area. In the summer, the entire house opens up so there's a fantastic sense of being inside and outside at the same time.

You don't see the house from the street, but as you come in through the front gate the house begins and draws you in. And it's a play of surprises as it opens up. It's immensely private, like a well-kept secret.

There's a real truth to materials in this house, a tenet of modernist architecture. There's no fuss, no concealment; the materials show themselves and what they are doing. The house resists decoration, because it doesn't need it. The space quietly sings. It possesses a sense of calm and privacy. When you live in a house of this caliber, you're not so much the owner, but rather the guardian of something.

I had the task to breathe life back into this mid-century gem. Restoring a house is a different process to renovating. Somehow you don't want to introduce too much of your own personality into it, but rather tease out its original feeling. It's a nice process to respect what is there are find out what used to be there. It's about capturing the right tone and letting the architecture speak a process of delicate discovery. Only by living in a space, being in it all the time, do you get a true understanding of what the architect intended.

Marco Chiandetti

2

Early Years in the United States

1973-79 Rice University
1979-81 Graduate School of Design, Harvard University
1981-89 Graduate School of Fine Arts, University of Pennsylvania
1980-89 Practice: Adèle Naudé Santos and Associates

After the productive period in Cape Town, the transition to the United States was stressful. Selecting a meaningful location to live and work, and adapting to a new educational institution and a new cultural context took more time than anticipated. Finding clients to work with was even more daunting.

Rice University
Houston, Texas
1973–79

In 1973, Tony and I were hired as tenure-track associate professors at Rice University. My role was to develop seminars, lectures, and graduate studios on housing design. Tony was asked to develop a series of lectures on the history of the modern movement and on architects with relatively contemporary practices. In addition, we were both teaching graduate-level studios. I put extra effort into developing my housing-focused coursework. I created a theory course that researched the history of housing typologies globally. Each year, the students made primers of focused research to be shared with fellow students. Over the years we collected an impressive library of housing proposals. My studios, mostly housing-based, engaged more adventurous developers to challenge their sociological assumptions. The discussions and debates were informative and demonstrated ways in which spatial complexity could provide better choices for many households, making significant impact.

In 1977, I taught a graduate architectural studio looking at the plight of low and moderate income homeowners in a large low-income neighborhood in Houston. Seventy percent of their houses were estimated to be structurally unsound by the city. Driving through these areas we noted an astonishing number of uninhabitable houses. Because these areas were considered remote, this condition was invisible to most people. Both faculty and students felt strongly that this should be a matter of public concern. My colleague James Blue, an award-winning documentary filmmaker on the faculty, was the obvious person to introduce to this subject. He had already done a film on the Fourth Ward, a low-income neighborhood near downtown Houston, and was looking for another local opportunity. This was an exciting continuation of his investigation into landscapes of poverty. I applied for a grant from the Texas Committee for the Humanities to make a film on our findings. We quickly received funding to produce a film series on public television in 1979, called *The Invisible City*.

I gathered humanists from Rice University, the University of Houston, and other organizations to be discussants in the series. James Blue designed the format and led the process. Given the budget we were a low-tech crew using super eight film and handheld microphones. This was an act of public engagement, and salaries were low. I had not initially intended to be working on the series full-time but the philosophy of this documentary team was absolute transparency, with all of us in view. Since I was the person with the best knowledge of the story, I became the lead narrator. This experience was priceless, watching my appearance critically each day as we logged in film episodes. From that time onwards I never had fear of public speaking again.

The film series was intensely provocative. We invited the audience to respond with comments at the end of each episode and then we responded in the next show. Viewers had to phone into a call center, which was my house; their call would be answered by my friends who repeated the caller's question or comment, which was filmed. This gave anonymity to the caller but recorded the conversation. The last show was filmed live at the University of Houston where PBS was housed and interviewees came with their families. We voted on an assessment of what had gone wrong, which was inevitably linked to the lack of adequate policies to control the city expansion.

The Invisible City series won a Certificate of Award from the Southern Educational Communications Association (SECA) and was shown internationally at film festivals. Most recently, it was shown again at Rice University in 2020.

At this time, I also decided to experiment with other creative pursuits, such as fabric and clothing design. Fabric design was particularly intriguing to me. Using simple lines that changed width, spacing, and formation, I was able to change the graphic reading of color and intensity. I also used rhythmic progression from calm to dancing patterns to change the reading from the top to the bottom of the dresses. The garments were long and simple to emphasize the graphic ideas. These designs were hand-painted on cotton. I produced a collection of "pool" dresses for a local department store in Houston.

I also had a contract with a Brazilian textile mill to design terry velour fabrics to be woven there and shipped to the East Coast. These were more complex in color formation because of the weaving process. I designed bathrobes for the Neiman Marcus department store for men and women that were featured in their famous Christmas Catalog. A local contractor produced the garments in New York. I also trained to be a silversmith and enjoyed the intense focus in making carefully finished silver products. This was a great, brief creative hiatus from architecture!

After seven years at Rice, Tony and I were both tenured full professors, and our lives had diverged. The fruitful practice from our Cape Town years had not made the transition to the United States. We both were offered teaching positions outside of Houston.

83

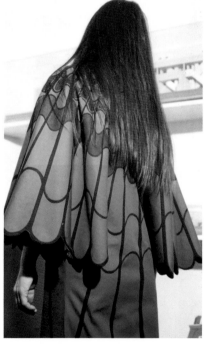

The Invisible City

I perceive a real crisis that exists, you know. and a worse crisis that is possible is going to occur unless something is done about it. The affected people really are the low and moderate income groups, who seem to be in a no win situation. And I then describe to him what we've been doing in my studio at Rice University, where we've been looking at the facts and the figures, we've been driving the neighborhoods.

You know, And I think the first thing we discovered is that the problem is endless..." [Describes overlying maps detailing households with income below poverty line, housing units needing major repair, to demonstrate intersectional causes with compounding effects] "Which astonished me only because this is a new city. How could we have such a large inventory of substandard housing when most of the city is post 1940."

James: "These are video cassettes. There are almost 180 on these shelves, about 75 hours of programming. And in each one someone in Houston has told us something or showed us something about an aspect of the city that is invisible to many of us. Now what I thought that if we could probe through all of this material, finding the pieces and putting them together somehow, we could make the invisible city, visible."

Adele Naude Santos.
Professor of Architecture

Houston's low and
moderate income areas.

Ken Austin, Mayor's Office
Planning Co-ordinator

FACTS
YOU WON'T
WANT TO KNOW
ABOUT HOUSTON
HOUSING.

Mrs. Willie Shelton
Fidelity

William McClellan
Director, Housing Authority

Roberta Burroughs
City Planning Department

Bob Fields, builder,
looks at Settegast

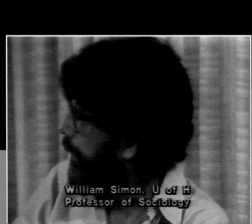

William Simon, U of H
Professor of Sociology

Hazel Patten
Third Ward

ACCORDING TO CITY PLANNING
REPORT JULY, 1973........

Maria Martinez
Magnolia

Maria Luisa Urdaneta
Medical Anthropologist
U of T, San Antonio

CITY OF HOUSTON
HOUSING ANALYSIS:

LOW-MODERATE
INCOME AREAS

So we will be visiting many of these communities in the process of looking for this [....]. That's a large part of the city. Yes I was going to say, that approximately half of the city lives in these areas. We are going to start off, with really having a series of facts on the screen, that some, somewhat alarming, but indeed they are. People in navigation telling us that people are living in automobiles, they're living 9 or 10 to a room, they're living in attics, they're living in garages, people are living in tin sheds without any running water.

Dave Johnson, Administrator
Housing Code Enforcement

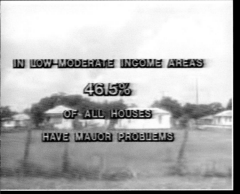

IN LOW-MODERATE INCOME AREAS
46.15%
OF ALL HOUSES
HAVE MAJOR PROBLEMS

102, 771 HOUSES
WITH MAJOR
PROBLEMS

AT LEAST
20%
OF ALL HOUSTONIANS LIVE
IN THESE CONDITIONS

Adèle Naudé Santos and Associates, 1980
An architecture and urban design practice

Working again in practice, my design process had changed. The Cape Town years were heavily oriented toward the integration of buildings and environments with landscapes. Making artful plans was critical to this. Our explorations were also volumetric and spatial. Now most of my work, however, was urban and devoid of the inspiration from nature. As the following two loft projects demonstrate, recreating artificial topographies started as a formal concept. With this, cross-sectional exploration became focal, often starting before I drafted plans. Space to be designed from an experiential point of view also led to a focus on staircases where the cross section could be experienced literally. This change in spatial experimentation continued through many iterations and spatial typologies over the following years and projects.

Graduate School of Design, Harvard, Cambridge 1979-81

I had spent several years teaching at the Harvard GSD previously, but in 1979 I was hired as a visiting Professor in architecture. This was not a tenured position, and I considered this an interim step. At this time there were only two women on the faculty full-time: Anne Spirn in the Landscape Architecture Department and me in Architecture. Moreover, at this stage, the Landscape Architecture Department had never tenured a woman. Thankfully, Anne and I quickly became good friends and produced an important study funded by the Oak Ridge National Laboratory through the Landscape Architecture Department. Called "Plants for Passive Cooling," the study investigated concepts that engaged architecture and landscape, which we both designed and illustrated. The study began with a thorough analysis of literature. Describing the process of energy transfer, setting principles for passive cooling design were produced with landscape students. Design applications for passive cooling were designed in tandem by me and Anne with a teaching assistant, Mark Rios, who investigated relevant plant material applications and an assessment of relative values to our proposals. This was a preliminary investigation and was never formally published.

In the architecture program I was asked to rethink the GSD's first-year curriculum with a new team. Most of the courses were already planned, but the structure of the design studio needed to be reconceptualized. I found curriculum development to be intellectually stimulating and pedagogically interesting. This was an important experience and helpful for my next career opportunity.

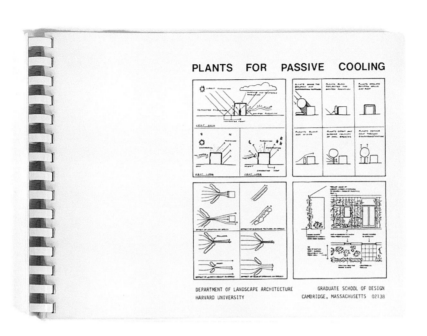

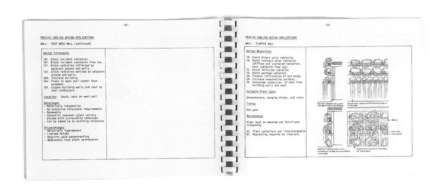

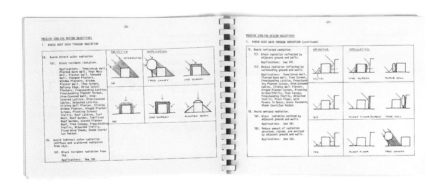

"Well, my dear, it's a good thing we like each other because here we are, alone," Adèle observed at the end of our first meeting in 1979. The only two women on the faculty of Harvard University's Graduate School of Design, we were surrounded by a multitude of male faculty. I admired Adèle's assurance and flair, her unusual clothes and jewelry. She had a bracelet with lethal-looking, inch-long spikes. A male colleague confessed that others were intimidated by Adèle. The occasion for our initial meeting and first collaboration was a research contract to produce a handbook for the use of plants for passive cooling on small buildings. I did the research and wrote the text; Adèle produced a series of drawings depicting her ingenious designs for ways of using plants to shade walls and roof. The result was *Plants for Passive Cooling*, a report that was circulated widely.

Two years later, Adèle abandoned me. The University of Pennsylvania had recruited her to chair their Department of Architecture. "You're next!" she said, as she took her leave. Five years later, I moved to Penn to chair of the Department of Landscape Architecture and Regional Planning. Adèle was on the search committee. As two chairs, we were co-conspirators. I joined Adèle in canceling our departments' classes for one week in the fall, which we called "Elective Week," where we each hired a diverse group to teach one-week classes, including Alex McLean, who taught a course in aerial photography.

In 1990, when John Meunier, president of the American Collegiate Schools of Architecture proposed the subject of Landscape and Architecture for the ACSA's summer conference and asked me to organize it, I invited Adèle and Glenn Murcutt, as architects for whom landscape was integral, to give keynote lectures. It was wonderful to see Adèle again. "I'm Queen Bee number one, you're Queen Bee number two," she announced to me at the opening reception.

Many years later, I had moved to the Massachusetts Institute of Technology and was on the search committee for a new Dean of the School of Architecture and Planning. Adèle, by that time a professor of architecture at the University of California in Berkeley, was high on our list of candidates, and I offered to give her a call. I made my pitch. "Why would I want to do that?" she said. "Why would I want to be a dean again." As a friend, I didn't want to press her into something she did not want to do. But the others refused to give up. They flew out to Berkeley to meet with Adèle and persuade her to reconsider. They succeeded. She agreed to visit MIT. I was delegated to give her a tour of MIT and to sing its praises. At first, Adèle was not impressed. The School of Architecture and Planning did not have its own building; it was immersed in an enormous complex of interconnected buildings. "The School has no front door," she complained. "But its front door is the main entrance of MIT, the words 'School of Architecture' are engraved in the entablature to the left of the entrance," I said. "And the dean's office is down the hall from the offices of the president, provost, and chancellor. There's no clear boundary between the School of Architecture and Planning and other Schools, but that's an advantage. Walking through the halls, you can peer through windows into other worlds, and you never know what you will encounter." A few minutes later, a robot came walking around the corner in front of us. "You arranged this!" Adèle accused. I had not. "Welcome to MIT."

134 Beach Street Loft
Boston, Massachusetts
1980

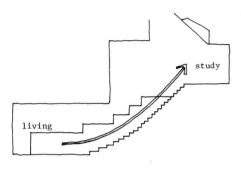

the gradient of the
steps becomes steeper
towards the private
study zone

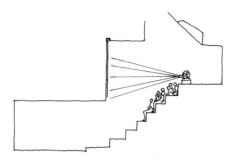

the middle terraces
form a theatre for
viewing films

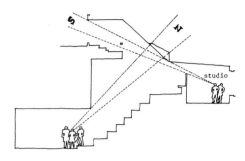

the stepped terraces
form an interior land-
scape viewed from the
livingroom with the vista
culminating in a large
north skylight and a view
of the sky

warm light from the
south filters down to
the study and studio

With Andrea Leers, a colleague from Harvard, I planned the renovation of two floors of a former leather warehouse into four two-level lofts with an addition on the roof. We both intended to live there. A central corridor divides the space into units that face the street and units that face the rear. These are all two bays wide and twelve feet high. On the second floor, one bay from each unit crosses over to the opposite side to become two bays deep. Double-height spaces are used for spatial continuity which also allows for cross-ventilation. All the units face south at roof level with large decks and city views.

My loft was treated as an interior landscape with stepped terraces that rose up to a study. This area was sky lit from a big north-facing window. I was still making films and created an informal sitting area from which film projections were possible on a blank surface of my neighbors' wall. I added numerous interior trees and plants.

Bookcases and sitting areas are built in. The pitch of the stair becomes steeper as the uses become more private. The top level is a room on the roof and the skywindow allows views of the city to the rear. The central idea of the loft is to create intimate spaces but also to stress the large spatial reality. There

are no interior doors other than to the bathroom. Lower walls separate the dining area and kitchen from the living space. A bathroom under the platforms has a sensual curved countertop with a sunken round sitting tub. This was perfect for relaxing at the end of the day. The walls of the whole loft were painted in shades of gray, like shadows, which deepened in hue at night and transformed spaces like the dining area to become more intimate.

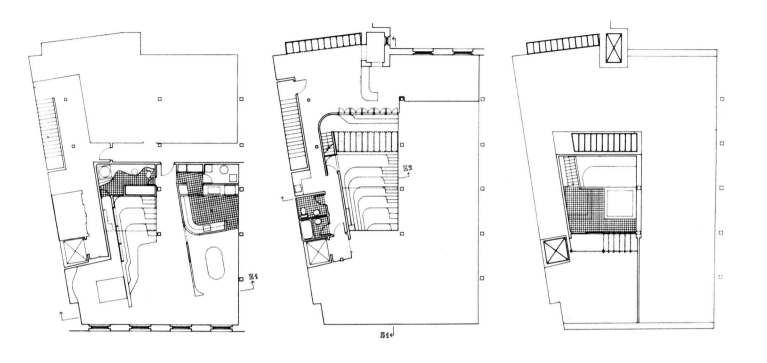

134 Beach Street Loft

Right The cross section
shows the spatial flow
between the three
levels and stair profile
and bookcases.

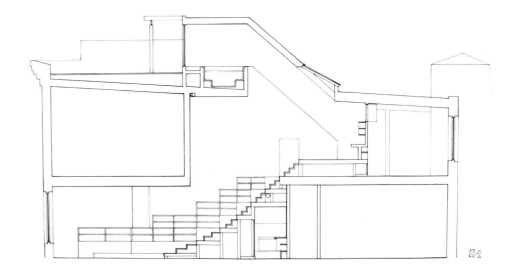

S1

Early Years in the United States

134 Beach Street Loft

Graduate School of Fine Arts
University of Pennsylvania, Philadelphia
1981-89

In 1981, I was offered the position of chair of architecture at the University of Pennsylvania, a school I knew well and in a city that had been home to me. This was a perfect opportunity to start thinking of combining my academic career with an architectural practice again. By now I had also become a registered architect in the United States.

My first tasks at UPenn were academic, and I chose to teach in the first year to understand the culture from within. Like many institutions, the school had been hiring many of its own graduates and the same exercises were being repeated. There was little debate or self-critique. I began with a collective review of all aspects of the curriculum. As a result, I brought in new visitors, funded summer workshops, and introduced collective experiences to be shared by all levels.

One of the more radical ideas was to have one week each semester when the curriculum was suspended. In the fall, we introduced mini courses related to the discipline but widened their scope. Students could attend five courses each, taught by related faculty in history of art, real estate, planning, landscape photography, and others. In the spring, visiting architects from around the world taught the same studio problem defined by us but within their own philosophical and methodological frameworks. Each day we had a lecture from one of our visitors for the whole school. Students could choose who to work with, and the subjects we chose were thought-provoking but not complex. On the final day, the debate revealed how different the outcomes were, based on methodology and theoretical positioning. These semester breaks were exciting, provocative, and brought students across years together. Very quickly all the departments joined this semester format. Anne Spirn followed me to UPenn to become the chair of landscape architecture and joined happily in this collaboration.

I also began a summer workshop with Balkrishna Doshi, well-known for low-cost housing and urban development in Ahmedabad, India. He had founded the interdisciplinary Centre for Environmental Planning and Technology (CEPT) and designed the first buildings on campus. He was also the director of architecture. This was my first attempt to make a workshop in a foreign context and choosing the students was critical. For students to visit a culture so vastly different was important but all had to have traveled outside of the United States. Housing the students in the minimal dormitories did not work well in the beginning but there were many empty housing units in the city. The next year the school rented several units and a cook who made dinners in one of the kitchens. The neighbors were friendly, bringing dishes for them to try. Being part of a community was also rewarding.

Our workshops started with a focus on housing problems in local contexts that could be visited. For the students this was an amazing learning experience, understanding a new culture and new building technology simultaneously. Many issues that would be taken for granted, such as privacy, functioned here quite differently. Open space critical to community building had its different rules; space sizes and room arrangements had different priorities. Importantly, students had to listen and absorb the cultural meanings with humility! How to formulate an appropriate aesthetic was a difficult task. The work was spectacular and the learning curves were impressive. Doshi was an amazing teacher.

I launched these first workshops for two years with other UPenn faculty teaching part of the time. In our planned third year, we were not able to visit because of an outbreak of illness in Ahmedabad. At the same time, in Colombia, a volcanic eruption covered the town of Amero in a mudslide overnight. Former students from Rice University called on me to bring a workshop to Colombia to help plan a new settlement for the survivors. I could

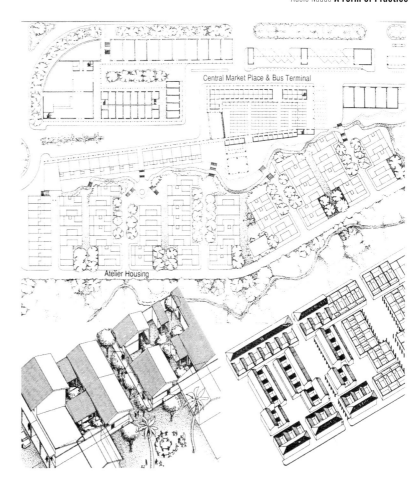

Central Market Place & Bus Terminal

Atelier Housing

do this, fortunately. Most of the students in the school applied. After many interviews I selected sixteen students and two assistants to join me. The former Rice students chose Honda, a town near the disaster but also close to Medellin, a narco capital. I rented a large walled hacienda, owned by a local hotel to service the facility. We set up studio space, hired a cook and a security team. We had weekly meetings with our local colleagues, and every two weeks the director for the project flew to Honda to give us a critique. Over the course of six weeks we designed new housing typologies, a marketplace, and new settlement plans, using local building materials. The work was serious, economically challenged, and had to be culturally relevant. Much of our design was built, and another UPenn team followed up the next year. This work was highly publicized by the *Philadelphia Enquirer*, who sent their architecture critic, Thomas Hine, to report on this development.

When I accepted the department chairmanship I never expected to continue as an academic leader. G. Holmes Perkins, the dean at UPenn when I was a student there, was considered to be a really successful leader, generous in promoting his faculty and host to an amazing gathering of all faculty at his home and garden each year! In my memory he was building a community of scholars and believed in creative dialogue. Building a sense of community by creating joint events and social occasions was to be one of the characteristics of my leadership. The special weeks each semester were aimed at bringing the classes together, finding interests in common and creating an interactive student group. Visitors for Design week for example, from many contexts were part of this, bonding over a special meal at my loft, and later promoting their experience at UPenn to their worlds. This set an example for future positions to be elaborated later.

REPLACING A BURIED CITY

The destruction of Armero was one of the world's worst natural disasters. Some University of Pennsylvania architecture students found an unusual way to help the people who survived.

Our proposal for the rebuilding of Honda showing the housing and marketplace we developed.

The article in the *Philadelphia Enquirer.*

2009 Naudain Street
Philadelphia, Pennsylvania
1981

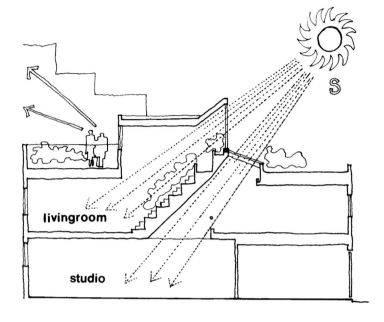

Above Light strategy: the spatial flow is emphasized by the staircase, and the deck features downtown views.

The Beach Street Loft in Boston was barely completed when I moved to Philadelphia. Here, I sought to create a similar live-work situation, designing a house and office for myself. This was once again to be a loft in a renovated industrial building. I found a low-rise workshop in a neighborhood of small, three-story houses for workers. The industrial space had one of these houses embedded in the property and it had access to a communal courtyard.

This was spatially a conceptual development from the Beach Street Loft. From the street a stair leads to the living room above, entering into an unusual double-height room. From here, a stepped garden with sculptures and flowering trees rises upward toward the south light. The lowest level is a sitting area that joins bookcases to form a comfortable space for conversation. The kitchen and dining area are connected to this level spatially, though placed to the side. The stepped wooden terrace leads to a garden room above, which opens to a big deck with downtown views. The private areas of the house on the second floor are hidden by the terrace formation and contain areas for sleeping. A back stair goes down to the studio on the ground from here. This concept has another reading from below because the inclined wall that backs the terraces creates an opportunity to scoop up to a window bringing southern light into the studio. Creating a double spatial idea with the same elements was always exciting.

The ground floor had been a garage and a storage area. It was repurposed to be a studio, a rental unit with access from the courtyard en-suite with the house, a storage area, and a garage for two cars.

2009 Naudain Street

2009 Naudain Street

Early Years in the United States

Reflections
An Appropriate Architecture

Ideologically, "postmodernism" was in full assault on the profession, and the idea that there were "no rules in architecture" was being proclaimed by influential architects such as Frank Gehry, among others. As the chair of a prestigious architecture department I had to clarify my position, which I first did with the following brief essay, "An Appropriate Architecture."

An Appropriate Architecture

Most architects will claim that in the design of their buildings they search for an appropriate solution. By appropriate I would mean that it satisfies both the functional aspects of the program but transforms solutions from the pragmatic dimensions to the poetic. It is not enough to solve the problem at hand but the enhancement of the experience is key to transformation of the act of building into the creation of architecture. An appropriate architecture finds a deliberate fit with the context, through incorporation or deliberate opposition. Response to context includes working with the microclimate, suitable use of local technology, and response to the context in cultural terms. Appropriate solutions have to be satisfying in formal and visual terms as well.

Architecture is an art in which a key ingredient is inhabitation. Buildings have to be comprehensive by their external form, imagery and contextual fit, but the success of the structure by those who commission it is more often measured by its inhabitability. Resolving the internal and external forces is part of the process of making architecture, and the question is one of balance, to what extent form and external gestures take precedence over the buildings functioning. In my work I start with the design of experiences, with spaces that support the building's intent. The qualities of space that can enhance pleasurable experiences is more important than functional fit, which I regard as a given. Buildings should work as intended, but the transformation of pragmatic issues to be poetic solutions is what we strive for. The design of space includes the shape and volume, the sound, and the quality of light but it is not static. Spaces are designed to be enjoyed singly or sequentially, mostly inhabited in different ways, requiring one's imagination to narrate probable experiences. Having set the spatial narratives as the foundation for the solution I enter into a dialogue with issues of form and context. Through this iterative process an architectural product is proposed. Other architects place their emphasis first on exterior form because they assume this to be more important!

Housing Competitions

From 1982 to 1985, eager to develop a practice again, I entered housing competitions, a subject I knew well. Harlem Housing comprised several city blocks for 450 units of affordable units. This was an intense two-phase competition, and our entry came in third. I developed a thorough urban design and architectural approach with illustrative principles that refined the street grid to include semi-public spaces and walk-up housing on five floors. Later, this was useful for teaching purposes.

We won the competition for Infill Housing for twenty-four affordable units in Camden, New Jersey. We developed a new typology, a zero lot line twin house responding to a local housing aesthetic. The idea was for the twin house owner to rent the second house to a low-income qualifying household. There was a back lane which gave access for parking, allowing the twin house to have two parking places, one off the street and one to the rear. The houses were proposed to be factory-built and shipped to site where a brick facade would be added using typical windows and a shared porch. This typology was promising, but the agency in charge lost their funding.

Finally, a competition for ten houses on an ecologically sensitive hillside in Cincinnati was another new typology, using interlocking panhandled lots. We wished to avoid vehicular driveways on this special landscape. Complimentary houses near the street with city views were paired with upslope houses with city and park views. All had direct private paths to the shared hillside park and direct access to parking off the street. We received an honorable mention for our proposal.

Opposite The basic housing typology on the main streets includes walk up houses plus an upper level walkway and a common open space at upper levels. Mews housing crosses blocks with semi-private space and a controlled entry.

Harlem Housing

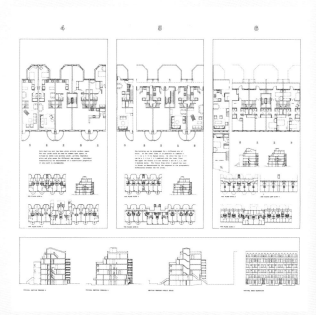

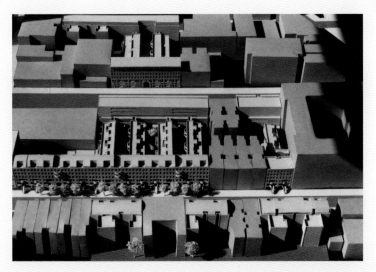

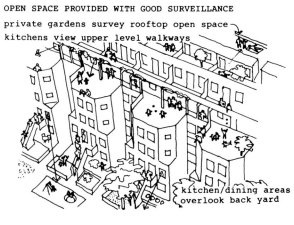

OPEN SPACE PROVIDED WITH GOOD SURVEILLANCE
private gardens survey rooftop open space
kitchens view upper level walkways

kitchen/dining areas
overlook back yard

Camden Infill Housing

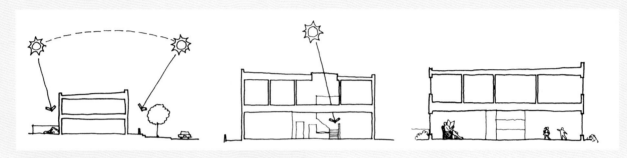

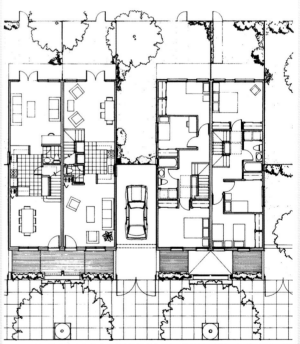

Zero lot line twins to be sold with one rental house for low-income families. The back alley allows parking for one car, the second from the street. Prefabricated modules with a brick facade made in situ match the neighborhood character.

All residents park off
the street with their
own direct access to
their unit. All units also
have their own access
to a shared park at the
top of the site. The
houses have a low roof
profile in the center
with the roof sloping
up to the park for
upper units and to the
city for street-facing
units. View corridors
are left open for views
in both directions.

Cincinnati Housing

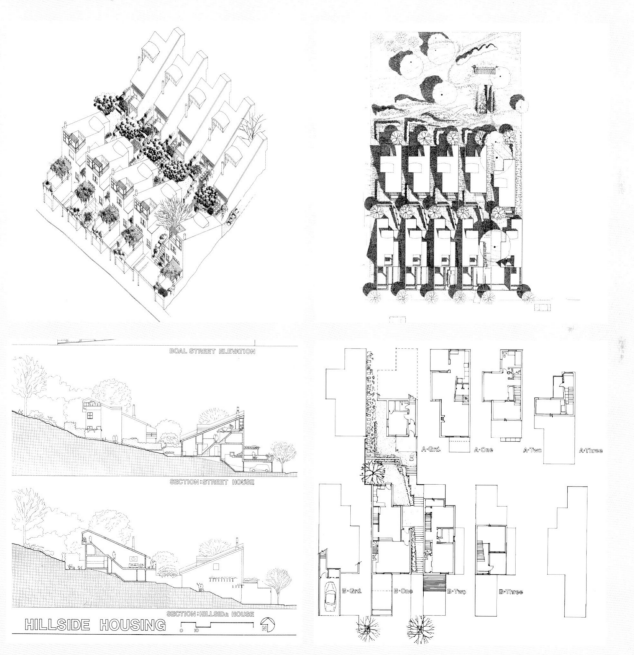

BOAL STREET ELEVATION

SECTION: STREET HOUSE

SECTION: HILLSIDE HOUSE

HILLSIDE HOUSING

A·Grd.   A·One   A·Two   A·Three

B·Grd.   B·One   B·Two   B·Three

Working in Japan

In 1984, I visited my friend and colleague Andrea Leers in Tokyo at the house of Taeko Matsuda, a business person who headed the Japan Housing Foundation. Andrea had hosted Matsuda's daughter when she studied at Wellesley and became part of the family. Now Matsuda was trying to persuade Andrea to design a building for her. They both insisted that I get involved as well, although I was there for a vacation. In six days, Andrea and I made a schematic design for a mixed-use building with two units at the top for Taeko and her son and retail on the ground floor. She insisted on no changes after I made the exposed columns round. The next thing we knew, it was built! Perfectly? Not quite!

Matsuda thanked me for the work by introducing me to a developer friend, Shingo Nomura. He hired me to design a small office building for him in Tokyo, and later a house overlooking Tokyo Bay and several other projects.

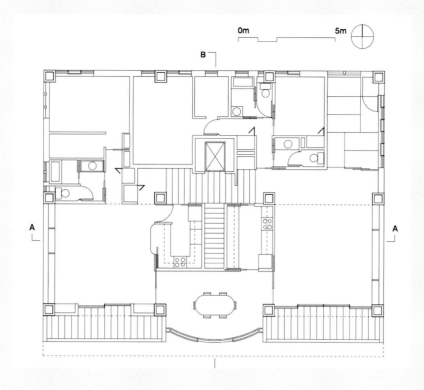

0m 5m

B

A   A

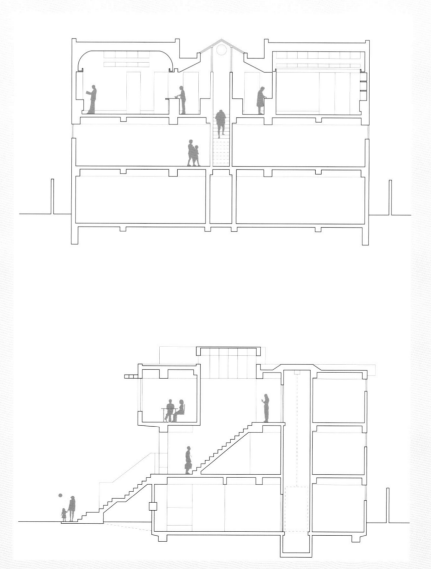

Above The units have separate entries and feature the dining room as a shared space with sliding doors to either side. The units are expressed with bay windows on the facade.

SDC Corporate Headquarters
Toyko, Japan
1988

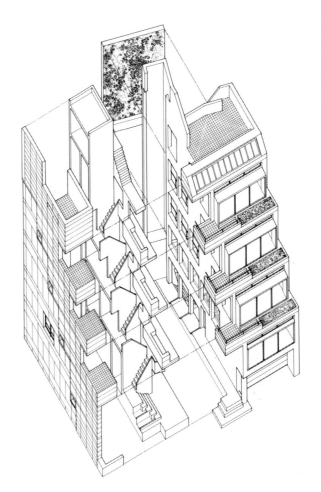

In Tokyo, the neighborhood of Ichiban-cho features narrow streets. The small sites are typically occupied by buildings of five floors, with natural light only possible from the street. In this area, I was commissioned by Shingo Nomura to design the headquarters for the SDC Corporation, to house the company's president and his immediate staff.

The site required light setbacks from the street which created terraces for offices. The internal stair in zigzag formation steps back-ward to work with the required setbacks, creating a dramatic circulation element. Services such as bathrooms are housed out of sight in this setback. The elevator is placed on the back wall. The building has

a street level entry, but the reception area occupies the whole second floor. This is where most public events take place. On the roof we created a special night event space for moon watching. In the basement there is a full catering kitchen.

As part of the design process, they asked me to incorporate large paintings by the Japanese artist Imai throughout the building. The first large painting occupies the back wall of the lobby, which is a triple-height atrium space with natural light from above. The floor is granite but is com-posed of small pieces which change color from totally black at the painting to orange at the window wall. The reception desk is

made of glass so that the floor reading is continuous. The desk appears to float in the space. The building is called Kachofugetsu-kan, which refers to the unity of the four seasons expressed in the large mural.

Our engineer, Norhidei Imagawa of T.I.S., was responsible for the structural design. The rules for spanning space were very tight and cumbersome. To span the void of the atrium, he proposed a new engineering concept, which had to be authorized. He was a real inventor who continued to work with us on many projects, including in the United States.

SDC Corporate Headquarters

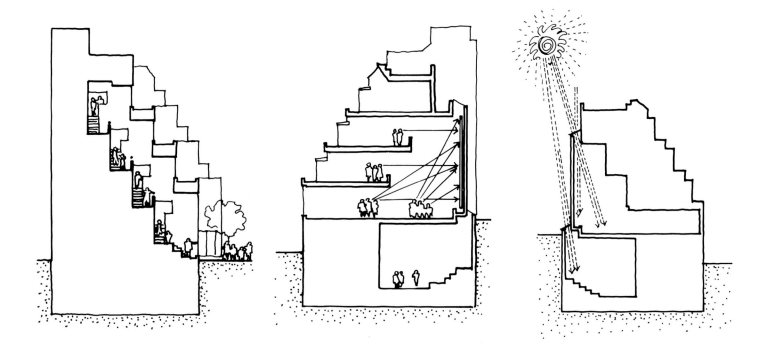

Above Cross sections of key features: the stair, the surprising painting viewed from each interior level, light brought into exhibition spaces from rear setbacks.

Early Years in the United States

115

116

Early Years in the United States

SDC Corporate Headquarters

SDC Guest House
Ninomiya, Japan
1988

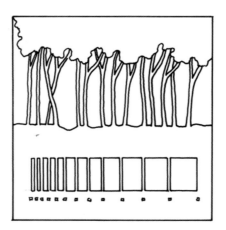

The client for the SDC Corporate Head-quarters also commissioned me to design a guest house in Ninomiya, a seaside town near Tokyo, with south-facing views of Tokyo Bay. The site was a remnant of a natural preserve, covered with mature cypress trees. Given this history, we started by minimizing the loss of trees, and we selected an existing clearing with a moderate slope.

The design reflects a desire to create a poetic response to the forest, learning from the existing natural rhythms of the trees, of the dappled light, and the irregular pattern of light and shade. The house invites the forest to enter the interior dramatically. Tree-like columns with branching struts support a large sky window which allows glimpses of the leafy canopy above and permits the dappled light to become part of the atmosphere of the house. The sky window forms the axis of the house from the chimney to the outside pool terrace. This window is shaded with wooden slats that echo the pattern of light and shade in the forest.

The home's public spaces occur on three overlapping levels which step down the slope and increase in size. The study and fireplace on the upper level, dining room and kitchen on the middle, and a large living room on grade extended to a large outdoor deck. Full-height sliding windows move into pockets to open the space completely to the garden and pool. This axis also defines levels of privacy and links the place of winter—the fire—and the place of summer—the pool.

Entering on the middle level of the house, the view to the bay is impressive as are the views up and down the sky window axis. The bedroom wing is on the middle level and features ocean views. The primary suite ends this wing with an exit to a private patio and a car parking area.

The roof is covered with copper to blend with the forest. The slope decreases in pitch from the chimney to the large overhang, shading the living room. The sky window breaks the roof into two parts. Metaphorically this roof is seen as a large leaf protecting the inhabitants from the weather.

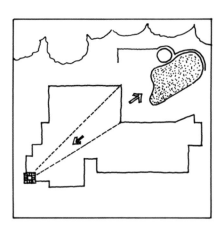 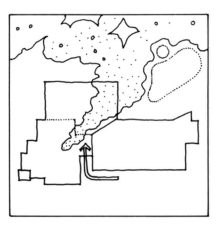

Opposite Concept diagrams expressing lessons from the forest: the irregular patterns of light and shade created by varying tree spacing, the privacy of boundary walls opening gradually to full forest views, a glazed diagonal window giving views of the tree canopy from inside, linking the place of winter—the fireplace—to the place of summer—the pool.

119

SDC Guest House

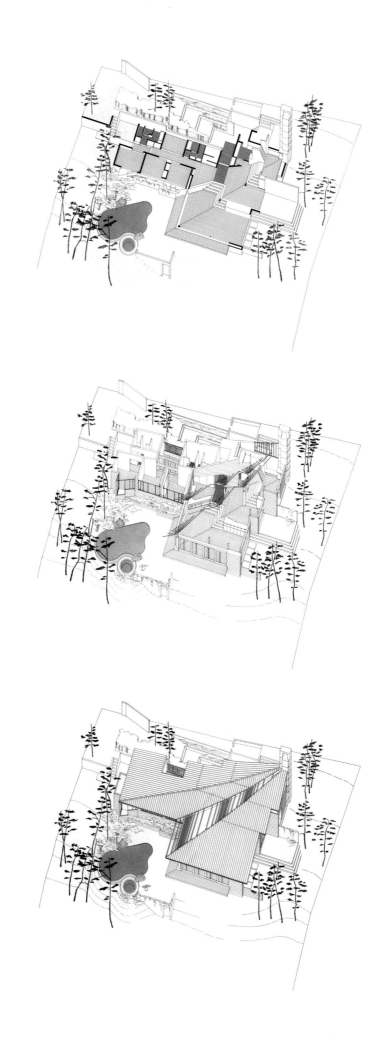

Early Years in the United States

Opposite The roof pitch is gradual—it is at its peak next to the chimney and flattens downslope. It was likened to a leaf protecting the family from the weather.

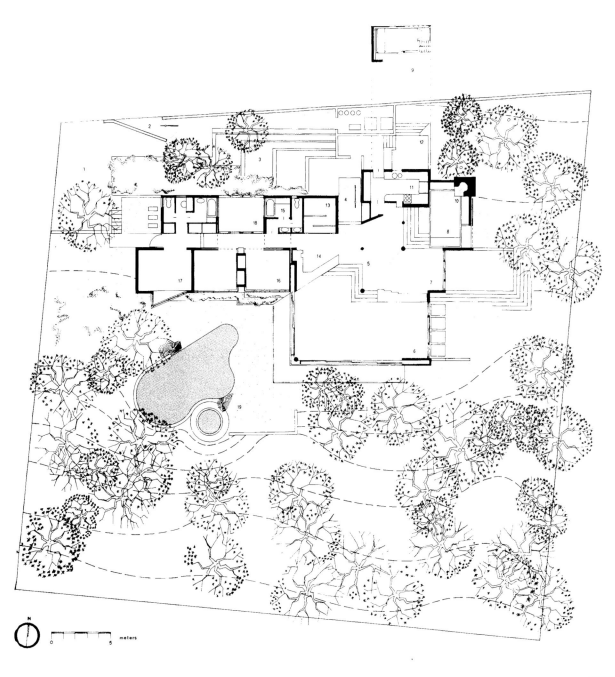

Early Years in the United States

SDC Guest House

124

SDC Guest House

Tokyo Fantasia
Office Building
1988

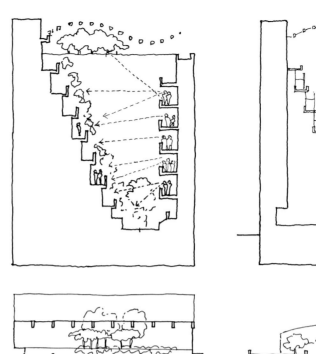

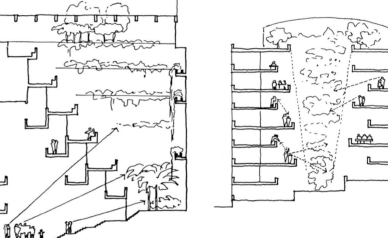

The SDC Corporation had been assembling land parcels for a larger office building in Tokyo's Tsukasa-Cho neighborhood. For this project, the client requested that the building have a public walkway woven through the ground floor, but privacy was important as well. An internal stair leading to roof gardens became a mediator between the public and private experiences of the building.

We developed several atrium scenarios to bring light to the office floors. A zigzag stair

joined alternate floors together with sitting areas for tea and relaxation. Planting boxes for seasonal flowering plants enclosed the space with transparent materials like woven mesh. We wanted the steel stair to feel lightweight and transparent.

We detailed the facade to make it as transparent as possible with good light penetration. On the roof we worked to include a design by artist Alice Aycock. This spatial idea was an exciting original concept for the client who was committed to building.

We prepared complete documentation for public approval. However, in the end Shingo Nomura was not able to buy the last portion of the property as it had escalated in price to an unreasonable level. At this time in Japan, low interest rates suddenly rose, bankrupting numerous companies, including the SDC Corporation.

Early Years in the United States

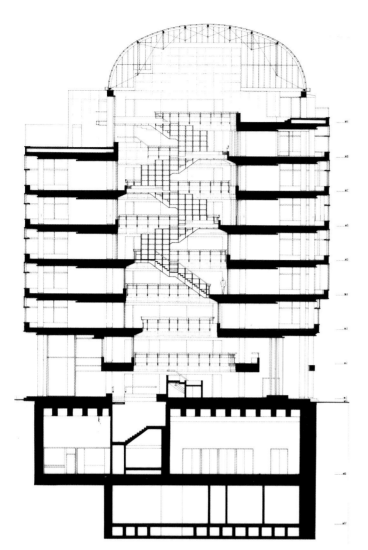

Above The garden stair contains planters and the landings are sitting areas shared by each side of the atrium. The stair rises diagonally to separate a pedestrian passageway from the private interior garden. This wall is transparent allowing the uses of the passageway to glimpse into the garden paradise.

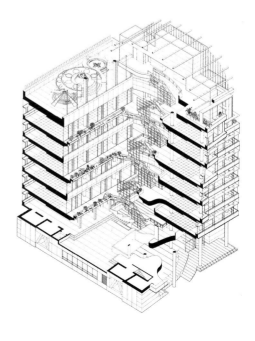

Tokyo Fantasia

Reflections
Spatial Continuity, Special Stairs, and Volumetric Experiments

The work-live loft projects and the works in Japan placed the use and experience of space at the center of the design process. They required experiential design thinking, combining plan and section together. Modest lofts led us to design more spatial complexity like atria and unusual staircases linking different levels. Staircases continued to evolve formally from this early beginning.

In the Beach Street Loft, the central stair changes pitch; it gets steeper towards private areas, it gets wider as it becomes more inhabited, and it becomes more gracious as one moves to the living spaces below. Lit from a large window bringing north light from above, the stair and stepped platforms bind the two levels together.

Closely related to the Beach Street project is the Naudain Street Loft in Philadelphia, in which the stair matches the rhythms of the planted display shelves, starting as a sitting area before spatially moving up into a high garden space. Like the former example, the stair serves to bring the two floors together. In addition, the canted surface under the steps has a stair below going down to the first floor, and scoops up to a window above bringing light to the lower level.

The Ichiban-cho office building in Tokyo features a new stair typology that follows the setback for light required by zoning. It zig-zags upward and hides service facilities. The view from below is dramatic and sculptural but going downward, offices display their work or artifacts in windows for view. The stair also frames the triple-level atrium allowing a better view of the three-story painting by Imai.

In Tokyo Fantasia, the stair performs multiple agendas. Firstly, it links offset double-height office floors around an eight-story atrium. As the stair zigzags backwards, the landings become wider and form sitting areas for tea breaks. They feature planting boxes for flowering plants that vertically extend the garden motif to the roof. Second, this stair separates a ground level public passageway through the building, bringing in diffused light and allowing visitors to glimpse the garden paradise created in the atrium.

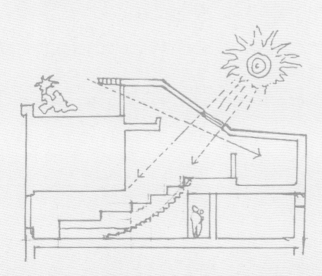

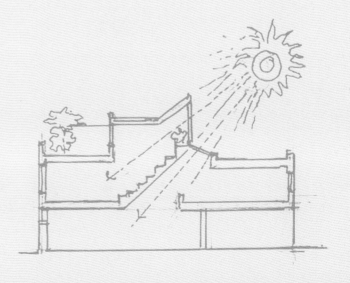

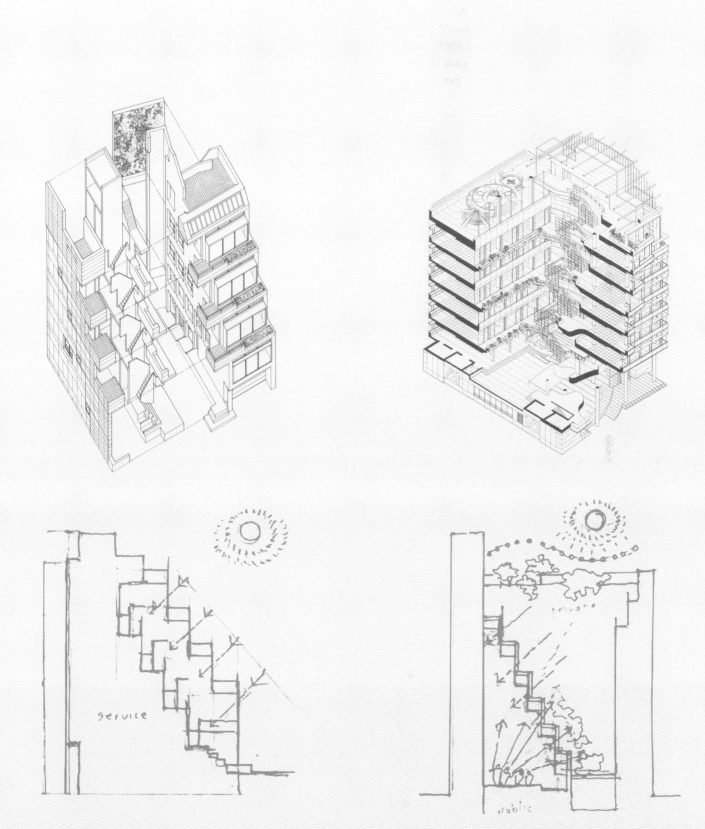

service

private

public

Pacific Center for the Media Arts
Hawaii Loa College
Kaneohe, Hawaii
1986

Opposite The site was dramatic topographically, part convex part concave which we used to separate public functions and academic ones. The Art Department courtyard focused uphill at mountain peaks and the public gathering for the theater occupied the valley and the entry.

A multilevel bridge crosses the valley joining the two sides while a circulation ring gives access to performance gardens set in the hillside. This also joined the existing buildings to this complex and a proposed next site.

In September 1985, Hawaii Loa College in Oahu announced an open international competition for the new Pacific Center for the Media Arts. I entered the competition over the end-of-year break. Architect Kinya Maruyama, who was visiting from Japan, joined us part-time and in three weeks had a bold entry. The purpose was to demonstrate our ability to design for the arts in an inspirational way. Winning this was a big surprise! I visited the campus, gave talks, met alumni, and reviewed our design ideas.

Early Years in the United States

Unfortunately, and to the surprise of the sponsors of the competition, this project never got built. There was not enough money to build the project and the school's president was terminated for fiscal irresponsibility.

The program had very public functions including an enclosed stepped theater, a black box theater, outdoor amphitheater, cafe, and lobby area. The teaching components included several arts classrooms and outdoor teaching spaces, which made use

of the topography and allowed separation of academic spaces by level from the public. We also made a bridge that crossed the valley to link the existing facilities with future proposed extensions. We were committed to work with the form of the land which was spectacular and viewed the whole complex as a verdant tropical garden.

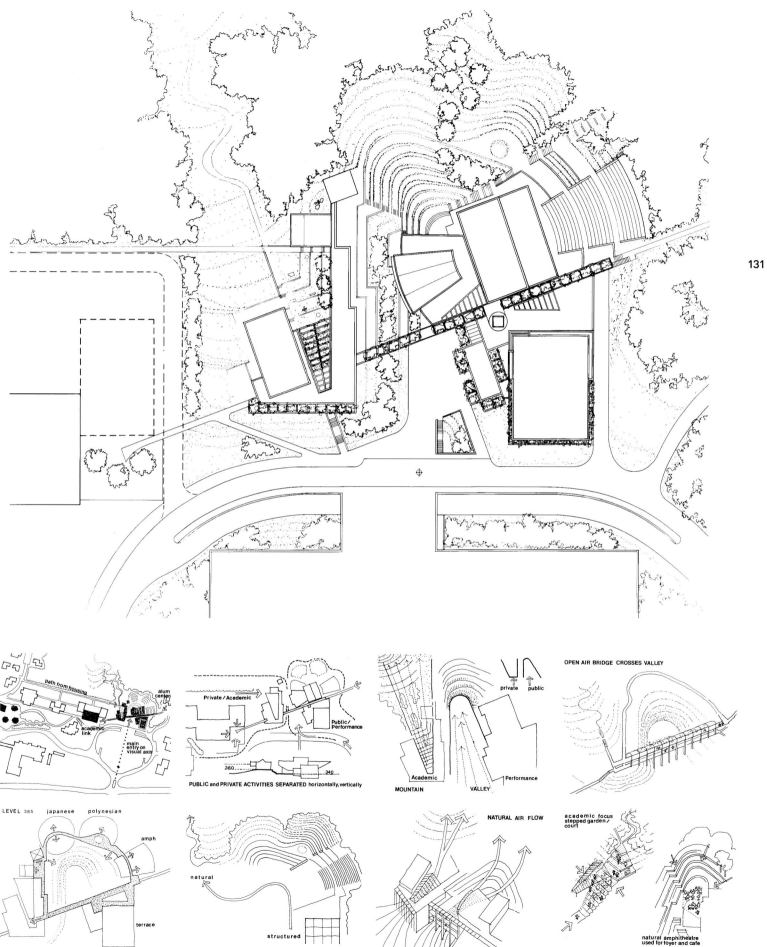

path from housing

alum center

academic link

main entry on visual axis

Private / Academic

Public / Performance

PUBLIC and PRIVATE ACTIVITIES SEPARATED horizontally, vertically

private   public

OPEN AIR BRIDGE CROSSES VALLEY

Academic

MOUNTAIN   VALLEY   Performance

LEVEL 385   japanese   polynesian

amph

terrace

natural

structured

NATURAL AIR FLOW

academic focus
stepped garden /
court

natural amphitheatre
used for foyer and cafe

Pacific Center for the Media Arts

132

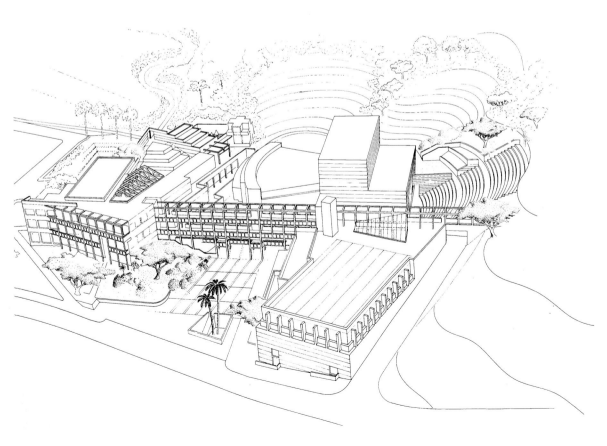

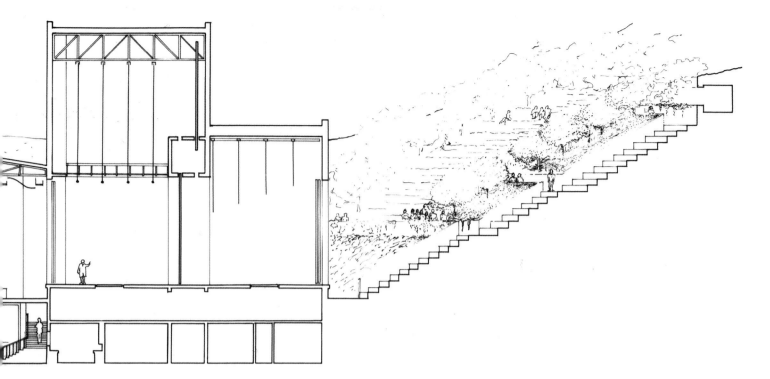

Above The indoor theater and outdoor amphitheater share the indoor stage and back stage functions. The potential size of the audience in this remote location plus the unpredictable weather made this program questionable.

Albright College Center for the Arts
Reading, Pennsylvania
1985-90

I was approached by Albright College in Reading, Pennsylvania, to be interviewed for an extension and renovations to their spaces for the arts. This was a competitive process and I had just won the international competition for the Pacific Center for the Media Arts in Oahu, Hawaii. We got the contract and served as design architects, while bringing on board Jacobs Wyper as executive architects. Encouraged by the arts director, we applied for an arts grant to include an artist on the team as well. After a series of studio visits, I chose Mary Miss, who was working with landscapes in spatially interesting ways.

Key to the design for this project was the creation of an entry space to the campus as well as to the Center for the Arts. This became the intellectual focus of our arts collaboration. The new building was to be located on a part of the campus with several buildings of different ages, including an old house which was set geometrically at odds with the other buildings.

Our design created an entry into the complex through a circular space, bringing the old house into the composition and allowing the pathways from this point to splay out at different angles. Mary Miss had been exploring circles that locationally shifted centers, which was a concept we used here. The entry space has a lower circle that looks like a clock mechanism referencing the passage of time. I added a shade canopy, designed by structural engineer Nori Imagawa from Tokyo, which shifts the oculi off-center in the spirit of the gestures below. The shadow of the roof moves throughout the day, expanding the experiential impact of the entire space. The building has a second floor with a walkway that surrounds this, offering another way to view the artifact. The circular motif expands out into the quadrangle where steps and seating create an amphitheater.

The entry circle joins the art studios and the gallery which can be accessed from this space. From here a major stair links to the existing theater on the second floor as well as parts of the campus upslope. The stair passes through the glass facade from inside to outside, joining the amphitheater to the lobby. On the first floor new spaces were added for music practice rooms.

This entry building with an arts emphasis changed the image of the campus stressing the importance of the creative arts and this college as an inventive place for the liberal arts.

Early Years in the United States

135

Albright College Center for the Arts

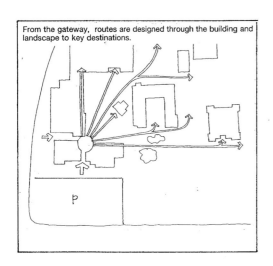

From the gateway, routes are designed through the building and landscape to key destinations.

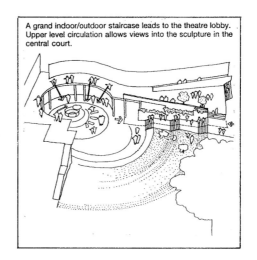

A grand indoor/outdoor staircase leads to the theatre lobby. Upper level circulation allows views into the sculpture in the central court.

136

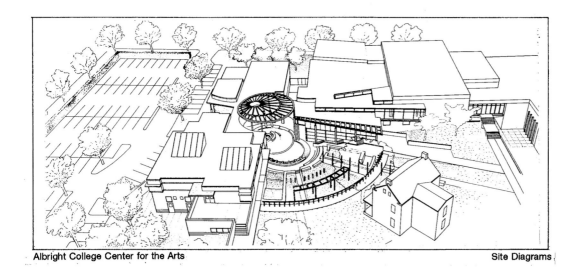

Albright College Center for the Arts   Site Diagrams

Above The Center for the Arts shapes a new formal entry to the campus, and identifies routes from this center.

The defined space gives entry to three separate programs: the new art studios, the Friedman gallery in new space and the reconfigured music and theater program.

Artist Mary Miss responded to the roof canopy's offset oculus with a complex form cut into the earth.

Early Years in the United States

137

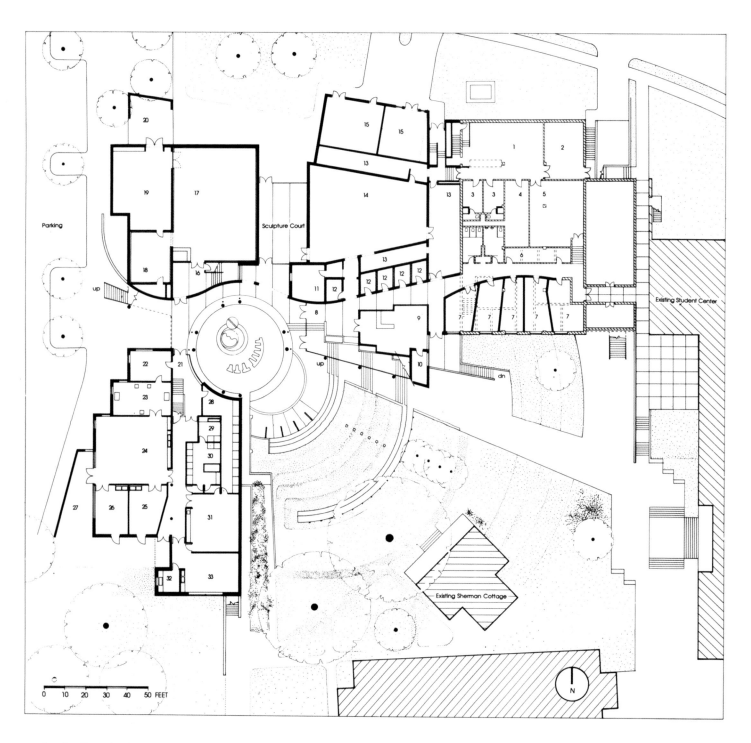

Parking

Sculpture Court

Existing Student Center

up

up

dn

Existing Sherman Cottage

0 10 20 30 40 50 FEET

N

Renovation of Campus Center Theater

1 Rehearsal Room
2 Mechanical Room
3 Dressing Room
4 Make-up Room
5 Costume Shop
6 Storage
7 Music Faculty Studio

Theater and Music Facilities

8 Foyer
9 Reception
10 Print Room
11 Electronic Piano Laboratory
12 Practice Room
13 Storage
14 Music Rehearsal Room
15 Mechanical

Freedman Art Gallery

16 Foyer and Stair
17 Main Gallery
18 Small Works Gallery
19 Gallery Workshop
20 Delivery Yard

Art Department

21 Foyer
22 Faculty Office
23 Wood Workshop
24 Sculpture Studio
25 Ceramic Studio
26 Metal Studio
27 Court
28 Film Studio
29 Color Darkroom
30 B+W Darkroom
31 Classroom
32 Fume Room
33 Graphics Studio

138

Albright College Center for the Arts

Early Years in the United States

Left An indoor-outdoor stair passes through the glass almost seamlessly joining the access to the theater lobby and the stepped garden.

Institute of
Contemporary Art
University of Pennsylvania
Philadelphia, Pennsylvania
1989

142

Office level can overlook upper gallery

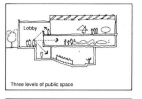

Three levels of public space

Visual link to sculpture garden from lobby

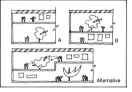

Alternative

Garden can link to upper gallery and other roofs

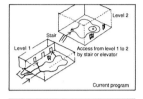

Access from level 1 to 2 by stair or elevator

Current program

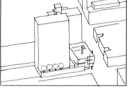

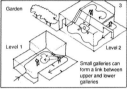

Small galleries can form a link between upper and lower galleries

The site for the Institute of Contemporary Art (ICA) overlooks the intersection where the University of Pennsylvania Campus meets the city of Philadelphia. The area is small and functionally challenged. Previously, it was used as the handicapped entry space to student dormitories. It is overshadowed by the adjacent dormitory towers, underlain by subway tunnels, plus dormitory windows open onto part of the site perimeter. The building footprint is very constrained, limiting solutions to issues like vehicular access and servicing.

The building is organized to maximize visibility on street edges and increase its apparent size. The entry at the corner of 36th and Sansom Streets is very prominent and the double-height lobby encourages entry. The site had two distinct zones for building. The gallery spaces could be located along 36th Street, where there was enough space to construct a large cubic volume, while along Sansom Street, the lobby spaces could occur on two visible levels. Along the wall of the dormitory block, one floor of service spaces was possible with a sculpture garden above. Service access was limited to the end of the sculpture garden.

The basic diagram of space distribution was clear. The galleries would be divided across two levels, including one quadrant of thirty feet high. Visitors would access the spaces from lobbies at both levels, which included a large elevator. Since there would be no windows on most of the 36th Street facade, we used a glazed ramp from the lower floor to the upper level to display art works and give visitors a view of the campus. This became an important display opportunity for artists, and it prominently features the ICA logo.

From the corner entry, a large splayed stair gives focus to the upper lounge and sculpture garden beyond. The lobby has a desk, some display areas, and gives access to the main galleries. There is also a meeting room which is open for use by the public. The tallest gallery is in the north west corner, surrounded by thirteen-foot-high galleries. On the second floor the southwest corner has another tall gallery lit from clerestories with flexible shading. The gallery spaces are simple with clean walls for showing art, but also spatially diverse linking double-height spaces together and deliberately securing more intimate viewing opportunities. Structure and services are exposed, and the space has hosted both elaborate constructions and more traditional work.

The second floor lobby leads to the sculpture garden and cafe. A projected bay window

Opposite Early
sketches used in the
interview show how
this very tight site
could be used. Key to
this was the location of
the galleries, the entry
at the corner of the
intersecting streets,
and the low-rise
service building with
a potential sculpture
garden on the roof.

143

Institute of Contemporary Art

facing Sansom Street gives views back to campus. The third floor is dedicated to staff offices, archives, and work space. On the ground floor, a loading area and shop is provided back of the meeting room for preparation for shows.

The transparency of this building ran counter to structures on campus. Most are made of brick, and they seldom invite entry. There was a lively discussion about the chosen materials, such as the metal panels, the extent of glazing, and color. The limestone base did make reference to the materiality of the surrounding campus. Finally, since this was the Institute of Contemporary Art, not an academic building, the formal discussion subsided and work proceeded. Over the years, ICA directors have given different foci to the use of space, which has proved to be flexible to different forms of subdivision. During the recent pandemic, when the building was closed to the public, the transparency was exploited to showcase the work of artist Na Kim. Viewed through the ramp on 34th Street, the double-height glazed entry and the windows on Sansom Street, the playful graphics transformed the building and re-engaged public viewing.

Above, Right
Transparency was an
important concept
to avoid a black
box concept. Along
Sansom Street stairs
to the upper lobby and
roof terrace are visible
through continuous
glazing.

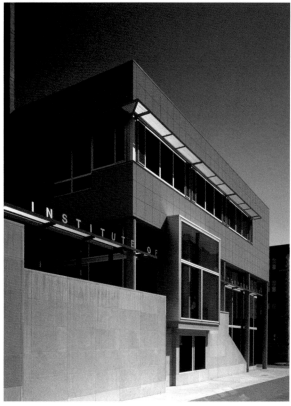

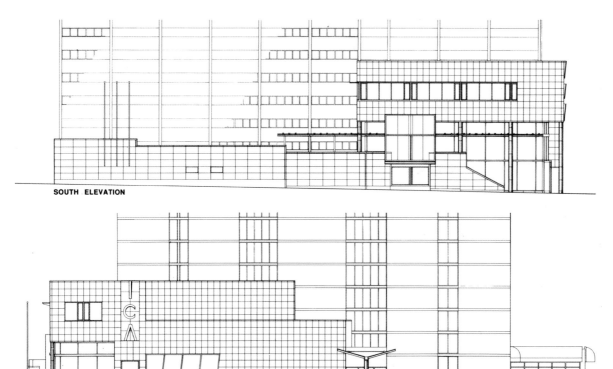

SOUTH ELEVATION

146

EAST ELEVATION

Left Gallery sizes, heights, and light conditions were stacked on two levels. The ramp between gallery levels becomes a window to the street revealing visitors in the museum who can look out, often showing part of the current exhibition content. The landing window was designed for display.

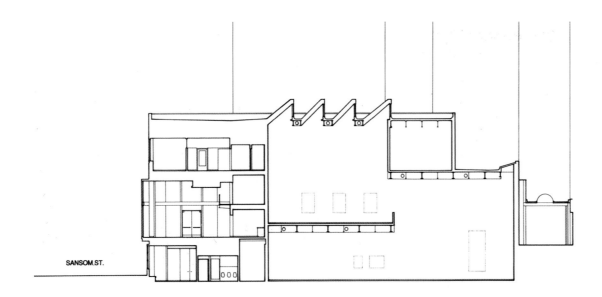

SANSOM.ST.

Early Years in the United States

148

149

Early Years in the United States

Opposite While the museum was closed during the Covid-19 pandemic, curators commissioned graphic artist Na Kim to use the transparency of the building to display works that could engage the public.

Reflections
A Focus on the Arts

While the Pacific Center for the Media Arts, the Albright College Center for the Arts, and the ICA Philadelphia were very different in scope and ambition, these proposals highlight arts education and the inspirational quality that arts reflection can give us. In each case public and private experiences needed to be calibrated since the public was always invited to be included. Our challenge was to create spaces and places where individual creativity or reflection could take place naturally. Display of art in a variety of forms was essential.

Winning the Pacific Center for the Media Arts competition was very exciting and showcased the transparency of the building on a difficult site topographically. The location offered great views, challenging cross sections and functional complexity. The college was relatively modest programmatically which surprised us given the ambitious and exciting academic program. Given the somewhat remote location the public outreach was very ambitious with functions, such as a cafe and dining facility needed to support visitors. This also included a large indoor theater, which would share a stage with an outdoor amphitheater. To allow for the best public experience at ground level, we located all teaching facilities on the upper levels of the site.

More emphasis could have been given programmatically to their unusual multicultural teaching program. The teaching spaces, which were set in garden rooms around the hillside, including the stepped garden room at the center of the arts complex, would have been unique and possibly inspirational to artists if built.

For Albright College the public focus was on shaping a thoughtful entry sequence. The client saw the design of the new Center for the Arts as an opportunity to engage visitors in an art-focused entry space that changed public perception of the College. The circular space serves as a welcoming courtyard but also creates the origin point from which several routes cross the campus. At the center of this, Mary Miss sculpted the ground with a time-themed piece shaded by a complementary roof structure, designed by Nori Imagawa. This space extended into stepped sitting areas in the garden and has been used for public events. A paired indoor-outdoor staircase linked this entry space to the theater lobby and communal facilities beyond.

The ICA Philadelphia located at the intersection of campus routes and city streets, needed to be very compact. Giving this building a public presence and inviting visitors in was an essential concept. Our solution to give visibility to this black box museum from the street was to create a window on a ramp joining upper and lower galleries. The window shape is unusual. Here, art can be displayed and visitors in the galleries can view the street below and be viewed by passersby. The two-level lobby, entered at this intersection, is very dramatic with full height glass to the sidewalk. The main stair, which leads to the upper galleries, creates views through to the garden on the second floor. A bay window juts over the small pedestrian street to give views of the campus beyond. The ICA'S open policy, allowing free access to their galleries, perfectly aligned with our desire to open the museum spatially and visibly to the public.

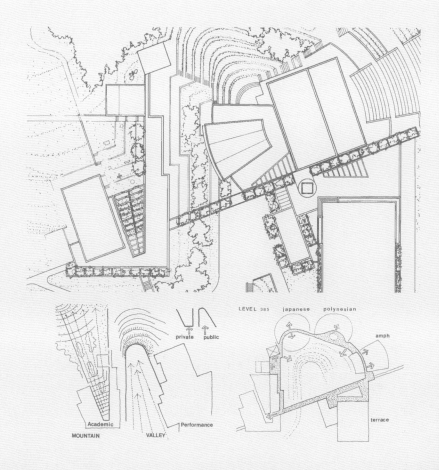

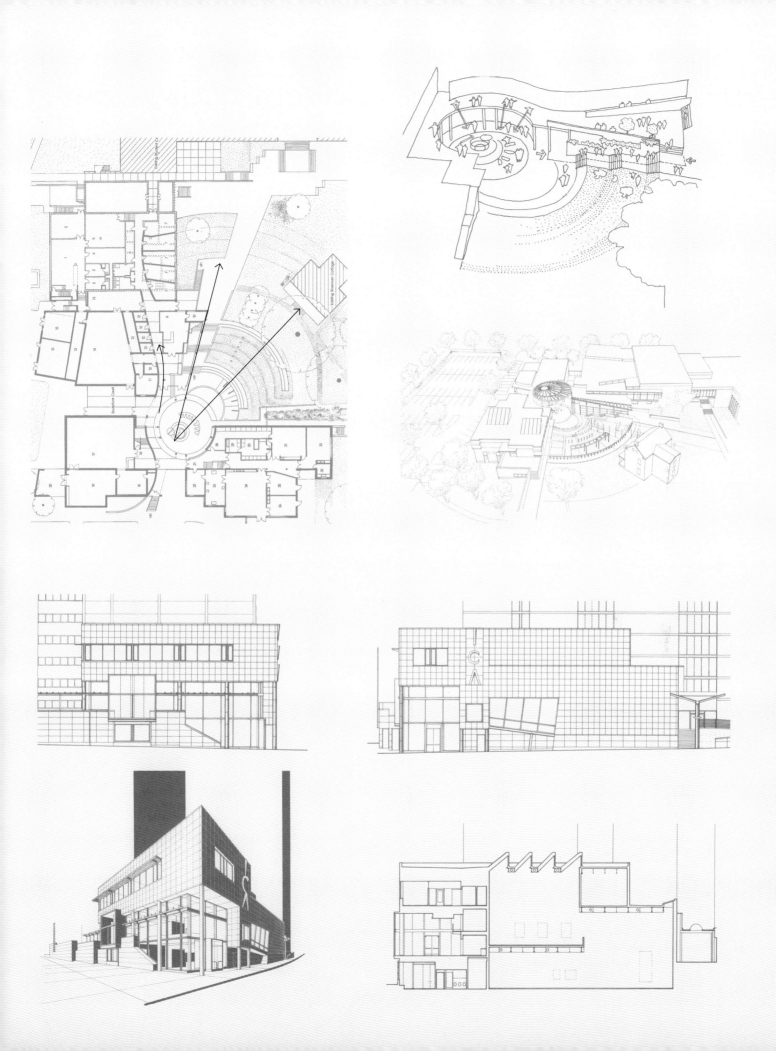

Franklin LaBrea
Family Housing
Los Angeles, California
1989

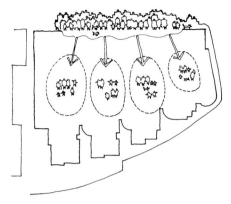

The project creates four small communities of approximately eleven households, small enough in scale for the inhabitants to know each other. A representative cross section of households is included in each grouping.

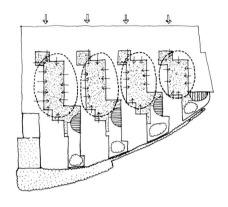

The community shares a series of common spaces including the garage, laundry/lounge, play area and covered porch.

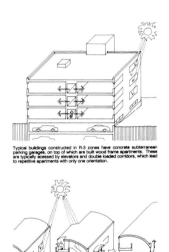

Typical buildings constructed in R-3 zones have concrete subterranean parking garages, on top of which are built wood frame apartments. These are typically accessed by elevators and double loaded corridors, which lead to repetitive apartments with only one orientation.

We propose to construct several small, naturally-lit garages with courtyards above providing access to house-like units. Dwellings have dual orientations and through ventilation, with individualized entry conditions.

In 1989, when the Museum of Contemporary Art and the Community Redevelopment Agency of Los Angeles announced an international competition for an affordable forty-unit housing project, I had just won a competition to build affordable housing in Camden, New Jersey and I had come third in a two-phase competition to build 450 infill units in Harlem, New York. We knew that we were considered eligible for this competition. Pre-selected firms with housing experience were invited to meet potential developers in the Museum of Contemporary Art boardroom. We each gave short presentations on our work. The developers voted on which firms they saw as eligible. There were several chosen including ourselves but

few developers were willing to join this effort. In the end only three firms signed on and we were selected to join the competition. We were at a disadvantage as a Philadelphia firm and were paired with the lesser-known development team. These developers had only recently met each other and had never worked together; one was in finance and the other was a builder. We were also assigned a Los Angeles-based representative to work with us.

The competition was formulated as a part of the exhibition *Blueprints for Modern Living*, sponsored by the Los Angeles Museum of Contemporary Art. The show focused on the "Case Study" house program run by *Arts &*

Architecture Magazine years prior. The exhibit, with a design by Craig Hodgetts, took place with much applause. The competition projects would form a postscript, updating innovative thinking from that time.

The competition was to consider the urgent problem of high-density affordable housing on a Los Angeles site. The program consisted of forty units of housing of different sizes for households with low and moderate income, eligible for financial assistance. It required parking for one vehicle per bedroom, as well as laundry and lounge facilities, playgrounds, sitting and picnic areas.

Our scheme won the design competition and

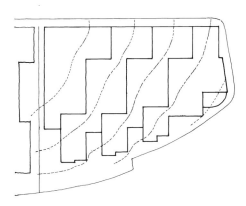

The parking structures step downward with the natural grade to the South and East. The platforms above form the basis for the housing grouping.

Opposite With a concept of creating a village rather than an apartment building, smaller groupings of families share space including a community porch. Smaller scaled garages have easy access to ground level gardens. Laundry lounges are placed next to play areas for observation.

155

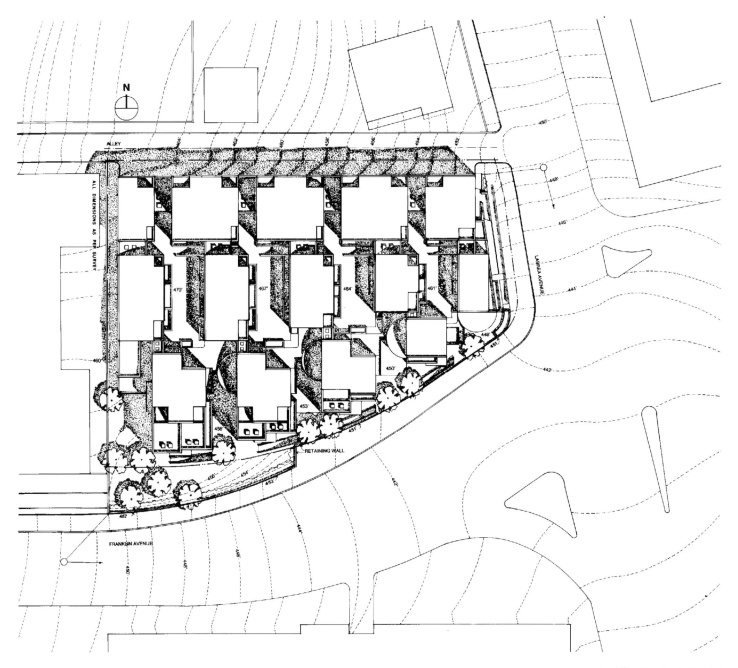

Franklin LaBrea Family Housing

Early Years in the United States

Opposite A change of use in level of the site creates taller living rooms with dining above, and a back balcony. The upper courtyard two-bedroom houses have two floors and one floor on the lower courtyard. This allows for related family members to be linked to the upper level but be independent or be a three-bedroom unit.

Left All units have private entry gardens with a weather protected front door. They share well planted spaces including a community porch

Franklin LaBrea Family Housing

was shown in the exhibition. Unfortunately, the winning developers were later discredited financially. The museum had to look for another developer to build the project. The council member of the district wanted this built as designed. This selection process took years, but Thomas Safran & Associates were finally designated as developers, on the condition that we would work with them to refine our design based on their experience with affordable development in Los Angeles. In addition, in the time that had elapsed since the competition, a new edition of the building code was published, allowing greater height for wood-framed construction and making some of the strategies we had adopted in the competition unnecessary.

From the beginning we wished to develop high density low-rise housing organized around garden courtyards with good ventilation and dual orientations, offering private outdoor space for each unit. In stark contrast to the tall surrounding properties which featured central corridor access, one orientation, stacked units on many floors, and underground parking, our scheme would feel more like an urban village.

We wished to reduce the numbers of grouped units to encourage families to know each other and collectively oversee the safety of their environment. We avoided corridors, all units have deck access and private patios. Included in each grouping, we designed sitting porches with barbecue facilities and downslope city views overlooking play areas.

The site slopes gently to the south and east allowing house groupings to be separated by a half floor in section; larger units have split levels with taller living rooms. The dining area overlooks the living space and opens to a balcony. The combined space feels very generous. The predominant unit type, a townhouse, crosses courtyards with entries to both levels. At the lower level a one-bedroom flat can be occupied as an independent unit or join the upper level two-bedroom townhouse for multi-generational households.

The stepped site also creates better light conditions, lowering the eastern building and opening up mountain views to the townhouses. The original proposal used ramps to separate courtyard levels and the entry to the complex. This was eliminated in the built scheme. Handicapped units are placed at the garden level with easy access to parking and common facilities such as laundry rooms and lounges.

Aesthetically, we wanted this complex not to be identified as subsidized housing, hence the curved roofs and lavishly planted public spaces. The garden area facing Franklin Avenue was created to be a tall green screen and sound buffer. The complex can be viewed from the street as large houses with curved balconies set in well landscaped gardens.

Franklin LaBrea Family Housing

Franklin LaBrea Family Housing

Reflections
Affordable housing provision is key to urban living

In Cape Town, a significant self-housed population occupies flat lands susceptible to winter flooding. My family was involved in aiding these distressed households by creating affordable units. Much of my teaching, starting at the University of Cape Town, also focused on housing, particularly affordable typologies. At Rice University my role was to create courses and studios that explored the topic both as a design problem but also as a social issue.

For my practice, Franklin LaBrea Family Housing was the first built affordable housing project. This project led to other commissions and, ultimately, affordable housing became an area of expertise in our San Francisco office with built work both nationally and outside of the United States.

Housing supply is a serious global issue, and the rise of "the right to housing" movement was an inevitable step promoted by successive UN Housing Conferences. Most nations have pledged to support this concept even as they struggle to do so economically. The notable exception is the United States of America, which has rigorously refused to do so. This growing issue by now includes middle-income households in many contexts. Using "Design Workshops" as an international teaching tool, I have continued to work with community groups to solve seemingly intractable housing problems.

By the time I first met Adèle in 1978, I felt I already knew her. Former students and faculty from South Africa, who admired her talent and passion for architecture, had been telling me for years that as two women pushing the boundaries in our field we were certain to become immediate friends. They were right, and we quickly became not only life-long friends but professional and academic colleagues and design collaborators.

While Adèle's teaching and practice has spanned continents and cultures, a through line is her intense interest in the idea of live-work space. I learned this as we embarked on a project together in Boston to convert a former leather warehouse into a series of multi-level lofts for ourselves. It was the first of a series of live-work spaces Adèle built for herself in each phase and location of her life—from Boston to San Francisco. These spaces became her personal laboratory of experiment. A microcosm of her work, these projects demonstrate a common core of design elements—section-driven, fluid vertical space, and interwoven interior and exterior landscape space.

Beach Street, Boston, Massachusetts

I had accompanied Adèle in her search for a living space in Boston in 1979 when she began her appointment at Harvard. We found an unrenovated former leather warehouse, and although I wasn't looking for a new place to live, the idea of developing the building together with a small group was compelling. Suddenly, I found myself delighted to be imagining a project with my remarkable friend. The design for the Beach Street loft began over my dining table, and it was then that I first appreciated Adèle's spatial genius. She proposed the creation of four two-story lofts fitted together like a puzzle, each with a double-height space facing big south windows and with access to the roof. For her own unit, she built an extraordinary stepped terrace of spaces rising to the roof with living space below and work space above leading to a roof patio.

Naudain Street, Philadelphia, Pennsylvania

The paint was hardly dry on the Beach Street lofts when Adèle was invited to be chair of architecture at the University of Pennsylvania. Undaunted by the change, she set about finding an industrial space in Philadelphia where she could continue her experiment in creating a new kind of live-work environment. She found a suitable property and— retaining the one-story structure for studio, rental unit, and garage—she superimposed two more floors with terraced vertical space facing a lush garden. The expansive light-filled space was a breath of fresh air in the narrow row house and light industrial environment of Naudain Street. The notion of a combined living and working environment had made another step forward.

Zoe Street, San Francisco, California

In the 1990s, when Adèle moved to San Diego and then San Francisco, we kept in touch despite the distance. She told me she had found an unreinforced concrete printing/warehouse structure she intended to convert into several lofts and a studio. By then I was unsurprised. This was a challenge of another sort, and there were many anxious calls about the long process of reinforcing the structure, making it compliant for seismic requirements. Undaunted, Adèle persisted in developing a series of live-work lofts, adding twenty feet in height (the maximum allowed) to the existing twenty-foot-high structure. In an exuberant variant on prior spatial ideas, Adèle stacked the double-height living space above the studio space, all open to a large palm-filled garden.

Village Street, Somerville, MA

Adèle returned to the Boston area in 2004 to accept the deanship at MIT's School of Architecture and Planning and, of course, planned the next in her series of experiments. True to form, Adèle discovered a former foundry in Somerville, near to Cambridge, which had been largely destroyed, discouraging development by anyone of ordinary imagination. Perfect for Adèle. The outer walls remained and two small enclosures at opposite ends of the footprint contained minimal artist's living space and an ad hoc children's theater. Once again, her anxious calls to me about discovered existing conditions that threatened the project were punctuated with ecstatic reports of the spaces emerging. Adèle restored the outer walls defining the enclave, built a double-height living space at one end of the property, and a two-level studio and apartment at the other. In between she created a trellised magical garden overflowing with flowering trees, plants, and furnished for outdoor living. The fluid vertical space in both structures recalled her earlier lofts, but the dominance of the garden as the force uniting the whole emerged as a fundamental priority.

Wall Street, Gloucester, MA

It was a cold late autumn or early winter day, as I recall, when Adèle asked me to visit a site with her in the seaside town of Gloucester that she was considering for development of two or three weekend houses for herself and others. The site, with a stunning view of the Gloucester's working harbor, was a wall of sheer granite rising some fifty or sixty feet above the street. At a glance, it was unbuildable. Adèle, of course, was energized by the challenge. The hurdles of gaining abutters' acceptance, utility permits, and construction complexities were all overcome in time, and Adèle once again created a beautiful retreat and workplace for herself as well as a second two-story unit for sale. The two houses step down the steep slope in an echo of the many stepped terraces Adèle had created in her former lofts, and like the previous experiments the dynamic spaces are interwoven with gardens and a spectacular view.

Adèle occupies center stage wherever she stands. Her exuberant personality, her outsized talent, and her deep care for the human experience have made her a widely acknowledged teacher and designer. For myself, I value her as a committed friend, an inspired colleague, and a sister on the frontier of our chosen profession.

In 1985, I was in the M.Arch program at the University of Pennsylvania, while Adèle was the chair-person. She had transformed the program and created an enlightening environment for architectural education at Penn. She brought her knowledge as an architect with international experience to the classroom, and pushed us to discover our own creativity and develop our skills.

Students were encouraged to take overseas summer studio to explore different cultures, broadening their knowledge and insight. Classmates went the Soviet Union, India, Mexico, France, and Italy, while I was selected to go to Colombia with Adèle to work on the design of the new city of Lerida to house the survivors of the tragedy in Amero, the city destroyed by a volcanic eruption. Adèle insisted on sensitivity to the culture and humility on the part of the design, which had to be affordable and use local technology. Our work was greatly appreciated and much of it was developed further and built. This experience was a highlight of my architectural studies.

From 2008 to 2010, the "MIT+SCU international workshop" was held in Shih Chien University (SCU) in Taiwan. Students and faculty from both MIT and SCU—mostly from the architecture program but also from urban studies, the Media Lab, industrial design, media communication, and fashion design—came together, forming an exciting cross disciplinary creative workshop which produced astonishing works and sparked interest and excitement for the reviewers.

Adèle was the commander among all. Students and faculty were inspired by her energy, charisma, and passion for teaching.

A Magic Treasure Box Maker
In 1986, Penn students from the Colombia studio were invited to a party in Adèle's home. We entered through a small obscure door from a deserted alley. Through the passage there was a workshop, a museum-like space for living and dining upstairs, another spacious living space on the top floor with an outdoor deck overlooking a swimming pool. The students marveled at the neat studio, colorful wood carved snakes on a stepped wall, reflecting lights from swimming pool, delicious seafood soup from the kitchen—a string of joyful spaces.

In 2008, I visited Adèle's home in Boston, a unparalleled palace she renovated from a ruined theater. A marvelous double-height living space, a unique studio, and a magnificent courtyard garden in between. I was entranced by the splendid sunlight, trees, blossom flowers, art collections, books, music, friends, cats, parrot, cuisine flowing through the house. Adèle certainly is a magical expert in conjuring up the lively spirit from opaque ruins.

All the students from the programs Adèle created in academia,
all the inhabitants living in the housing she designed,
all the people who worked in or passed through buildings she built,
all the friends who have gathered around her...
all are inspired and benefitted from her magic.
I was lucky to have her as my role model and mentor.

Ann Yu-Chien

Reminiscing about my time spent in the United States very early on in my career brings back such fond memories of my dear friend and colleague Adèle Santos. Years ago, we taught together at San Diego and Philadelphia as well as at Rice if I am not mistaken.

Adèle's perceptive way of approach to resolve design problems made me realize what a great teacher she is. She would be forthright with her opinions and yet encouraging at the same time. That I believe is Adèle's greatest strength. An insightful and wise teacher I would say!

Teaching together with her has been some of the most memorable times for me and what connected us throughout was our interest in affordable housing. Such great memories of dialogue, discussions, and celebrations, and I hope the two of us can someday conduct a studio together!

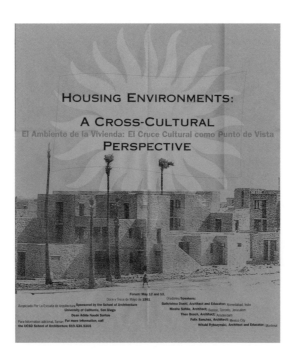

Balkrishna Doshi

Working with Adèle for the last thirty years I have seen how collaboration and team building are among her greatest skills. Adèle trusts her collaborators but has a way of leading the design process with an inspiring idea that makes the work hers. In the studio, Adèle assigns a high level of responsibility to each project manager for the day-to-day progress of projects, and then tracks the progress of each by circulating among the desks, sketching and discussing the details under consideration. One of the joys of working with Adèle is hearing her stories; in that spirit I offer a few, starting in Philadelphia:

For my first project with her, the Tsukasa-Cho office building, that which came to be called "Tokyo Fantasia," Adèle had started with project with a strong idea that caught the client's interest: a two-sided atrium that has a public component and a portion reserved for occupants of the building. Carrying on a dialog with the collaborating architects and structural engineer in Tokyo via faxed diagrams we determined the code constraints and structural system, and with a few months of work I was on a plane to Tokyo to present the schematic design. Our Japanese collaborators were fascinated by Adèle's ability to conceive of space and then shape the structure of the building around it; to start with the aspirations rather than the constraints of a project.

The Franklin La Brea family housing project in Los Angeles was pivotal to this era of the studio. After an intense short-listing process that catalyzed a reorganization of the office archive and collation of a new portfolio, we were selected to prepare a design for the competition. The project itself became a statement of principles coalescing Adèle's academic housing research with the realities of building codes and construction techniques.

Adèle and I traveled to Los Angeles to see the site and meet the developer we were to be teamed with to ultimately build the project if we won the competition. As we visited their existing projects, a vision began to form in Adèle's mind that the key to the project was to reinvent the relationship between the apartments and the required parking. Some creative interpretation of the Los Angeles Building Code set us on a path to create a series of small garages rather than the large "podium" that conventionally preconditioned the form of housing at the time.

The effort to produce the competition entry, which was to be exhibited at LA MOCA and included ten large boards of drawings, two large-scale models, and a narrative booklet further illustrated Adèle's ability to organize and motivate a team. While teaching at the University of Pennsylvania, she knew some of the of the most talented recent graduates, so she offered short contracts to an exceptional group to produce the required material, with a regular staff architect in charge of each main part of the labor. Meanwhile, Adèle sat down and drew the fifty narrative diagrams that tell the story of the project. The diagramming process had been used in previous competition projects but came into focus with the Franklin La Brea project since we had to explain a very complex thought process to the jury.

The studio was filled with activity and Adèle kept everyone motivated with good food and good stories. The diagrams were compelling to the jury, and we won the competition. This process was to repeat several times over the years, and the ideas formulated in the intense process of the competition continue to inform the housing work of the office.

Getting the project built required a feat of endurance, another of Adèle's defining traits. The developers we had been teamed with were not able to fulfill the financial obligations for the project, so the MOCA organization asked another developer to step in. The new developer had no understanding of the concept of the project and had their own architectural staff make several changes that would have made the project completely conventional. When the revised scheme was sent to us for approval, Adèle rejected it and was able to convince the MOCA curators that a new developer should be pursued.

After many discussions, Thomas Safran and Associates agreed to build the project, but only on the condition that we rework it to meet their programmatic needs. In the meantime, the building code had gone through its three-year update cycle, which allowed us to keep the concept generative idea of the project intact but accommodate the larger apartments required. We teamed up with Los Angeles-based Carde Ten Architects to complete the project, seven years after the initial competition win.

The Franklin La Brea project tracked the evolution of the office over a ten-year period: though the competition was done while we were in Philadelphia, the project was ultimately completed after the studio had moved to California. The move allowed us to be more involved in the construction documents and administration and being on-site deepened our understanding of California construction techniques that contributed to the development of the firm as we designed more housing in the state.

In Philadelphia, Adèle had also developed a connection to the arts community, which lead to our selection as architects for the Institute of Contemporary Art at the University of Pennsylvania. The project had a complicated background with a previous scheme made unworkable by budget overruns so we were tasked to work quickly and to deliver the project through a design-build process in which the design contract by the builder.

Adèle produced a series of diagrams during the interview process for the project that showed how the ICA's goals could be accomplished, and those became the guiding principle as we developed the project in an intense process that led to a start of construction within six months of the initial commission.

The fast-track process forced our hand on some decisions, for example an early programmatic decision to condition the lobby to the same environmental criteria as the galleries required a tinted glass that is darker than we would have liked, whereas a more circumspect process might have allowed for reevaluation of the program in light of the HVAC requirements, once it was clear that the visual connection to the street was more important for the lobby than the ability to display delicate art work there.

The ICA opened on time, just as Adèle and I left for San Diego, in retrospect making the building a parting gift to the city. The success of the intense design and construction process gave us both the confidence and the portfolio to pursue more complex projects such as the Yerba Buena Gardens Children's Center and the Perris Civic Center.

Work in Japan continued after our move to San Diego. A key project from that time was the Rokko Island competition, a design-build competition for 3,000 dwellings and associated services on a human-made island off the coast of Kobe. We were invited by the home builder Misawa to work with them to prepare their entry.

The generative idea for the project came from the large mounds of earth that were piled on the site to consolidate the fill from which the island was made. We proposed to sculpt the remaining fill into a hilly landscape and dubbed the project Green Hill Town. A significant design effort went into meeting the programmatic requirements including parking and compliance with the residential code that requires sunlight reach each living space for s specified number of hours each day, as we knew that the project had to get past a technical review committee before being seen by the competition jury.

As in other competition projects, there was a huge production effort required to prepare the drawings and models, but in the Rokko Island project the complexity of the design problem required a more diverse design team as well. Drawing on her simultaneous experience in formulating the multi-disciplinary curriculum at the UCSD School of Architecture, Adèle invited collaborators Ignacio Bunster and Laura Burnett from Wallace Roberts and Todd as landscape architects and new UCSD faculty member Susan Ubbelohde and her firm Loisos-Ubbelohde to work with us on landscape design and to joined the team to consult on energy and sustainability. The effort concluded with a whirlwind trip to Tokyo where Ricardo Rabines and I worked with the team in the Misawa office for a week finalizing the drawings, cost estimates and models for submission.

Although our team did not win the competition, the design proposals caught the attention of the housing authorities in Kitakyushu in southern Japan, who were interested in replacing outdated public housing in their city. They commissioned us to develop a master plan for several sites and then to design the buildings for one of them, a project that became Kadota Housing.

Beginning 2005 we had another opportunity to develop the ideas initially proposed in the Franklin La Brea project. Carde Ten Architects asked us to collaborate with them to pursue a project in Ventura, CA California, sponsored by Artspace Projects. The project was to be the first new affordable housing in Ventura in many years, one of the first to implement a newly develop form-based zoning code and was to be designed in a community process with a group of artists who would ultimately live in the project. The biggest challenge became convincing the design review committee to approve the project, as they had a wide purview and the committee represented differing viewpoints.

By this time Adèle was at MIT, while I managed the office in San Francisco. She would fly to the West Coast for design charrettes and then we would go together to Ventura for major presentations. As had been the case 20 years earlier, a clearly defined set of design concepts, set out in a series of narrative diagrams brought the client, artists, and regulators along on the design journey and ensured the project was approved and ultimately constructed.

Like Franklin La Brea, the project had a pause in the middle of the design process when Artspace reevaluated the project and decided to step out as developers. Fortunately, the project manager was able to start a new development company, PLACE, and take over for as the developer. The revised project, now called Working Artists Ventura (WAV) had to be adjusted to match available funding opportunities and was expanded to include not only the original program of affordable live-work spaces but also supportive housing units both for families and for transitional age youth and thirteen for-sale market rate condominium units.

Treating design as a journey has enabled Adèle to guide her projects through often challenging situations. The process of diagramming combined with the collaborative approach that welcomes differing perspectives roots each project deeply in its context while simultaneously making the ideas embodied in the buildings relevant to the continued development of architecture a wider discussion.

Had Adèle, whose Brobdingnagian appetites and ferocious work/pleasure compass spun nearly every event into a frenzy, been appointed Master of the Universe, she may have aspired to that, but been willing to settle for the Galaxy. Because behind the larger-than-life personality I knew, there lurked a practical, no-nonsense leader whose approach to everything—cuisine, decor, personal adornment, architecture, and friendship—was super-scaled and unsullied by compromise of any sort. When our paths crossed, as they often did, it was often over a Close Encounters-scale mountain of shellfish, surrounded by a raft of smart and smarter faculty and students whose access to Adèle was a closely guarded perk.

In a life defined by the question "why not?" Adèle often applied her considerable creative gifts to the places she would call home. She moved crates of African statuary, bangles, and spears at a minute's notice from her Philadelphia digs to San Francisco, and finally to an abandoned foundry in Cambridge, along with her free-ranging parrot and a coterie of cats, where they would nestle among colorful tribal blankets thrown over brawny chairs in a Hellzapoppin' cloud of visual clamor.

Nothing about Adèle was small or cautious or careless. In her reign at the University of Pennsylvania's School of Architecture, she brought faculty from around the world, including Wolf D. Prix, Álvaro Siza, and Michael Sorkin, and old goodies like Aldo van Eyck, and treated them like visiting royalty, transferring her passion for their work to the students and framing their presence with baroque dinner parties, hearty laughter, and rowdy toasts. The resonance of those events spilled into the studios and lecture halls where students eagerly sought out those that Adèle had knighted. It was, in its way, a feast of ideas presented as a bouquet of creativity and world-changing architectural visions.

Adèle's architectural vision was rooted in Team 10. She had shaken off any early formalist tendencies by the time I met and worked with her. With her bravado and extraordinary persona, she would present profoundly humanistic work to clients, couched in a design language which avoided alignment with the isms of the day. Each project would emerge from her studio as a total surprise to those that knew her, bounding from her competition-winning apartments at Franklin and La Brea in Los Angeles to vaguely institutional modern at San Francisco's Moscone Center (with a merry-go-round, no less!) to a palatial residence in Japan.

As an architect, Adèle tells stories. Always attentive to space, events, and a flowing narrative, she is at her best in large-scale urban environments where the transitions from place to place can be transformed by a canopy, and the experience is in the journey rather than an imposing view of an imposing object. She designs comic-book style, directing attention to this or that view, often interspersing diagrams with the same hand, which I found irresistible. In her hands, such a fluid approach to the environment dispenses with "style" as an unnecessary crutch, focusing instead on knitting together satisfying spatial sequences with a special sauce of surprise, humor, and good manners that adds up to a profound knowledge of how people behave.

That same attitude pervades her teaching, which often dethrones stuffy academic protocols and plunges directly into the heart and the chemistry of teaching itself. In her leadership of a virgin architecture school at UC San Diego, she restructured the curriculum around short-term immersion in a particular subject, in which all students, regardless of grade level, were expected to participate in a charrette-style, high-impact, week-long session with an invited guest. Subject matter ranged across the conceptual spectrum, from obscure histories to avant-garde computing, which, at the time, had barely made it out of the labs, much less into the rusty halls of academia. In that, once again, Adèle's talent for turning conventions inside-out in search of new ways of building and learning was controversial, disruptive, but deeply meaningful.

There, I've said it. Adèle's approach to design is profoundly, positively, and admirably out of step with mainstream architecture. With her emphasis on experience rather than eye candy, her work must be visited in order to appreciate the depth of her humanity. Her projects tend to be contextual and inclusive, embracing the surroundings while illuminating them with a new, charismatic presence that, like her dinner parties, makes everything look good.

3

California

1989-95   University of California in San Diego
1996-04   UC Berkeley College of Environmental Design
1989-95   Practice: Adèle Naudé Santos and Associates in San Diego
1989-93   Practice: Adèle Naudé Santos and Alan Levy in Philadelphia
Two associates joined the firm in San Diego: Bruce Prescott and Ricardo Rabines

The move of my life and practice to California was prompted by the offer to create a new School of Architecture for the University of California in San Diego. The city was expanding rapidly and the need for a professional school had been under discussion for years. Members of the related professions of architecture, landscape architecture, and city planning had been very engaged in discussions about environmental issues and the lack of a vision for the urban quality of the built environment and streetscapes in San Diego in particular.

The offer was very attractive, particularly the challenge to create a better model for architectural education, which I felt was mired in the past. I also enjoyed the prospect of being part of an interdisciplinary school where Planning and Landscape were closely integrated. Adding to the temptation to move, the micro-climate was spectacular, and the flora and fauna reminded me of Cape Town. The idea of living in a comfortable climate amid flowers all year was compelling. Nevertheless, accepting the position and moving to another coast was a difficult decision because my Philadelphia practice and life were doing well.

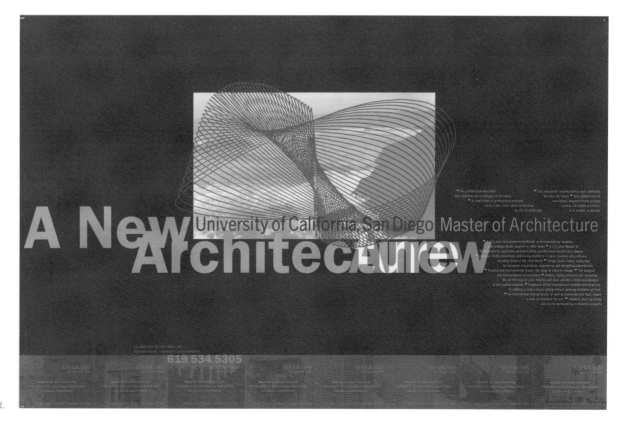

A poster announcing the new program by renowned graphic designer Lorraine Wild.

University of California in San Diego
New School of Architecture
1989–95
Founding Dean and Professor of Architecture

Taking on the position of founding dean and professor of architecture at the University of California in San Diego (UCSD) was an enormous task. The university wanted a research-based School of Architecture that would be internationally recognized. The new team had to conceptualize a new form of education as the Internet was presenting opportunities for transforming traditional forms of teaching. Recruiting faculty, renovating facilities, expanding the capacity of the library, and dealing with new politics as the state was moving to new budget realities. We had less than three years to do this. This was very time consuming, and I still had an ongoing architectural practice.

I had four full-time tenure track positions to fill. I had an usual recruitment process, inviting potential candidates to a "salon" for two days of retreat to be my proxy faculty. We were loaned a spectacular house on the cliffs overlooking the ocean. These days were well catered, too. There were three of these: History and Theory, Architectural Design, and Building Technology. The invitees represented different points of view. The debates were very stimulating and helpful, and led to applications to join the faculty. I also had funding for part-time faculty, not all were to be local. The planning for this addition to the UCSD campus had taken years and at the time the initial budget appeared adequate but not generous. We had no way to anticipate that the state economy would falter badly in a few years.

The faculty hired by UCSD were Craig Hodgetts, architect and technological wizard; Dana Cuff, theorist and scholar of architectural practice; Susan Ubbelohde, architect with a focus on technology; and William Curtis, architectural historian. Together, these individuals were to create a new curriculum. Part-time input came from legendary teacher and author Edward Allen, whose prolific books on building construction were widely used in architectural education.

With the new faculty, our first research challenge was to find a better model for architectural education and to create more productive lives for faculty and students. We proposed team-taught studios with divergent but complementary faculty expertise. We had a construction yard and a workshop where projects could be mocked up. We also had good computer tools and ways to experiment visually. Teaching modules were short but required full-time attendance by faculty. After this they had the equivalent time off to do their own work. The studio was the focus with subjects integrated into this; design and technology were blended together. The only stand-alone subjects were from our historian. We were experimenting with being in touch via the Internet so students could be critiqued virtually. At that time, it was too early for this concept to work smoothly, but we were on the right track. The University did not like us breaking all their streamlined rigid rules. However, our proposed curriculum was assessed by selected experts and was accepted at the state level—a requirement prior to admitting students. Students arrived as planned with twenty-two in the first professional degree and eight at the master's level.

A very significant element in building a new Department of Architecture was to cultivate an audience for this new entity. Fortunately, the start of this school was eagerly awaited by local practitioners in architecture, landscape, and planning. Building a community around the new school was important politically and economically. To begin we had an exhibition of internationally significant affordable housing with Balkrishna Doshi as the keynote speaker. This was followed by a conference called "Converging Lines," looking at collaborative interdisciplinary practices. This event brought brilliant thinkers together—from Disney imagineers and automobile engineers to landscape artists, showcasing artistic collaborations. We had an active program of lectures, exhibitions, and public events to engage professionals, often with parties at the school or my house afterwards.

We started the new school year with an event at the famous Salk Institute designed by Louis Kahn. Jonas Salk was very supportive of this addition to UCSD and attended the event. We began with the setting sun shimmering on the water course down the length of the courtyard. This was a thrilling and optimistic moment symbolically.

Unfortunately, in the middle of our first academic year, California's state economy showed drastic signs of failure. My administration reassured us that the future of this new school was safe. However, not very long after this it was shockingly clear that the last program to arrive at UCSD would be the first to be dismantled. There was an enormous public outcry led by local newspapers. Students had

to be transferred to the University of California Berkeley or UCLA. The two-year students could finish their degree, and the faculty could join other UC departments. This was an unforgivable mess. I continued to resolve what I could and would finish off the second year with the advanced masters students. I also intended to show what a School of Architecture could contribute to thinking about the future of the city if it had survived.

Building a New Department of Architecture in a Public Institution

During my time at UCSD, significant research took place in a course entitled "Urban Futures." In San Diego, an area called Center City East had become a place for homeless people to live on the street, in overcrowded low-rent hostels, and close to services for the urban poor. This was unfortunately located adjacent to the historic Gaslamp District, the recent revival of the center city, serving visitors and locals with new restaurants, shopping, and entertainment. The core of downtown included modern office buildings and Symphony Hall. Center City East, by contrast, was flat land with relatively low-rise buildings—primarily warehouses of one and two floors—and eighty-foot-wide streets and small urban blocks. The area felt quite deserted, with rundown buildings, some historically important ones, low-rent housing units, and overcrowded hostels. The freeways leading to downtown also passed through this zone. The condition of this neighborhood had become a potential hazard. The area was not considered safe.

Besides the area's overall environmental quality and the social problems, there were many long-term desires for the planning of this zone: the Convention Center needed to expand but without blocking views of the harbor; a new sports arena was needed; the central library was in need of a new building; and there was talk of a multicultural center catering to the cultural mix. In addition, there was a design to engage the waterfront with new attractions including a naval amphitheater with a maritime museum of old navy vessels. An older proposal, put forth decades before, was to physically and visually link the famous Balboa Park to the bay. This latter idea now gained enthusiastic support and "Park to Bay" became a fundamental component of the plans.

In discussion with the Planning Department, we agreed that our Urban Futures course could study several options for the renewal of the Center City East District, which would also influence plans for the whole of downtown. The city's participation in this would be very helpful.

We did this by staging three weekends in which visitors would join the students for an intense three-day charette. We worked spatially from overall planning alternatives to smaller scaled urban design concepts. These exploratory investigations included testing opportunities for the newly proposed uses, pedestrian environments like paseos and marketplaces, and better access systems for all movement systems including trolleys. This was collective collaborative work without designated authors.

Each week, the students summarized their findings, which were conveyed to the next team. The final weekend, housing typologies were tested for market rate and affordable units. Neighborhood support services and amenities were included such as local open space including reserves for seismic faults lines in the area that would create an unusual open space network. On the last afternoon, we hosted public, televised discussions. The mayor attended this meeting with key staff. They were thrilled with the work, and I was invited to make a visual presentation to the City Council. This was a great success and surprisingly the plan was proposed to be formally adopted by the city. A report was published, and this proposal was given several awards. Parts of this plan continued to be valid over time. This process was considered to be so influential, stirring up debate and critical discussion, that the mayor commissioned us to run another public process to debate the viability of connecting Mission Bay to San Diego Bay. This had become a favorite topic of the boating community. I organized this with remaining students, UCSD scientists and local participants in the earlier visioning process. We had easily proved what contribution an architecture school could make to the future development of San Diego.

Supporting our charette, at least twenty-five people flew into San Diego from other universities and international practices, to spend three days with UCSD faculty, students, and important local practitioners. These efforts were without compensation, made in academic solidarity and friendship, joining this creative challenge.

Reflections
Adèle Naudé Santos and Associates in San Diego 1989-95

One of my early tasks upon arriving in San Diego was to find a location for my house and design studio, preferably in a combined structure. There was no time to build one, so I purchased a large wooden house, part of an old estate with a coach house close to Center City. The exercise here was to eliminate rooms, cutting voids to open up vertical spaces such as the entry, and cultivate the garden and patio. The coach house became the studio with separate access, connected on the second level. Large Ficus trees and shade plants made a calm garden paradise.

San Diego was a beautiful city to live in and full of surprises. Living on a hill above downtown with a roof deck, my views included the coastline, planes landing at the airport, and high rise buildings lit up at night. I was close to Balboa Park and the famous zoo where I would walk each week checking out my favorite animals. Every few months a colorful swirling creature flew into my tall trees making curious sounds. Another escapee from the zoo had come to spend a few days!

Surrounded by deep canyons which harbored wild animals, each late afternoon a troupe of raccoons, babies included, walked up my driveway through the garden en route to the next canyon. This was clearly a well established old pattern.

Weekly, I would drive to Chino Farms known for cultivating heritage vegetables, tomatoes in all shapes and colors, and greens I had never seen before. Each visit contained a surprise, such as white strawberries, Huitlacoche in October, the precious Corn fungus used in Mexican cooking to make mole.

The most exceptional experience was to drive through numerous ecologies in a half Day. Beach, up to mountain top town, down valley and desert, palm groves, through horse farms, vineyards, back to coast. There are few places in the world that this can be experienced and none so easily.

Reflections
Narrative Maps; Concepts and Creations

In 1998, I had two important solo exhibitions—one at the Kitakyushu Museum of Modern Art in Japan and one at the National Museum Bloemfontein in South Africa.

Narrative maps had become part of our work process as we began to design more complex projects, with multiple agendas and issues to be understood. Narratives are descriptions of a project's most potent design issues—mini stories anticipating an important experience or observation. They reveal and record thought processes underlying design decisions, translated into a visual format. In doing so, key design issues are interpreted, represented, and integrated early into the design process. The diagram can best depict tangible ideas and explicit issues, recording their essence, but concepts that represent mood or atmosphere are best conveyed by vignettes. Making ideas visible by mapping them helps to understand the complexity of issues. As they are descriptive and subject-focused, narratives are easily categorized, prioritized, and organized in a comprehensible sequence. Such a visual text can be accessible to the non-designer, a strategy we have developed over time. This mapping process takes verbal or written texts and integrates these into design thinking, bridging the gap between program and design outcome. The quest to create "appropriate architecture" needs an explicitly transparent design process like this one.

If ever architecture education was going to change, it might have been at UCSD in 1990, when Adèle Naudé was named founding dean of the new architecture school. "I believe it is essential to create a new model for architectural education at this time; one which is more responsive to the changing social, environment, and technical issues facing our profession. UCSD, as a major research university set in a growing dynamic city, can be the perfect place to challenge the architectural status quo." So said Adèle in the university press release upon her appointment. Not long thereafter, she began assembling her founding faculty in the way she knew best: around a dinner table. Sitting in a spectacular modern house on the La Jolla bluffs that turned its back on the sea of pink stucco suburban fabric behind, Adèle talked and cooked a group of us into enthusiastically joining her on what seemed a pioneering expedition. UCSD was more science than the arts or humanities (notwithstanding the incredible, experimental Visual Arts faculty), and San Diego was more developer-oriented than architecturally driven.

Perhaps we should have seen just how precarious the idea was: a woman-run architecture program (one of only a few in American history even at that late date); running a resource-rich program of only graduate students, in small studio formats, with a lot of support staff on the payroll, and an impressive roster of visiting luminaries, in a science-oriented university. But anything seemed possible with Adèle at the helm.

A year after her appointment, the founding faculty was announced: myself, described as an architectural sociologist; William Curtis, architectural historian; Craig Hodgetts, architectural designer; and Susan Ubbelohde, an architect specializing in environmental technology. Composed to have all the genetic material needed to give birth to the next generation of architects, the five of us set about building a school from scratch with the luxury of a full year of planning. Craig Hodgetts and I drove the freeway from LA, William Curtis flew in from France, and both Adèle and Susan moved to San Diego.

One year later, in 1992, the first group of twenty-four graduate students arrived at our academic utopia, housed in former military barracks. The students seemed brilliant, and we led them into an innovative pedagogic model. There would be just one collaborative, cross-disciplinary topic per ten-week term, centered around the studio. We would begin with a two-week research or history-theory seminar customized to the studio's design project. The next six weeks were studio-only, when all of us might travel together to distant sites, give desk crits, and debate at Adèle's house after guest lectures. Each ten-week quarter would end with another two-week seminar that might advance the environmental approach or tectonics of the students' studio projects. One term the students focused on migrant farmworker housing; in another term, more advanced students collaborated with city agencies to propose urban vision plans for San Diego. Sitting so close to Mexico with over a dozen architecture schools on the other side of the border, we began research partnerships and hosted a major transnational symposium. Regular evening lectures came from world-renown architects like Balkrishna Doshi and Ricardo Legoretta or Chris Carradine of Disney Imagineers. Building experiments took place in the grassy courtyards, led by visiting faculty like Ed Allen from Yale. San Diego's urban decisionmakers became regulars at our juries. Each quarter, we modified our plans for the next term based on what we had learned. The two-week seminar, for example, didn't leave enough time for students to read and ruminate, so we tried starting both seminars in the first two weeks, and picked both back up again at the end of term.

Not long after the second cohort arrived in fall 1993, we were shocked to learned that our experiment had fallen victim to a UC systemwide financial crisis. We protested, litigated, and eventually accepted the status of academic refugees: students and faculty were offered shelter at either Berkeley or UCLA, the two other architecture programs in the UC system.

In retrospect, the School of Architecture did not have nearly enough time to test its experimental models, nor did the faculty have time to reflect on what had happened. Instead, we were absorbed back into the conventional modes of teaching architecture that continue to resist significant, let alone radical change. In 2021, UCSD opened the "Design and Innovation Building," an immense investment to leverage design for transformative change, but without an architecture or design program. San Diego needed the UCSD School of Architecture, the program was based on an alternative to the centuries-old architectural academy, and the faculty were distinctly cross-disciplinary idealists and practitioners. It may have been the right recipe in the wrong kitchen, despite head chef Naudé's best efforts. Had the school lived on, might it have pulled all architectural education in a slightly new direction? It was ahead of its time, and academia has still not caught up.

Dana Cuff

A Gift To San Diego

When Adèle Naudé arrived in San Diego in 1989, she was already a celebrity of sorts. Ideas about this new professional school had been percolating in the city for years, and it had become a repository of dreams for a professional community had longed for thought leadership and stronger connections with the University of California San Diego (UCSD)—the ivory tower in La Jolla. Under the leadership of Adèle, whose ideas about architectural education embraced real-world engagement as applied research, the school promised to not only draw top talent and vital intellectual energy in fields related to the built environment, but to enlist them in shaping the region at a pivotal moment in its development.

As Adèle settled into a new community, establishing her professional practice on the west coast and focusing her energy on her primary ambition of redefining architectural education—she was also at the top of everyone's invitation list. One of my responsibilities as her external relations officer at the school was to help vet her public appearances so that the community got a taste of the school as it was evolving without Adèle's calendar becoming overwhelmed with extracurricular activities.

The community was hungry. Not a week would go by without at least one or two invitations to evaluate. An AIA chapter or an advocacy group inviting her to lecture about architecture or urban development; a journalist or philanthropist eager to talk about her ideas; local practitioners interested to serve on the architecture faculty, and a wide range of nonprofit groups—ranging from Women in Construction to a local environmental powerhouse like Citizens Coordinate for Century Three—all curious about this exotic new dean whose influence would shape the city. Of course, time for community interaction was limited, even if Adèle's interest was keen.

The city itself offered a rich, real-world laboratory to explore urban futures. Situated at the US-Mexico Border, San Diego is subject to the multidimensional challenges of immigration and international trade. Despite the region's temperate climate and extraordinary natural beauty, San Diego's urban environment lacked gravitas. The downtown had few notable buildings and lacked the vitality of a significant residential population. With the exception of the Gaslamp District, a few blocks accommodating nightlife, there was not much of a "there" there. San Diego—both the city and the county—was characterized by low-density development patterns profoundly shaped by and for automobiles: wide city streets undermined a satisfying pedestrian experience and a vast network of freeways carved up and exacerbated a fragile ecosystem that was stressed by drought. For someone like Adèle, whose academic approach included rolling up her sleeves and working with students and faculty on current issues, San Diego offered a rich array of opportunities.

In the early days, Adèle's schedule would allow for the occasional personal appearance, but her initial strategy for community engagement was programmatic: lending a public dimension to the process of faculty recruitment. For each aspect of architectural education—e.g., history and criticism, design, materials and methods—Adèle would identify leading thinkers as candidates for her core faculty. She would then host a salon, inviting these candidates to the school for a weekend to advise and confer on their area of expertise and discuss how it could be taught better or differently. This would give her insight into pedagogical issues as well as an opportunity to interact with potential colleagues. The weekend activities would also involve these thought leaders presenting and participating in a university-hosted public forum on a topic that was both relevant to their expertise and to the region. Members of the public could attend and interact with attendees. It was a heady time, and these events created excitement and forged personal connections between the school and the city.

The most impactful interaction with the city came a couple of years later. In fall 1993, almost as quickly as the school ramped up, it had to wind to a close in the wake of the University of California's budget crisis. Adèle wanted to leave a gift for the City of San Diego in return for its support. In forging the school's final academic quarter, she created the opportunity to use the city itself as a topic for study. She surveyed city leaders and settled on the 300-acre Center City East in downtown as an area of inquiry. How might interventions in this built environment, at a variety of scales, improve this area and the city as a whole?

To answer those questions, the academic quarter was organized around a series of three charrettes, each building on the work of the one previous. The first charrette sought an understanding of how Center City East fit within the wider city framework. The second examined neighborhoods within Center City East. And the third charrette zeroed in on discreet interventions—at the block or site level—that would have important impact or catalyze greater change.

The goal was for the quarter-long exploration to be pedagogically sound and imaginative in ideation, while also taking into consideration actual projects proposed for this area of the city. Charrette findings would be documented with the hope that at least some of the ideas would be developed further by the city as part of its future road map.

In building the teams for these charrettes, Adèle partnered the core faculty members and the class of six M.Arch II graduate students with a team of local professionals to lend continuity throughout all charrettes. She then supplemented each charrette team with an array of leading academic and practicing urban designers from all over the country, crafting each guest list to foster compelling outside perspectives.

It bears mentioning that the world was primarily analog at that time. Digital tools that we now take for granted were barely on the horizon. So, the charrettes were anchored in the physical world, rather than on computer screens. Each charrette took place in person over a few intensive days, with participants committed to long hours, including sharing meals together. The charrette process followed a template. The first day was devoted to laying the groundwork. Adèle would frame the charrette purpose and scope, and then one of the city participants would present the agency's maps, diagrams, and plans for the area. The group would then survey the territory in question by car. These trips were instructive and full of lively, often funny, conversations, as participants got to know the city and each other better. Before the day's activities ended, a brain-storming session would clarify the themes to be explored the following day—and would contribute to a lively discussion at a group dinner.

The second day was primarily a workday, which often spurred more site visits in the vans. The studio space would be humming with activity—some people talking, others drawing furiously. Adèle and other faculty would walk the room, check in on the different working groups, and pause to draw out ideas. Late in the afternoon, the full team would reconvene for an analysis session to determine which ideas had most merit and to sort out the best way to represent them. Production work would then begin again and continue long after dinner. The morning of the third and final day was devoted to wrapping up the ideas, while the afternoon was dedicated to preparing the presentation narrative, the final drawings to illustrate it, and practice for a public presentation of findings in the evening.

While the charrette working process was methodical, participating in it felt intense and organic—like being part of a hive. Those of us who worked with Adèle would sometimes describe her as a sort of queen bee: she has this way of gathering people together and finding a way of drawing out the best of them. Her intellectual and design acuity is tempered by a disarming play-fulness and social joy. As each charrette progressed, participants would get so engaged that they would effectively shed their status, working with interest alongside others who might be more-, less-, or differently accomplished.

Group meals were always memorable, particularly when Adèle was hosting at her home. Cooking with Adèle was tantamount to a team sport played at higher level—exotic ingredients with un-usual preparations, gorgeously presented and always delicious. Each of the three charrettes had a similar trajectory but its own particular focus and flavor.

At quarter's end, a Vision for Center City East—a compendium of charrette highlights and rec-ommendations—was summed up in a booklet, complete with analysis, drawings, and ideas for the future. Adèle left a parting gift to the City of San Diego from the UCSD School of Architecture, which burned a bright light in its brief life.

Today, thirty years later, downtown San Diego is completely transformed, and Center City East reflects some of the changes proposed in the school's vision. But I'd venture Adèle's real gift to the city, the bigger impact, was in the human experience of the charrette participants, whose in-tense work—sharing ideas in real time, anchored in a real place, creating materials, and breaking bread together—yielded visceral insight about building community. One can only wonder how San Diego might have developed differently had the UCSD School of Architecture continued under Adèle's leadership.

A Vision for Center City East
San Diego, California
1993

The context was adjacent to the historic Gas Lamp District, recently restored, and an attraction for visitors. The retail and restaurant quality had improved vastly and frequent visitors from Tiaquana had started using this amenity. The core of downtown included modern office buildings and Symphony Hall. Center City East by contrast was flat land with relatively low-rise buildings, warehouses of one and two floors. Very wide streets, eighty feet, and small urban blocks, 200 x 300 feet. The area felt quite deserted, with rundown buildings, some historically important ones, low rent housing units, and overcrowded hostels. Social Service Organizations for the very poor, some giving free food, were located here. Unsurprisingly, a low income population came to inhabit the run down buildings and squatted on side-walks. The area was not considered safe.

Besides the overall environmental quality and the social problems generated here there were many long term desires for the planning of this zone. The Convention Center needed to expand but not block views of the harbor. A new Sports Arena was needed, the central library needed a new building, a Multicultural Center catering to the cultural mix and border access was desired. Engaging the waterfront with new attractions including a naval amphitheater with a Maritime Museum of old navy vessels, The oldest desire proposed decades before was to physically and visually link the famous Balboa Park to the Bay!

This big idea had enthusiastic support from the design team, and Park to Bay became a fundamental component of the plans.

Over the three weekends we worked spatially from overall planning alternatives to smaller scaled urban design concepts. This was collective collaborative work without designated authors.These explorative investigations included testing opportunities for the new uses proposed, pedestrian environments like paseos and market places, better access systems for all movement systems including trolleys. The final weekend housing typologies were tested for market rate and affordable units. Neighborhood support services and amenities were included such as local open space including reserves for seismic faults lines in the area that would create an unusual open space network.

Over the three weekends we got feedback from the public forums we planned, and responses to the university television recordings. The last meeting the mayor and her staff came and expressed enthusiasm for the work. I was invited to show the material to the City Council who later decided to adopt this work into their Master Plan. As to be expected only some of our proposals survived the test of time.

Supporting this charette at least twenty-five people flew into San Diego from other Universities and International Practices, to spend three days with UCSD faculty, students, and important local practitioners. These efforts were without compensation, made in academic solidarity, friendship, joining a creative challenge.

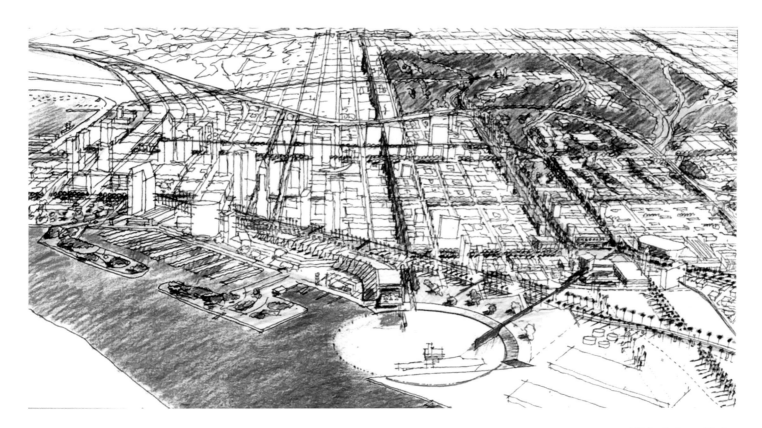

A Vision for Center City East

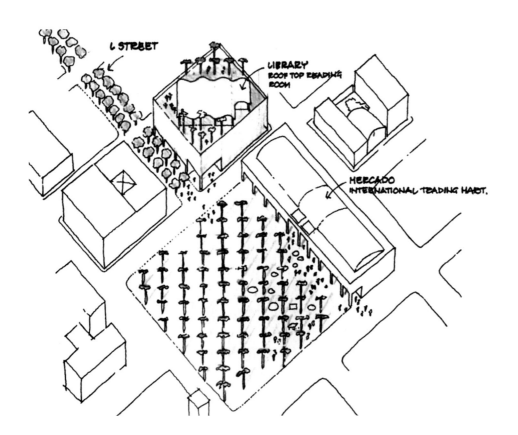

L STREET

LIBRARY
ROOF TOP READING
ROOM

MERCADO
INTERNATIONAL TRADING MART.

184

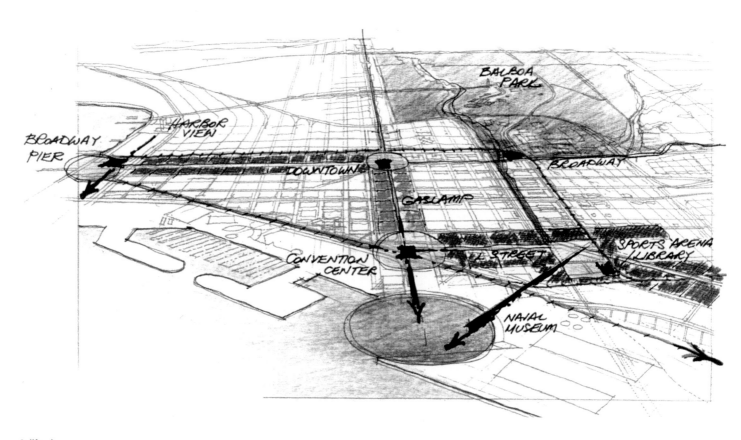

BALBOA
PARK

BROADWAY
PIER

HARBOR
VIEW

DOWNTOWN

BROADWAY

GASLAMP

SPORTS ARENA
LIBRARY

CONVENTION
CENTER

L STREET

NAVAL
MUSEUM

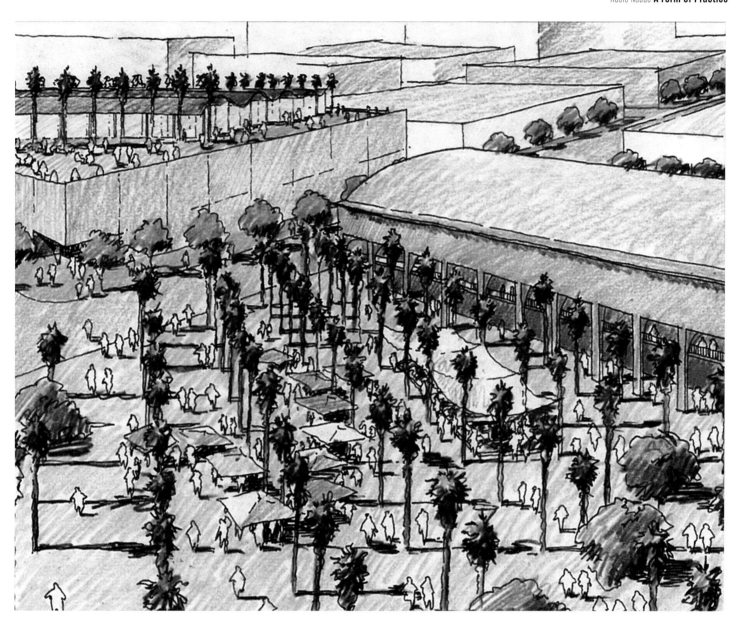

A Vision for Center City East

Arts Park
Los Angeles, California
1990

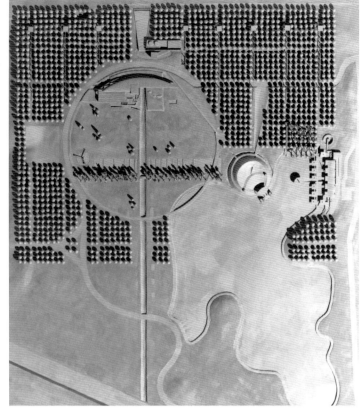

Opposite Citrus trees form a spatial grid, eroded to create outdoor rooms.

Irrigation lines become pathways using trellises to carry water pipes that shade the parking grid and other functions.
The circular path defines an agricultural demonstration space, and connects all facilities in the park. The Natural History Museum site is defined by this path which spans an important restored waterway.

Our design for Arts Park Los Angeles was the winning entry in a competition. We collaborated with Hodgetts and Fung Design Associates, Rios Pearson Inc., and artist Mary Miss. Our program included an amphitheater, a 1,000-seat restaurant, a Natural History Museum, and a concept for the master plan.

We started by researching the history of the park and discovered that groves of fruit trees, mainly citrus, had covered the land. These were being eroded as subdivisions for suburban growth made the land less valuable for agriculture. We reenacted this process conceptually, using the spacing of trees as spatial markers separating the facilities in the park. Water towers visible from the main access street revealed an irrigation system, which followed designated paths in the park. Parking was planned to fit into this grid to shade cars with elevated trellises carrying the water pipes.

An existing flood control lake created a setting for a waterfront restaurant and a place for performance. The Natural History Museum spanned a restored waterway. A space was cut out of the orchard to create an outdoor lobby and procession space to the amphitheater, which was hidden by a tall grassy hill. It had a mysterious entry space leading to a staircase but also a ramp on the outside, winding to the hilltop. From here, the space stepped down to the lake and the performance stage. The Ramada restaurant was also oriented toward the lake with shade canopies. At the lake's edge this pattern was transformed into docks for artist-designed boats for hire. We set an island bar in the lake, with access from a causeway. This was crowned by a large lantern roof, which acted as a night beacon.

Our master plan was selected by the client because it could integrate other projects. The Arts Park never went ahead, however, because the engineers in charge of the flood control lake had not fully understood what the concept would entail. Without much discussion, in disregard to all the efforts and costs incurred to prepare the competition and those incurred by the competitors, they withdrew their support for the park.

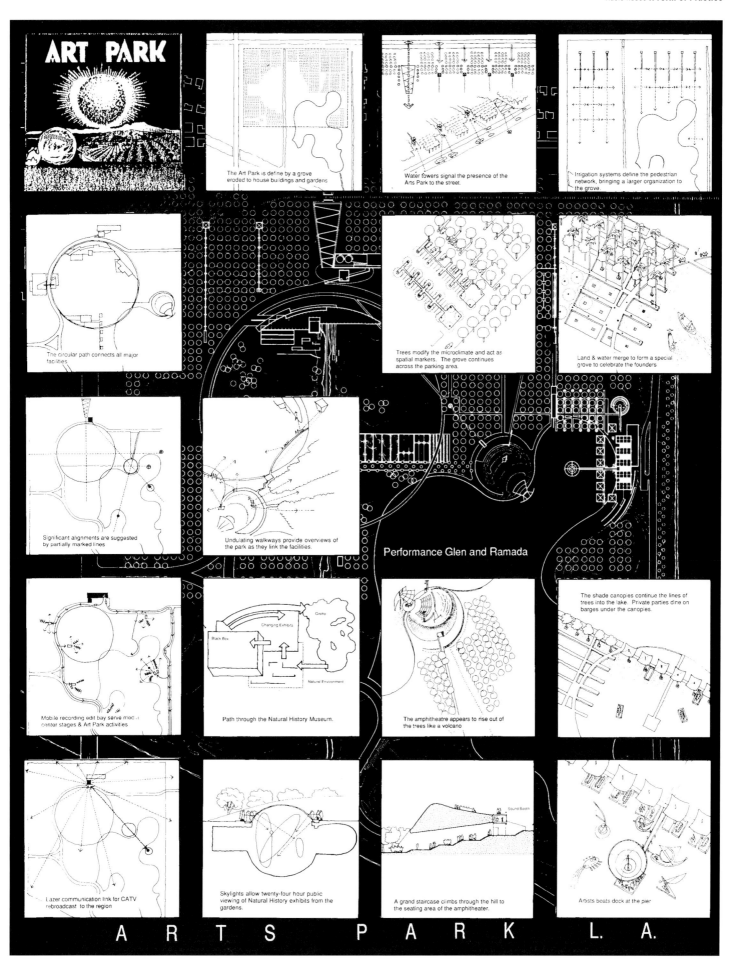

ART PARK

The Art Park is define by a grove eroded to house buildings and gardens

Water fowers signal the presence of the Arts Park to the street.

Irrigation systems define the pedestrian network, bringing a larger organization to the grove.

The circular path connects all major facilities.

Trees modify the microclimate and act as spatial markers. The grove continues across the parking area.

Land & water merge to form a special grove to celebrate the founders

Significant alignments are suggested by partially marked lines

Undulating walkways provide overviews of the park as they link the facilities.

Performance Glen and Ramada

The shade canopies continue the lines of trees into the lake. Private parties dine on barges under the canopies.

Mobile recording edit bay serve media center stages & Art Park activities

Path through the Natural History Museum.

The amphitheatre appears to rise out of the trees like a volcano

Lazer communication link for CATV rebroadcast to the region

Skylights allow twenty-four hour public viewing of Natural History exhibits from the gardens.

A grand staircase climbs through the hill to the seating area of the amphitheater.

Artists boats dock at the pier

A R T S   P A R K   L. A.

California

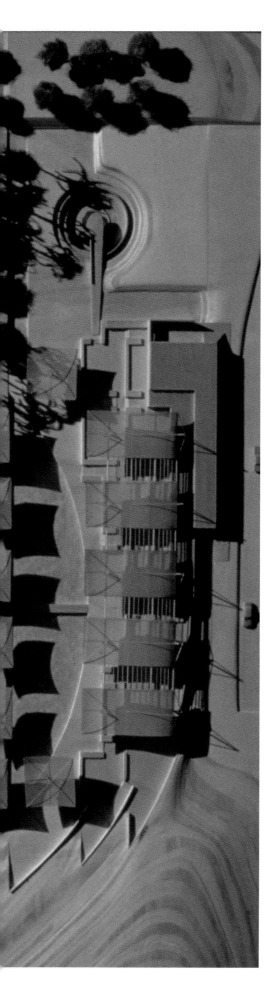

Below The amphitheater is a surprise element. From the park entry it appears as a hill rising out of the trees. The foyer, an open space is focused on a mysterious aperture in the hill. This is a staircase going through to views of the lake. Alternatively, a slow ramp takes visitors around the hill to join the amphitheater which rises out of the lake.

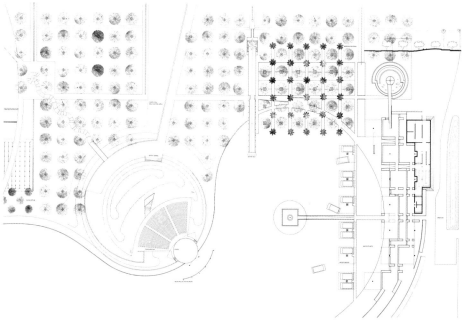

California

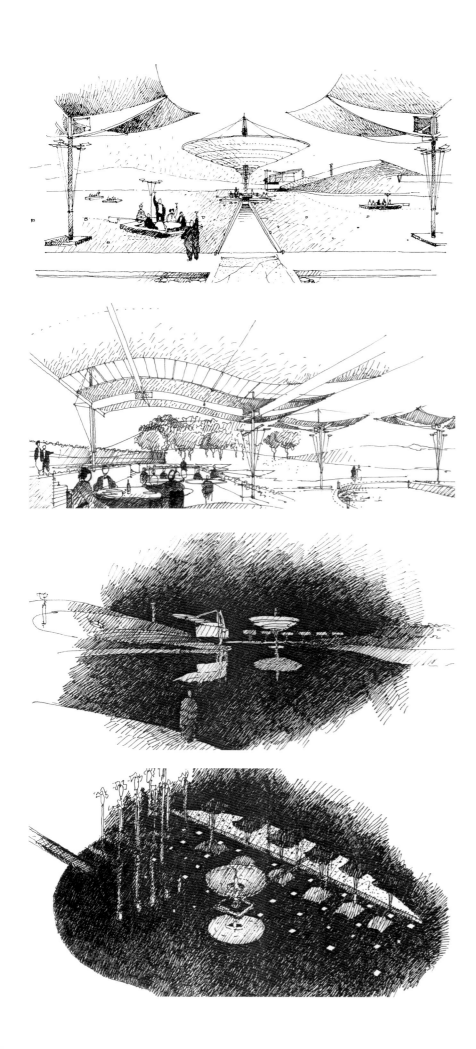

Opposite The Ramada restaurant is located on terraces with lake views with undulating shade canopies that replace the grid of trees. Piers line the lake edge with artist designed boats that can be hired for pleasure. An island bar floats in the lake with a translucent canopy that is lit at night as a dramatic beacon.

Left A causeway leads to the island bar.
Middle Dining in the Ramada restaurant
Below Night scenes of the lake

Arts Park

Perris Civic Center
Perris, California
1991

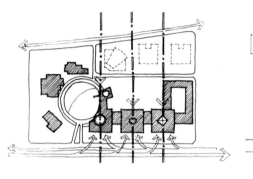
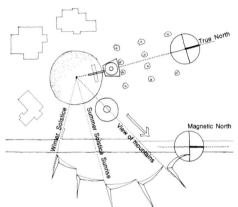
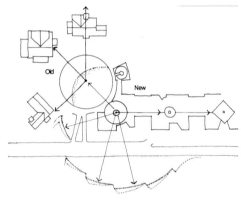

Perris is a typical town of the Inland Empire region and had no distinguishing features or buildings. While located on a prominent site in the center of the city, with freeway access and regional visibility, the competition for a new 100,000-square-foot Civic Center had no obvious anchor nor history. The natural environment, however, was beautiful and could be the inspiration for a new image. The valley was very fertile with crops like alfalfa celebrated annually with a festival. The surrounding hills had stone outcroppings. The sky was very iridescent, and hot air balloons were popular. Our research revealed that Indigenous American tribes inhabited this area, carving on rocks, leaving symbols that indicated sky watching, marking solar events.

We were one of four teams invited to produce a design. We intended to highlight the natural phenomena of the valley, making the Civic Center a place where citizens could explore their ancient history in this landscape, and learn how to live with the variable climate, including intense heat in summer. We were fascinated with the iridescent sky and saw it as a key link bridging the past and present.

The site included a series of existing buildings that were not of great quality. The first big issue was to create a prominent space within which these old structures and new buildings could be integrated. A circle was the best underlying geometry—large enough for the community to gather for different events, formal and informal, but not a typical plaza given the harsh microclimate.

We decided to create a mounded space referencing the convex and concave formations of the larger landscapes. This topography would include a grassy hill relating to the existing buildings and a convex granite plaza, oriented to the sky and the new buildings.

Civic centers typically contain visible clocks, but we wanted to mark the passing of time by creating a sundial in the granite plaza. The stair is a gnomon that ascends to an amphitheater above the Council Chamber. All the existing buildings open to the new space, anchored by the offices of the mayor and the Council Chamber.

The program was composed of different office groupings—the mayor, the administration, the police and the county jail. We designed these programs around a series of courtyards, each emphasizing a particular phenomenon of the valley. These spaces would be self-ventilating, water catchments, piped to a central storage for landscape irrigation.

The courtyard of the mayor was the Sky Catcher. Using a mirrored, splayed, conical enclosure, the reflected sky could be brought to the circular courtyard below. Public access

Opposite The Civic Center was given a site on Perris Boulevard. At that time it was modest road, close to a freeway entrance which could give this facility regional visibility. The land in front of the center was to be used for display of regional plants. Many of these are flowering or brightly colored.

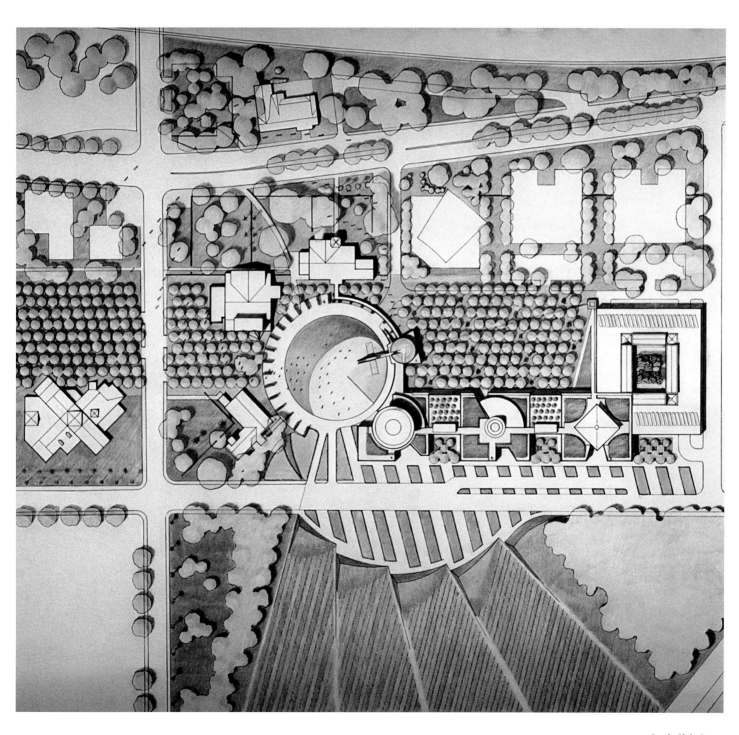

would be allowed. This referenced contemporary hot air balloon experiences as well as the tradition of Indigenous sky watchers who originally occupied the site.

The Earth Chamber courtyard was the focus of the administrative units. Here the rich soils and rocks of different colors were displayed on a central disk. Mirrored faceted glass formed a pitched enclosure, reflecting and fragmenting the image on display. When the wind blew it activated the rotation of the disc, turning the courtyard into a virtual kaleidoscope. This is where people paid their bills and would do so in an unusually magical place.

The police centered around the Wind Catcher courtyard. Wind was to be scooped down across a water cistern cooling the breezes. On the roof fragrant flowers would be grown, like jasmine, allowing the wind direction to be identified. We imagined this courtyard as a soothing place. Part of this cluster included the jail where people would be in residence. We proposed a water garden with shade canopies that included misters to grow exotic local plants.

The last important element was the Council Chamber, engaged thematically but expressed differently. A partial globe used as an amphitheater formed the roof. The location of Perris would be marked on the ceiling. Natural light would be brought into the space around the perimeter.

We won the Perris Civic Center competition. However, shortly after this the mayor lost her election, and the city manager who had steered this process was fired for complex reasons. There was a discussion of changing the site to a less prominent location but keeping the courtyard formations. This would have been difficult. Finally, fiscal reality ended their ambitions, and the project was canceled.

Below The needed program was partly built in three existing buildings on this site, none of architectural quality, nor placed together logically. The challenge was to integrate old and new structures together with a public gathering space with local character that could function in a very hot environment.

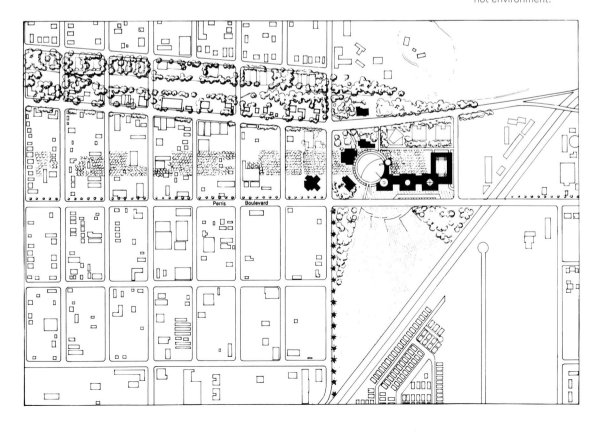

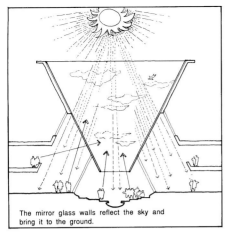

The mirror glass walls reflect the sky and bring it to the ground.

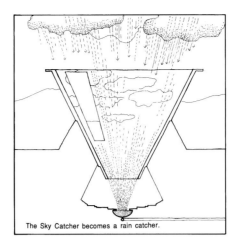

The Sky Catcher becomes a rain catcher.

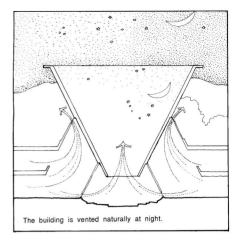

The building is vented naturally at night.

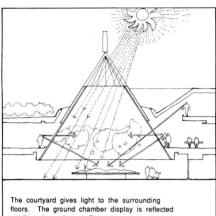

The courtyard gives light to the surrounding floors. The ground chamber display is reflected on the mirror glass walls.

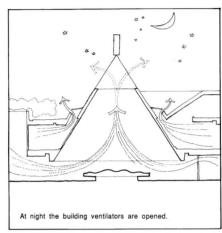

At night the building ventilators are opened.

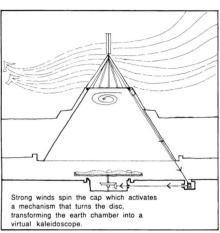

Strong winds spin the cap which activates a mechanism that turns the disc, transforming the earth chamber into a virtual kaleidoscope.

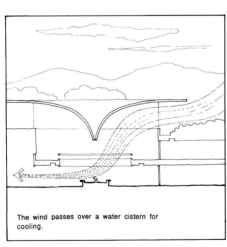

The wind passes over a water cistern for cooling.

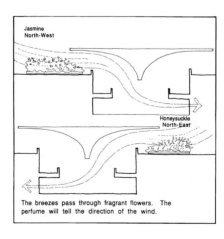

Jasmine North-West

Honeysuckle North-East

The breezes pass through fragrant flowers. The perfume will tell the direction of the wind.

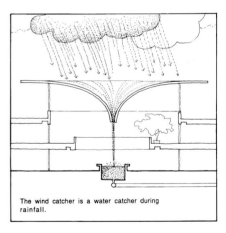

The wind catcher is a water catcher during rainfall.

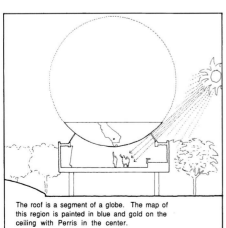

The roof is a segment of a globe. The map of this region is painted in blue and gold on the ceiling with Perris in the center.

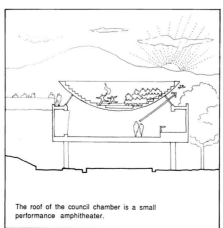

The roof of the council chamber is a small performance amphitheater.

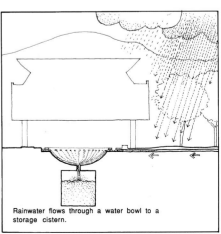

Rainwater flows through a water bowl to a storage cistern.

California

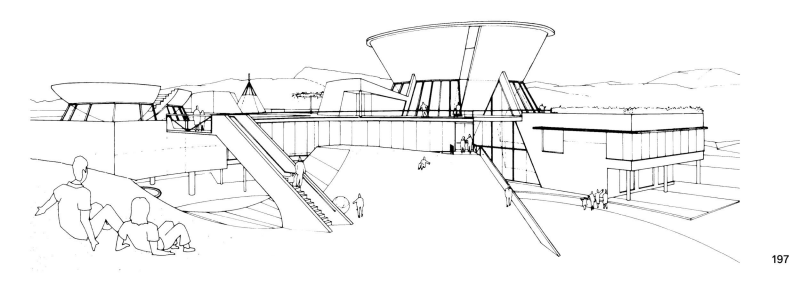

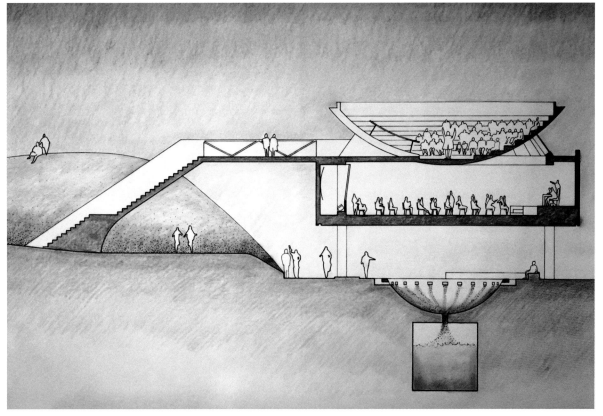

We chose a circular form which could relate to all entrances. This was not a plaza but a convex and concave form reflecting the larger landscape, and anticpating more informal gatherings. Grass faces existing structures and paving is integrated into the formality of the Mayor's complex.

The complex had three separate programs which face the Boulevard. To the rear parking shaded by evergreen trees was typical. We chose Jackeranda trees with purple flowers which were planned to continue for many blocks.

Perris Civic Center

California

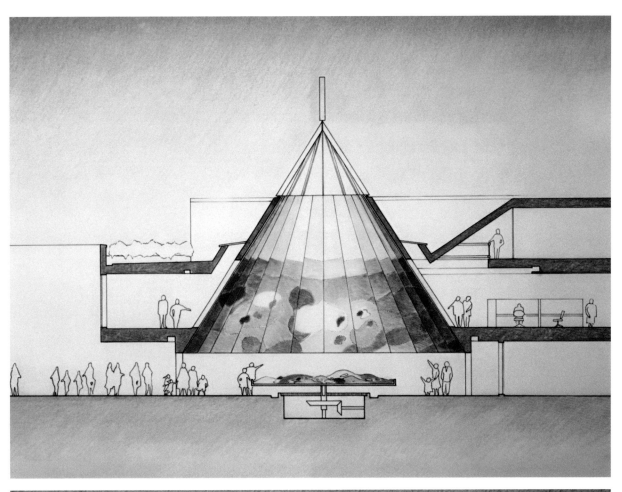

Perris Civic Center

Rokko Island
Green Hill Town
near Kobe, Japan
1991

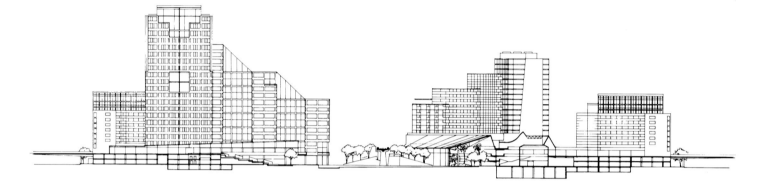

In 1991, we worked on a new project in Japan—a design-build competition for a large development of residential, cultural, and commercial buildings on a new island, off the coast of Kobe.

This was a fast-track competition entry. A consortium of developers, led by our previous client Taeko Matsuda, was independently working on their pro forma as we were following the directive, as they described, "to create a place for the celebration of life where cultural facilities promote interaction and care for the environment and human tradition." The housing blocks, consisting of 3,000 units serving many different age groups

and income levels, were to be surrounded by hilly gardens with natural amenities such as pools, a lake, and forests.

The land had to be stabilized, and the proposal was to add large amounts of soil to do this. Excavated earth was mounded into twelve-meter-tall hills, planted with native species. We were committed to integrating the buildings and the landscape, taking advantage of the formation of hills that could hide parking, create ramped pathways, and provide green roofs.

The current master plan surrounded a central axis with a monorail that linked to the main

coast. The site was segmented into three bays in the east-west direction. The central bay was reserved for the hotel and cultural uses, including a university. Housing, our main focus, occurred on land to the east and west of the center.

We designed the housing blocks to optimize southern exposure. Planned to define the site edges, and maximize landscapes, the housing form could protect against the impact of cold winds and encourage breezes from the south. There were four distinct patterns of housing. The blocks to the south consisted of five floors broken into smaller buildings to allow for summer breezes and ocean views from

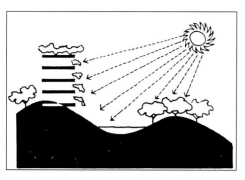
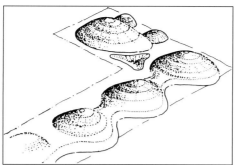
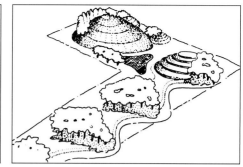

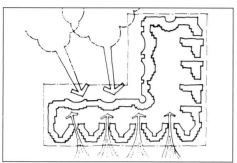
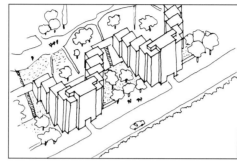
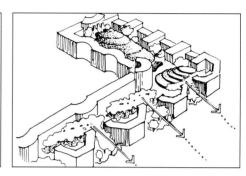

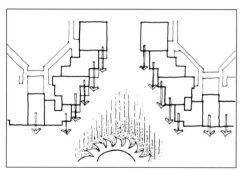
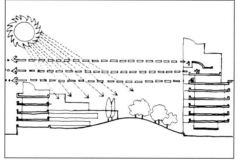
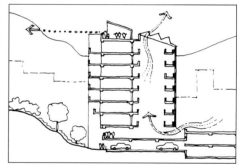

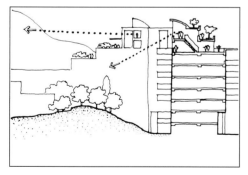
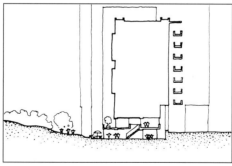
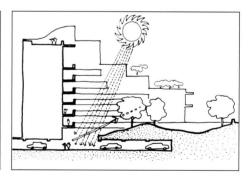

Rokko Island Green Hill Town

the rear. The northern and western housing gave protection from harsh winds. The lower levels were continuous but had variable heights up to eight floors. Blocks close to the center were stepped in profile with roof terraces facing gardens and breaks for paths to the center. High-rise towers were placed to have long views, as well as atria with public amenities and view terraces.

Although not programmed at this stage we suggested elements that could give the center a unique focus. The monorail link to the center could engage an artist to give their sculptural forms and energy. Discussion about a public greenhouse was greeted with enthusiasm and we proposed a three story curved space to edge the hotel. A spa and other indoor sports would be included. There would be full-sized trees and colorful plants with good natural ventilation and café and dining spaces with informal seating arranged to invite the whole community. Opposite to this we proposed a glazed arcade lined with stones on several levels. in the center of this there could be a cascading waterfall matching the central axis of the complex. The sound of water would be relaxing and the humidity would be welcome in most seasons. Here offices would be located in high- rise towers at the same density and scale as the adjacent housing blocks. The university would use this axis as its entry space. The center needed to be programmed to serve a mixed -income community, and many residents may have chosen to both live and work there.

The clients loved our project, but the competition was chosen on strictly financial and organizational terms. Our development team was based in Tokyo while our competitors were from the Osaka area. A local team won the competition and the rights to develop the property.

202

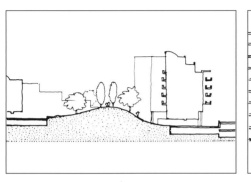
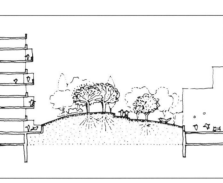
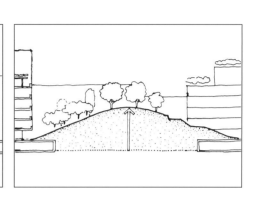

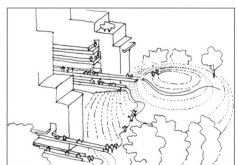
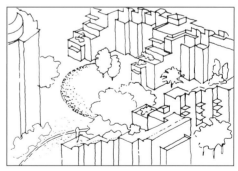

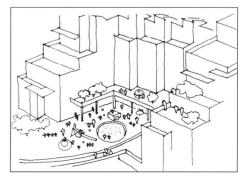

Rokko Island Green Hill Town

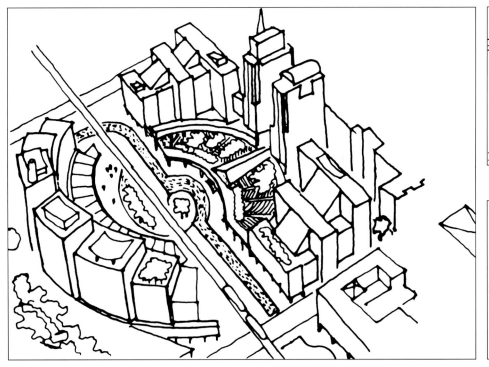
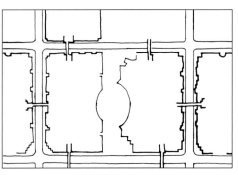
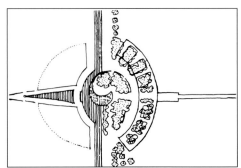
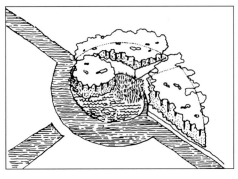
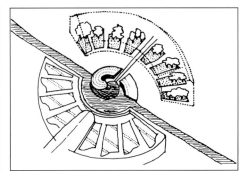
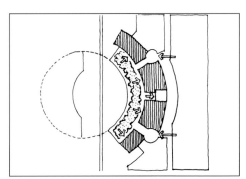
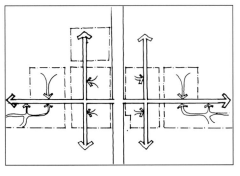
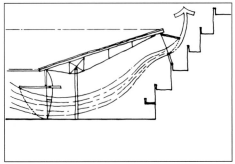
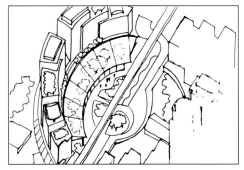
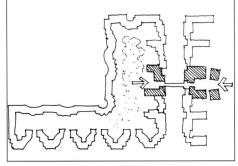

204

The office towers mark the entry to the complex through a glazed ramp from the artistic central icon. This leads to the arcade which rises in steps for two floors with a water fountain cascading in the center. The sound is the most important feature but humidity helpful in the very hot months. This covered street leads to residential areas and commercial development

On the opposite side a three floor high curved greenhouse is proposed with trees and exotic plants as a public space to relax dine and meet friends. The roof structure is playful with tree-like forms adding to the exuberance.This is ventilated through a space for hotel balconies to view the greenhouse.

Kadota Housing
Kitakyushu, Japan
1994

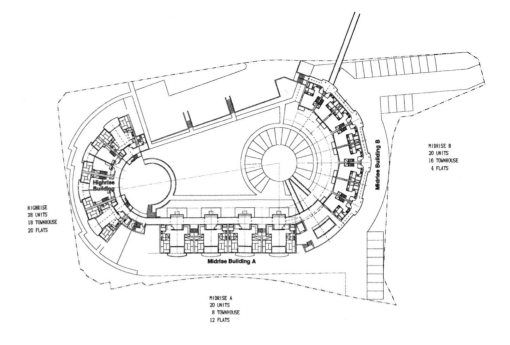

HIGHRISE
38 UNITS
18 TOWNHOUSE
20 FLATS

Highrise
Building

Midrise Building B

MIDRISE B
20 UNITS
16 TOWNHOUSE
4 FLATS

Midrise Building A

MIDRISE A
20 UNITS
8 TOWNHOUSE
12 FLATS

In the mid-1990s, we worked on two public housing projects in Japan. The first was a project with the prefectural government of Kitakyushu. A series of sites on the hillside above the city, served by narrow streets, could be developed. We were encouraged to connect them. Using a "street in the sky" concept, three sites could link together with local sidewalk access. The mayor found this concept really interesting, and we were assigned our first block.

This was to include a taller building for elderly units, family units with ground access and parking, and some senior units with patios. A "street" tied these dwellings together at level four, which also served family townhouses. This street was planned to cross the road to join the next block at level three. At grade, there were vegetable plots, a lawn, a playground, and patios for ground-level units. Four stairs gave upper units direct access to the ground.

The ten-story elderly building had a radial form minimizing the central circulation, widening the window wall. Two bedrooms and a terrace opened to the view with a compact plan centered on the living room.

The first two buildings were built as planned. The construction crew had never built housing where the stacked floor plans were not identical, although the ducts were continuous. Our Japanese partner tried to smooth this out, but to no avail. The local construction team redesigned the last phase of the block. They kept the principle of the street and the overall form but changed the housing units to be identical and gave no access to the garden from the ground level imagined for elderly units. The mayor moved on to another position and the larger plan for linked plots did not survive.

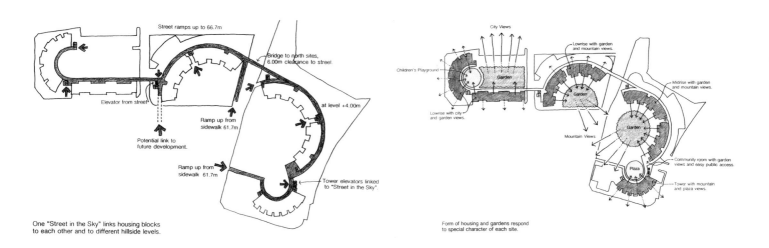

One "Street in the Sky" links housing blocks to each other and to different hillside levels.

Form of housing and gardens respond to special character of each site.

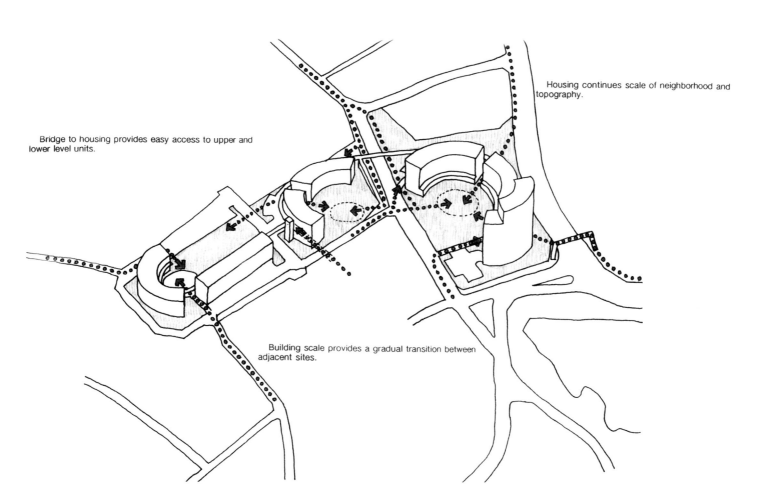

Bridge to housing provides easy access to upper and lower level units.

Housing continues scale of neighborhood and topography.

Building scale provides a gradual transition between adjacent sites.

Kadota Housing

208

Below Apartments at grade have patios designated for the elderly. Stairs link the garden to the upper walkway, feeding two units.

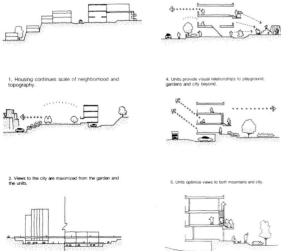

1. Housing continues scale of neighborhood and topography.

2. Views to the city are maximized from the garden and the units.

3. Continuous access system becomes a "Street in the Sky".

4. Units provide visual relationships to playground, gardens and city beyond.

5. Units optimize views to both mountains and city.

6. Use continuous access system as socializing space.

California

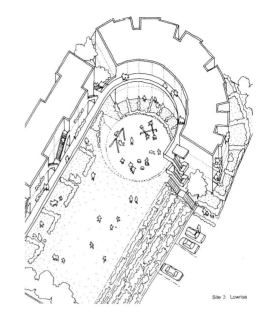

Site 3 Lowrise

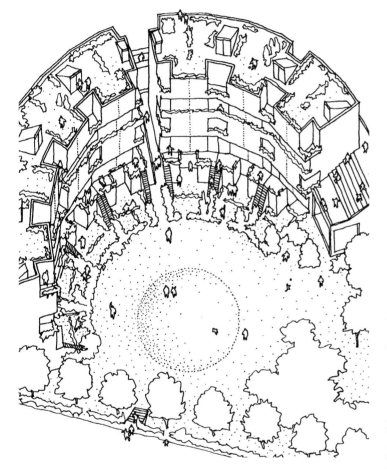

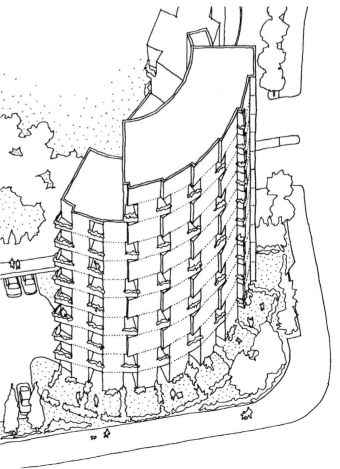

Kadota Housing

Dairi Nishi Apartments
Kitakyushu, Japan
1994

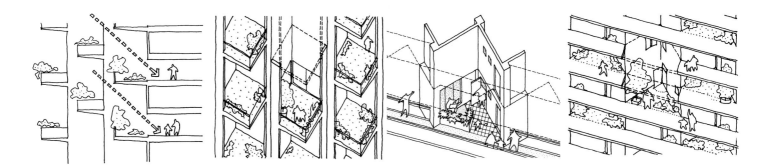

Opposite The shadow plot regulations designated the siting and volumetric limits for the building. Units were best planned in an offset pattern with terraces facing in two directions. To get sunlight deep into living rooms we made these double height and had alternating floor plans with continuous ducts. The entry space is also double height, allowing the small bedrooms to face a void on the upper levels. The patios function as outdoor rooms.

The same year as the Kadota Housing, we worked on another public housing project in Kitakyushu—107 units for the Fukuoka Prefecture. The site was on a hillside but facing north to the mountains. It had very stringent sunlight regulations which were calculated and plotted out before we began. The irregular pattern let us offset units to improve sunlight access to living rooms and patios. The size of predominantly three-bedroom units with tatami mats measured seventy-two to seventy-five square meters. We had learnt a strong message from

the Kadota Housing project about stacked units and, through experimentation, we found that there were spatial advantages to stacking two floors of plans with different arrangements but continuous ducts. This allowed us to build double high patios with increased sunlight penetration to living rooms. A "house in the sky," a concept built earlier in Cape Town, seemed to be buildable here in subsidized housing. The client loved the concept of patio houses which were a new idea and enthusiastically endorsed the project.

Outdoor access is typical in affordable housing in Japan, but bedroom windows on corridors are undesirable. Because of the geometry of the blocks, we were able to separate the windows from the access. The entry spaces to each unit are also double height, with downslope views. We expected that tenants would personalize these spaces. Management constrained this but only temporarily. Children's scooters, stools, and shoes were evident on a last visit.

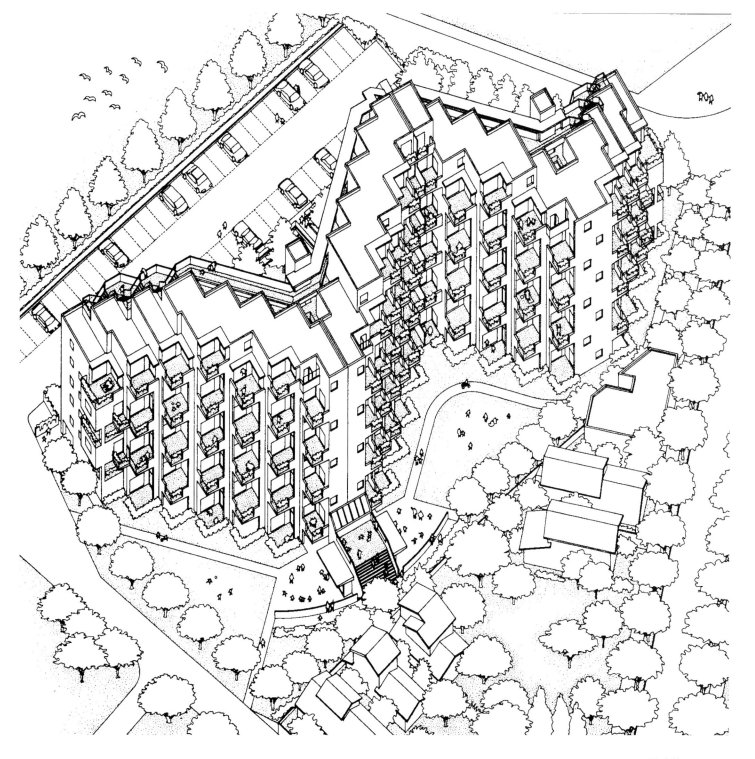

Dairi Nishi Apartments

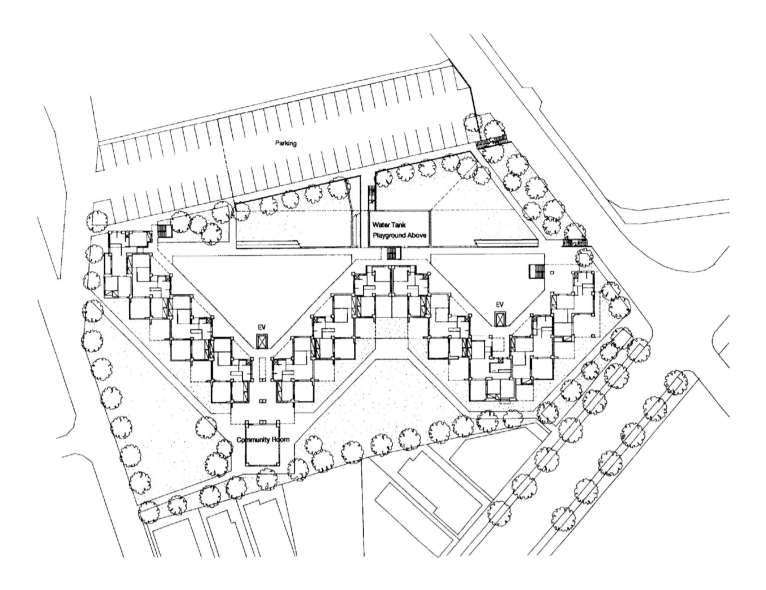

Parking

Water Tank
Playground Above

EV

EV

Community Room

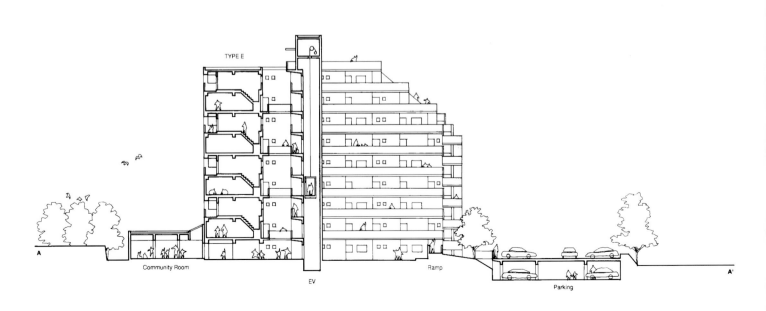

TYPE E

A

Community Room

EV

Ramp

Parking

A'

California

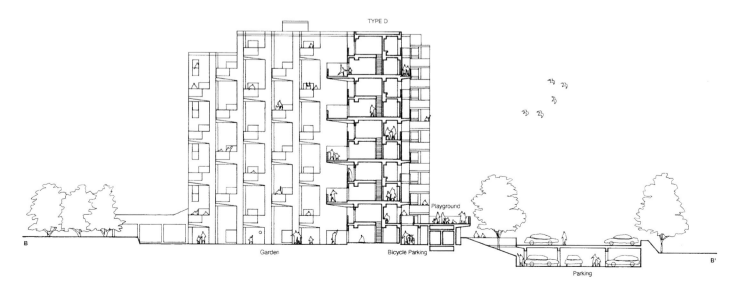

Dairi Nishi Apartments

214

California

Dairi Nishi Apartments

Reflections
Public Housing in Japan

I have often been asked why building housing in Japan was more attractive than doing so in the United States. One serious issue is that, in the United States, affordable housing has developed a set of standards and typical layouts that have become routine. Economics is the real driver, directed by the comparative data available, and local authorities have control over the building process. Given these stringent economics, developers are risk-averse to new or untested concepts.

Larger-scaled concepts appeared to be more experimental in Japan, driven by adventurous mayors, who are eager to be seen as progressive. Unfortunately, these elected positions are changed quite often. In reality, at a detailed level the construction is controlled by the building departments of the housing authorities with greater pragmatism, and their own rigid standards.

In my background, there were lingering ideas that had influenced my thinking about building housing at higher densities. Working with members of Team 10 during my time at the Architectural Association in London, two urban concepts remained in my mind. The "house in the sky" was an important one. I experimented with this concept in Cape Town but wished to repeat this for a more needy population. A "street in the sky" was a more complex endeavor. In Japan, however, both concepts had a good reception initially.

The concept for Kadota Housing, encouraged by the mayor, was to link land parcels together with a street that crossed one road but could be accessed from different levels of sidewalks on either side. The terrain was hilly and this was a practical concept, particularly for numerous elderly residents who lived in the area. Our original plan was to form a larger concept of several blocks as seen in the diagram.

Dairi Nishi Housing was perhaps the most important project we built exploiting the double-height patios and offset plans that responded to sunlight regulations. Pairing two floors with different plans but the same utility ducts is pragmatic but allows all units to have double high patios bringing sunlight light deeper into living areas. These patios are large enough to dine in and can be gardens. The access walkways are wide and used by children to play. Creating a recessed space off these for apartment entries also achieves a desirable area to be personalized, a place to sit and supervise children and enjoy the view. The geometry allows bedroom windows along the walkway to be recessed and private which solves another endemic issue

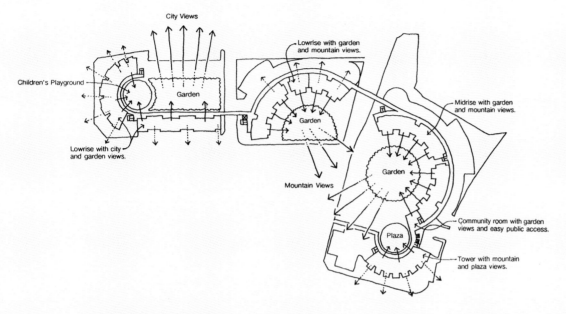

City Views

Lowrise with garden
and mountain views.

Children's Playground

Garden

Midrise with garden
and mountain views.

Lowrise with city
and garden views.

Garden

Mountain Views

Garden

Community room with garden
views and easy public access.

Plaza

Tower with mountain
and plaza views.

Form of housing and gardens respond
to special character of each site.

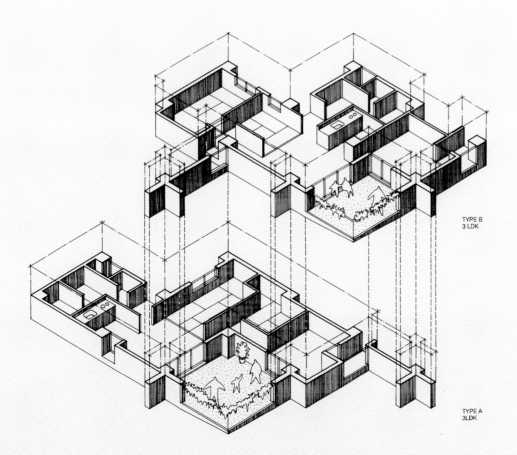

TYPE B
3 LDK

TYPE A
3LDK

UC Berkeley College of Environmental Design
San Francisco, California
1996–2004

My status in the University of California system continued in San Francisco. I agreed to take a part-time role, teaching one studio each semester at the graduate level. I also gave a course on housing design at the graduate level and taught undergraduate studios several times.

The move to UC Berkeley was inevitable. The first big decision was to live in the city and commute to Berkeley to teach. Loft living was my desire in an expensive context. Bargain seekers used the URMB list that revealed masonry structures that required steel reinforcement to survive, listed alphabetically. This was my tedious task. I decided to start with the last letter Z which led me to a vacant concrete warehouse near South Park. This property had two street facades on Zoe and on Ritch. Surprisingly, there was NO steel in the thick walls! This is what I bought and became my home and studio after extensive renovations.

San Francisco as a city was exciting from many perspectives. Living in a food obsessed city came with numerous affordable eateries. Festivals of all kinds took place including naked participants. A lively art scene and first class art museums and performance places. Parks with long histories. The waterfront as a public place and in particular the Saturday farmers market at the Ferry Building. This was a big cultural event each week with farmers bringing crops to sell, fresh fish and meat, international and local cheeses, mushrooms, pastries, and endless baked goods. A large

flower market brought color and more exotica. This
was a social gathering place to meet, enjoy good coffee
or lunch, and stock up on exceptional quality food.
I met friends there every week! The Ferry Terminal
functioned as a gourmet emporium during the week.

My participation at the university would not be full
time immediately to allow me time for my practice to
regroup. Thereafter I was willing to teach studios at
undergraduate and graduate levels and reframe my
Housing Theory course.

Yerba Buena Gardens Children's Center
San Francisco
1991

The Yerba Buena Gardens Children's Center was designed through an intense public process involving community interest groups and the San Francisco Redevelopment Agency. Public meetings were frequent at both small and large scales. Our services included programming, master planning, and architecture and interior design. We developed an explicit design process aimed at engaging participants in the evolution of the work and what issues were involved.

The site was the first issue—on the roof of the Moscone Convention Center, raised above the ground and possibly linked by a bridge to the adjacent site where the Esplanade, the central park, was located. The only ramp access was from the corner of Fourth and Howard Streets, which at deck level could join a bridge crossing to the Esplanade. On Howard Street, the volume of the Convention Center had been built and Third Street was dominated by the Moscone

Meeting Rooms under construction. The visibility of the project was confined to Fourth Street and part of Folsom Street.

The next challenge was to assign the extensive program to a location on the deck. The project would include the Zeum, exhibition and performance spaces dedicated to the needs of children, a childcare center, an ice-skating rink, a bowling alley, and a restaurant. In addition, we had to house an antique carousel. The carousel was not welcomed anywhere because of the noise and the potential vibration it caused. Yet, as a revered part of history, it needed great visibility. A welcome solution was the suggestion that the entry ramp could wind around this building. Childcare, an intensely private use, needed little public access and no visibility was consigned to the least accessible corner of Fourth and Folsom Streets. Due to its size and scale, the ice rink was located on Folsom Street with the bowling alley adjacent

but separated. Access to Folsom Street was important for the neighborhood and a public elevator could also serve the Childcare Center. The Zeum was placed in the most public position on Fourth Street, where the entry ramp and bridge to the Esplanade entered the deck.

Having placed the facilities on the deck through this deliberative process, we debated strategies to weave the various components together. As a public place, visitors and neighbors would be using the walkways to cross the blocks to downtown. There were many elderly living in the area who would use the gardens. A feature of the center would be views of children of different ages at play. Making activities visible in these facilities could be compelling. It also made sense for routes to be at two levels, more direct above and open-ended below. The gardens, designed in collaboration with landscape architect M. Paul Friedberg, started to take

Yerba Buena Gardens Children's Center

shape ahead of our work, and featured a large play circle, several other circular forms, and a potential amphitheater close to the carousel.

A covered walkway, defined by the edge of the buildings, would have views into exhibits, lobbies, shops, event spaces. A route above could serve the cafe above the bowling alley, viewing the gardens and downtown, as well as with views to the skaters in the ice rink. These ideas became very important. The Folsom Street elevator was an important component because it gave access to the deck and served this upper-level walkway.

The program for the Zeum was the only multi-story use, needing easy handicapped access. We chose to use a ramp around a lobby on several levels with an interactive video floor, a major endowed exhibit. Continuing to the roof, telescopes offered city views.

The ice rink faced the gardens with large glass windows and downtown views. The bowling alley was an internal experience, but the cafe terrace and shade roofs above made a perfect location to sit and enjoy the children's garden activities.

The childcare facility was scaled to meet the height of lower adjacent structures but sloped down internally to be more intimate for smaller children. Inside there were porches and a continuous playground. Patios facing Fourth Street formed outdoor rooms for preschool children.

The Zeum had flexible spaces of different heights to accommodate various programs. A permanent theater, in the round, had an independent lobby. Backstage spaces were adequate but small. A cafe was part of this lobby, serving both the audience indoors and anyone in the outdoor courtyard.

In the end, the facilities were built but with less durable materials than we specified. The metal panels were substituted by stucco on the walls facing the garden. As a new cultural facility, Zeum was finding its correct audiences and place in the complexity of San Francisco culture.

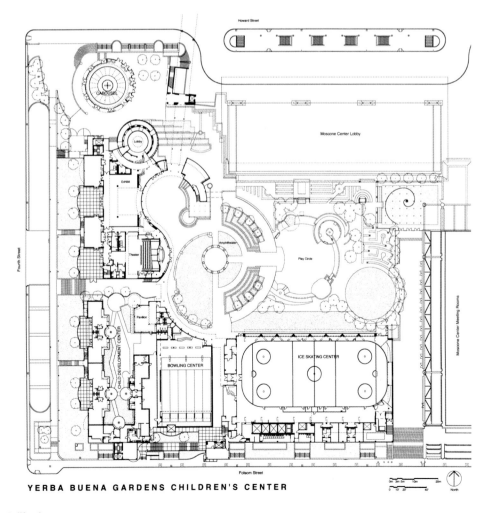

YERBA BUENA GARDENS CHILDREN'S CENTER

Opposite Located on the roof of the Moscone Center with only ground-level access, we had to fit mixed uses with different users, time of use, and different ages on top of meeting halls.

Developing a two-level circulation pattern across the site could be useful, a faster route and a meandering one. The upper level could become a protected system close to the building.

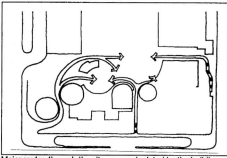

Major routes through the site are manipulated by the building forms.

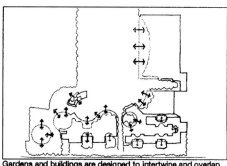

Gardens and buildings are designed to intertwine and overlap visually and functionally.

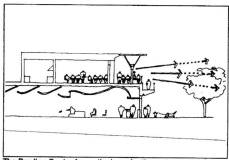

The Bowling Center forms the base for the restaurant and dining terraces above.

223

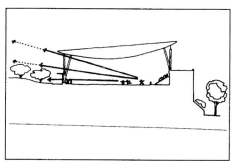

The glass wall of the Ice Rink affords views of the gardens and skyline beyond.

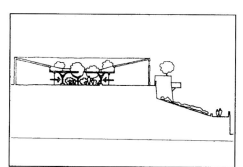

The Child Care building is high toward Fourth Street, where it has a civic presence. The roofs slope down to the courtyard to provide a more intimate, domestic scale.

The main pedestrian entry to the site is a gentle ramp from the corner of Fourth and Howard Streets.

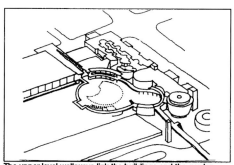

The upper level walkways link the buildings and the garden elements allowing for a continuous circulation loop.

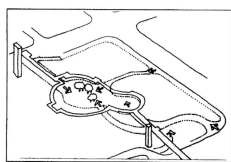

Two levels of circulation intertwine the buildings and the gardens and give access to facilities at both levels.

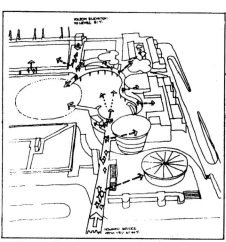

A bridge over Howard Street connects the site to the Esplanade and creates a pedestrian entry at an upper level. A walkway connects to the bridge and provides circulation through the complex.

Yerba Buena Gardens Children's Center

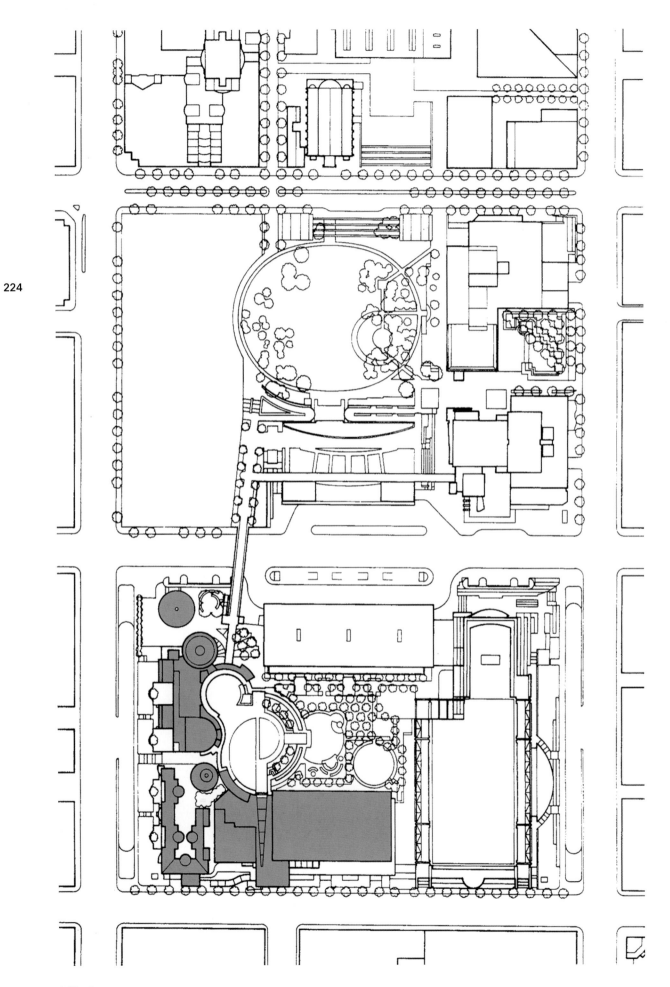

Yerba Buena Gardens Children's Center

226

Yerba Buena Gardens Children's Center

228

California

Yerba Buena Gardens Children's Center

California

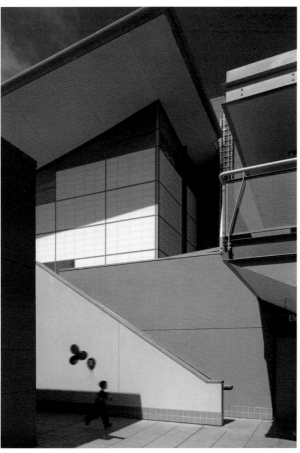

Yerba Buena Gardens Children's Center

Reflections
Three Public Space Designs in California

The design for Arts Park Los Angeles, Perris Civic Center, and Yerba Buena Gardens Children's Center occurred within the time period of 1989 to 1991. Arts Park and Perris Civic Center both started by excavating forgotten histories which became thematic starting points in the designs. The agricultural history of groves of fruit trees and the rhythmic spacing of these defines the Arts Park, and the history of sky watchers and contemporary versions with hot air balloons in addition to the landscape of rocks and agricultural landscapes were the focus in the Perris Civic Center. Including Yerba Buena Gardens in the comparison, all three projects were designed anticipating user experiences, views of activities, and journeys through space. Designing magical experiences link Perris with Yerba Buena through the faceted reflective glass walls in the courtyards and the reciprocal reflections in the carousel enclosure and the facetted lobby of Yerba Buena's Zeum ramp. In the courtyard between the Zeum and the store, one child is reflected dozens of times to become a crowd to their surprise and delight.

Neither Arts Park nor the Civic Center were built but some forms are given extended lives. The circular courtyards and conical glass roofs in Perris influenced the carousel and Zeum lobby grouping. Children are enchanted to watch the kaleidoscopic images of animals dancing past them from the Zeum ramp. The bar in the lake of Arts Park with the lantern roof is part of this set of iconic designed experiences.

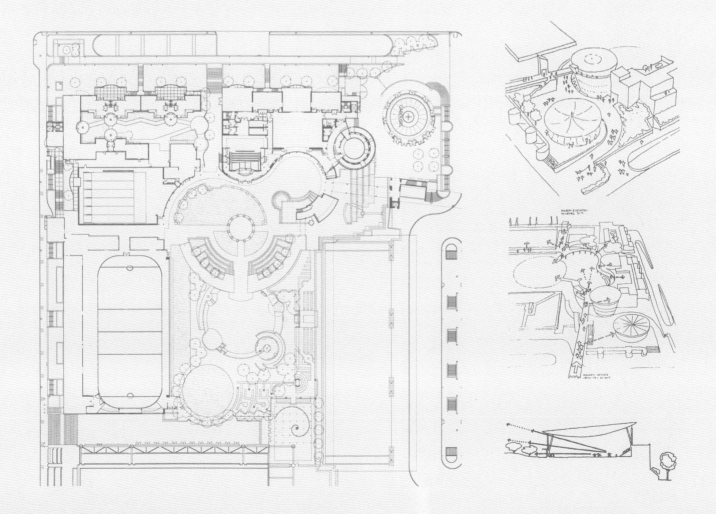

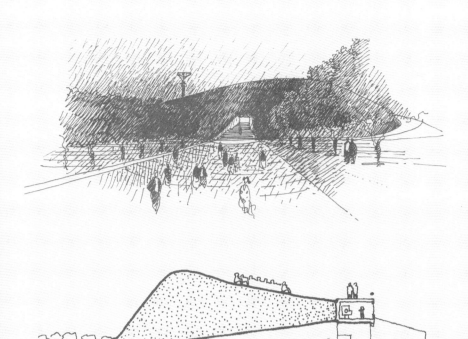

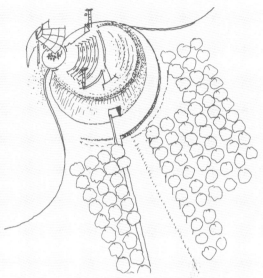

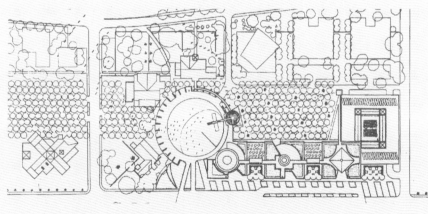

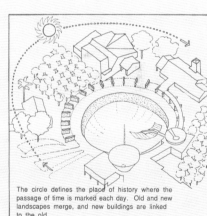

The circle defines the place of history where the passage of time is marked each day. Old and new landscapes merge, and new buildings are linked to the old.

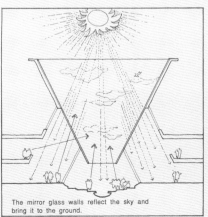

The mirror glass walls reflect the sky and bring it to the ground.

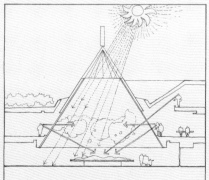

The courtyard gives light to the surrounding floors. The ground chamber display is reflected on the mirror glass walls.

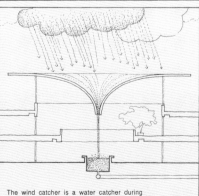

The wind catcher is a water catcher during rainfall.

John O'Connell High School
San Francisco, California
1995

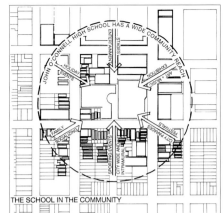

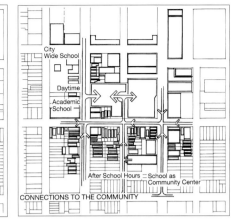

In 1995, we won a design competition for the John O'Connell High School in San Francisco's Mission District. The 120,000-square-foot technical high school serves predominantly hispanic youth. The concept was a significant departure for the San Francisco School Board. The school was designed to function academically as a high school entering from Folsom Street. After hours the building functioned as a community center, entered from 20th Street.

The elements of the plan were unusual too. From the academic entry, a three-story circulation spine covered in translucent glazing creates a gathering space for the students. From here, light can reach the classrooms and laboratories located on either side and cross ventilation minimizes dependence on mechanical systems. The classrooms also face gardens in the side yards. The window walls are offset vertically to maximize exposure to natural light.

The center of the spine widens to form an outdoor plaza with palm trees. The circular form creates a space for the cafeteria and auditorium to expand out to terraces. The library and art classrooms have expansive views above. From here, students can access the locker rooms and the gymnasium. The neighborhood field occupies the rest of the block.

This facility has an extensive community life. It is a good prototype in contexts that are overcrowded. Schools have outdoor spaces built into their programs for play and sports. By making these accessible to a wider audience, important community benefits could occur as demonstrated in this example. This is a wider community concept I have proposed before.

John O'Connell High School

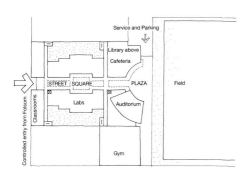

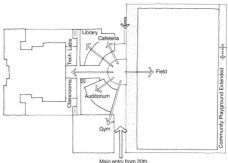

Left From the formal front door a daylit central spine leads to the community facilities. Gardens are located on the property edges and classrooms are stacked by size to maximize daylight conditions. Through ventilation is possible as the central spine is covered but allows air flow.

The community space has a semicircular courtyard with outdoor terraces for viewing events planned for the space.

The front facade is four floors high with a recessed entry and capped by a special vaulted room, the extension of the central spine.

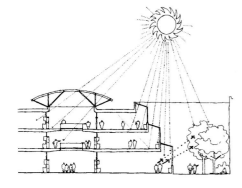

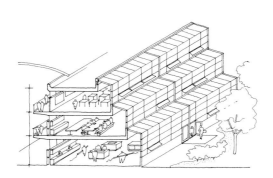

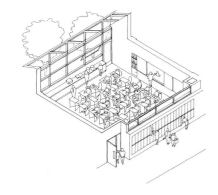

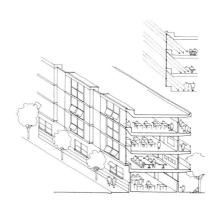

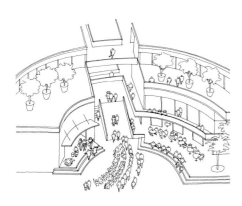

John O'Connell High School

California

John O'Connell High School

Ritch/Zoe Street Studios
San Francisco
1996

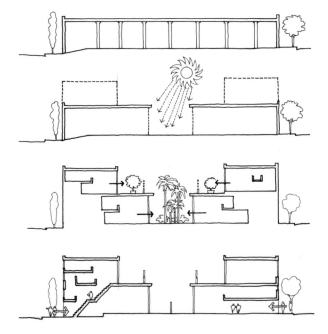

The area near South Park in San Francisco had become the locus for loft development with the park, a unique space, as a meeting place. It was also where many homeless people hung out, safety was not assured, and urban pioneers could buy property at reasonable costs.

I found a property fronting Ritch and Zoe Streets that had been a printing press recently but had previous lives as a warehouse. The twenty-foot-tall building was made of concrete with a timber framed roof. Surprisingly, the one-foot-thick walls had no steel reinforcement but few cracks.

I wanted to renovate the building, transforming it into five live-work lofts. The first task was to demolish the interior walls and floors and to reinforce the structure by adding more steel reinforcement and concrete to bring the building up to seismic standards.

The building is L-shaped and mostly 165 feet deep. A thirty-foot-wide courtyard was demolished in the middle to create gardens and bring in daylight. We added another twenty-foot-high floor above the existing building reaching the height limit. We wanted all units to have entry directly from the street and from individual parking spaces. Ground-level units all have private garden space, while upper units have wide terraces overlooking the inner courtyard, planted with palm trees. All living rooms are double-height spaces with plate glass doors opening to the gardens.

The two units on Zoe Street were initially merged to house our San Francisco office and with a residence on the two upper floors. Each unit has a separate entrance but are joined on the mezzanine level of the office where we had a conference room and library. The studio space has a forty-foot-long double-height glass wall facing the palm court. It was like working in an arboretum.

The upper unit is accessed by a stair that curves gently to disguise its length. The workspace on the second floor has a bathroom and is double-height at the window wall facing the street. This void connects with a dining space above. The workspace joins the office at the mezzanine. The living room on the third level is also a double-height space and opens onto a large deck. A stair, part of a bookcase, goes up to a study, bridging the space to the dining room and kitchen. Spaces are continuous but visually separated in this manner. The overall spatial effect on this level is complex with dramatic cross views down to the second level and up to the study. This was a perfect place to entertain faculty and visitors as had become my lifestyle!

California

Opposite The building was a one-floor warehouse about twenty feet high with access from two streets. For better light conditions a central courtyard was created. On the roof an addition was added facing each street with setbacks from the court for terraces.

Units are entered directly from the street. Parking garages for two cars are recessed and have private entries to each unit. These are live-work lofts with separate work spaces.

Ritch/Zoe Street Studios

California

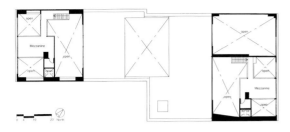

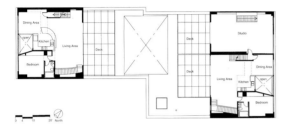

244

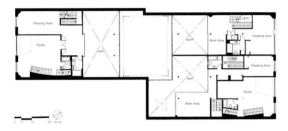

California

California

Bryant Street Lofts
San Francisco, California
1998

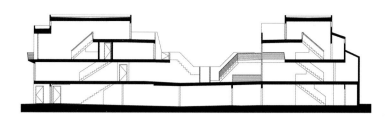

On Bryant Street we designed a live-work loft project with six multilevel units. The site was challenging due to its compactness, with only a window wall on Bryant Street. The surrounding streets were very noisy with frequent truck traffic. Neighboring buildings were mostly industrial, trending towards loft development.

All of the six units have an independent workspace with a separate entrance. The two street-facing lofts are entered from Bryant Street, while the three lofts on the rear boundary are entered through ground-level patios from the garage. The second floor above the garage has entrances to all living rooms with patios. Except for the middle unit facing Bryant Street, these are townhouses on four levels with two double-height rooms. To the rear, the building steps back twice to create skylights and bring ventilation to the living spaces.

Each unit is unique because abutting properties change the light qualities, and living patterns of the owners can be arranged differently. We assumed the room off the ground-level patios would be for work, but some owners use these suites for guests.

The generous garden balconies and patios are well-planted and maintained, making a very private oasis in the city. The street frontage blends with the industrial character of the neighborhood keeping this place a secret.

Opposite This formerly industrial property had no light access from the rear, nor from the sides. A central courtyard was inevitable. Six multilevel live-work units with two entries were built. All units have residential entries on the second floor with individual patios.

Light at the rear was created by stepping the facade backwards, shaping skylights.

Bryant Street Lofts

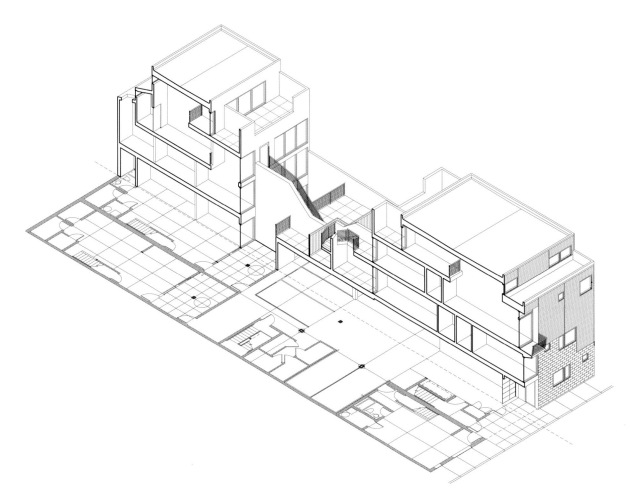

Bryant Street Lofts

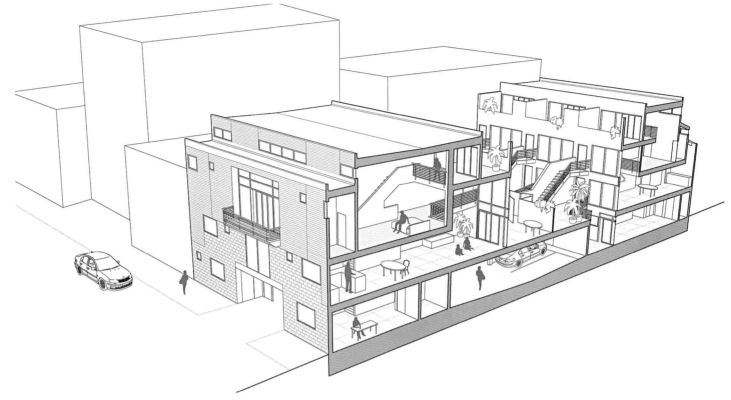

California

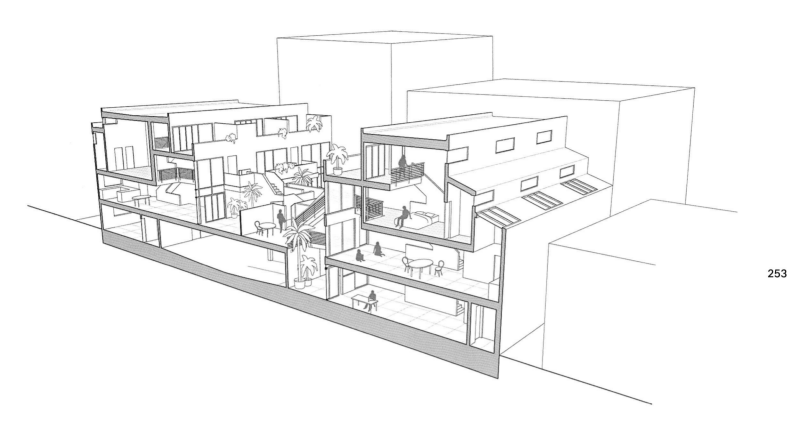

Bryant Street Lofts

Reflections
The House as Workplace

Even today there are few urban areas that encourage live-work environments; many contexts actively prevent this very attractive compact way of living. Having one multipurpose place is also economical and eliminates everyday commuting to work. Historically, women cared for children at home and earned income doing domestically condoned activities. Writers, artists, and scholars often found this way of life convenient as well. Since the pandemic, working at home has been well-tested, and being full-time in the workplace is under assault. Productivity levels while working at home are high, even higher than in a typical office by some estimates. There will inevitably be pressure to create zoning changes to allow more flexible mixed-use housing typologies and better choices for the work week.

Artists were early inhabitants of former industrial spaces. Their high ceilings and abundant natural light were considered glamorous. In cities like San Francisco, higher-income occupants loved these places too, pushing prices higher until these units were no longer viable for artists. A zoning fight was inevitable, and this land use was eliminated. I was living in San Francisco at the time and have always practiced this efficient way of living. I have converted industrial spaces and built new lofts units, always including a viable workspace. One of the legal obstacles for cities like San Francisco was verifying that work is taking place. This is no longer a credible factor.

Spaces for living face south.

Spaces for work face north.

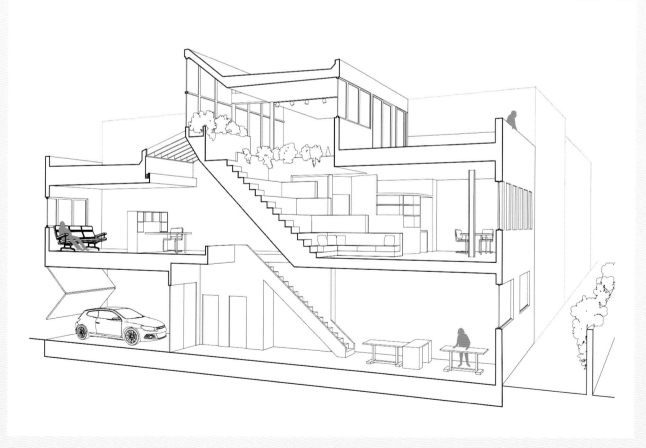

Mission Creek Senior Community
Mission Bay Development
San Francisco, California
2001

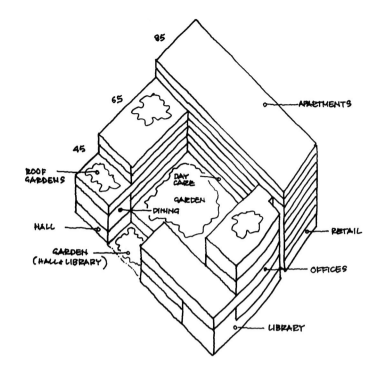

Along San Francisco's Mission Creek, we designed a mixed-use Senior Community complex. The block consists of 140 subsidized apartments for seniors, a branch of the Public Library, a community meeting hall, Adult Day Health Center, non-profit offices, and a corner coffee shop. We were appointed by the San Francisco Redevelopment Authority to serve as the design architects for the building and were the interior architects for the branch library.

The site had four distinct faces, which strongly influenced how we positioned the programming of the block. The most important and visible location was Fourth Street, and this particular site was considered the gateway to Mission Bay. In this publicly prominent location, it seemed appropriate to locate the branch library on the ground floor, with offices on the upper levels. The library's reading room occupied the prime corner of Fourth Street and Mission Creek. Berry Street was quieter and therefore most suitable as a frontage for housing. The Mews was a pedestrian street between blocks, connecting Berry Street to the walk along the river. The residential entrance on Berry Street, close to the Mews, was functionally in the best position to serve these units.

A sheltered, south-facing garden was placed in the center of the block. From here the water views are spectacular. The gardens terrace down to the ground extending views from the public walkway into the site. A common dining room and other social spaces face the garden, which is specially designed for the use of seniors. The space is shared by the Adult Day Health Center, which has an independent entrance. The social spaces of this facility face the creek.

The apartments are one-bedroom units, some designed for two people. Each unit has a small basic kitchen, handicapped bathroom, and a balcony for sitting and growing plants. Ground-floor units have patios. There are several lounge areas on each floor and many have city views and balconies.

This mixed-use block was very appropriate for the urban context and takes advantage of the different visual environments, relative noise levels, and safety concerns for the users.

Opposite This site had four distinct edges. Fourth Street was the major street for public functions while Berry Street is residential– a pedestrian mews for housing views and a boardwalk on the creek of Mission Bay for open space.

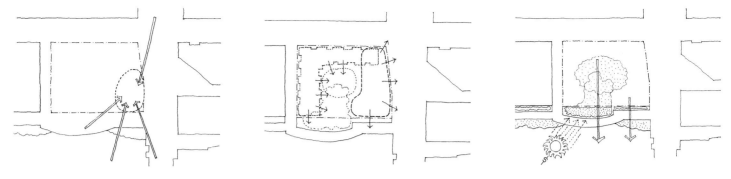

California

Mission Creek Senior CommunityMission Bay Development

260

Below The Public Library was a separately commissioned part of the project. The books were selected for this community. The easy covered walk for the seniors with a coffee shop on the corner of Berry Street was very popular.

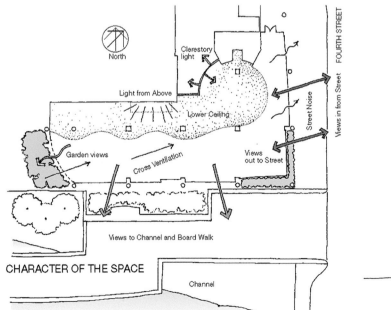

CHARACTER OF THE SPACE

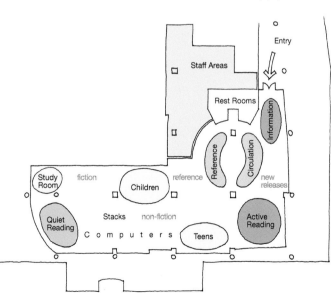

California

Rock Houses
San Francisco, California
2002

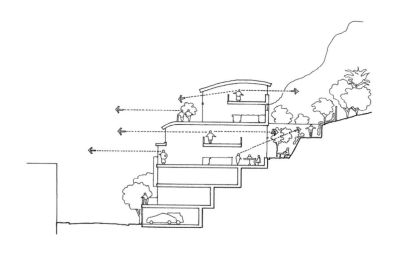

In 2002, we took on a design project for a site above the Castro District, where the land seemed too steep for development, but the views were exceptional. There was an unserviced shack on the site which could not be demolished until a replacement building plan was approved. We designed two stacked houses for the site with a small, shared elevator and two stairs. Rock gardens in the rear would be needed for ventilation, and we wanted to offer large balconies and roof terraces for viewing the city.

The site is a rock outcropping that rises straight up from the street edge to approximately 30 feet. A narrow staircase was the only access. Blasting was not allowed in residential neighborhoods. Luckily, the rock could be excavated for a twenty-foot depth needed to park two cars. The structure needed exceptional care with much steel reinforcement. The first habitable level area was at 30 feet and then continued upwards.

The upper house has two bedrooms, the lower house has three. Both units have double-height living and dining rooms. Outdoor balconies, generous terraces, and rock gardens address the special views. The upper house rises above the adjacent property to be a pavilion with views in all directions. The lower unit has three floors above parking plus a mezzanine. The upper house has three floors. The building has seven floors, the maximum height.

The complex was under construction when I was offered the deanship of Architecture and Planning at MIT. I was reluctant to sell this unusual property, but I would need to relocate to Boston and likely build again. I sold this to an eager developer who built this luxury building as designed and was richer in the process!

Rock Houses

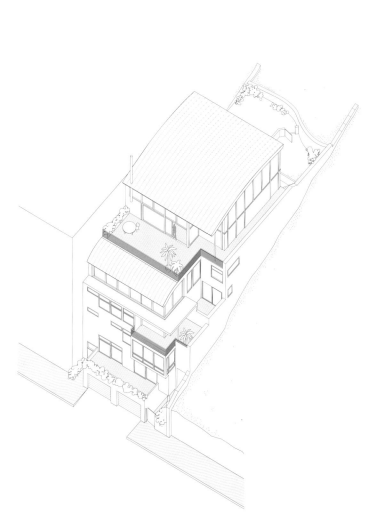

Above The site could be excavated to allow for parking, an elevator and two egress stairs on the ground floor, plus much steel reinforcing. Two stacked units were built with bedrooms on the lower two floors, and a living room, dining area and a study mezzanine on the third level. A rock garden was created at the rear for light and ventilation. The living room, mezzanine study, and deck views were spectacular as predicted.

Rock Houses

4

Massachusetts Institute of Technology

2004-15 MIT Dean of the School of Architecture and Planning at MIT
Practice: Adèle Naudé Santos and Associates, Somerville, Massachuse
Practice: Santos Prescott and Associates San Francisco, California

I was aware of the search for a new dean at MIT but was enjoying my life and work In San Francisco. Several attempts to engage me in this discussion particularly that this position was "Big Time" was useless. A deanship at a private university I knew would be more creative, possibly make an impact on architectural education but was this worth more time in my life? Finally I agreed to have a discussion on architectural education, made a date but then broke my ankle! Even some relief!! After this a search committee was dispatched to visit me at my house composed of bright, lively, energetic people of course. As soon as I could walk I went on a visit to meet the provost and wider Search Committee. By then it was clear that I was the top candidate.

What convinced me to accept this move to Cambridge? This was a place that I knew well and had lived in for many years. My MArch in urban design was from the GSD; I taught there several times over the years and had old friends still living there. I always felt at home in Cambridge. Leaving San Francisco was another issue entirely and one that I assumed would not be permanent. The discussion with MIT was a five-year commitment; I would not sell my property there but would need help in establishing a home and studio here. My practice would continue and be bicoastal with my long-term associate in charge of San Francisco. Unfortunately a deanship at MIT needs more than the five years I had hoped for, and despite the time San Francisco has never left my mind.

Taking on the deanship at MIT was an honor and a large task that occupied me for ten years. I was determined to continue my practice but scaled this down to fit into time available outside of my position at MIT. I was dean of Architecture, Planning and the Media Lab, which included the Center for Real Estate; Art, Culture, and Technology (ACT); and added the Center for Advanced Urbanism. As one of six deans at MIT, I also played an active role as advisor to the upper administration, and the deans worked together most Tuesday mornings. At this juncture, the Department of Architecture needed the most immediate help academically, although over time I had to be actively involved with all units.

A looming issue was space for all departments. They were scattered on campus and were not equal in quality, some even being sub-standard. The construction of the new Media Lab building was canceled shortly before I arrived.

My first task was to hire a new head of architecture to replace the person who had this position for fifteen years— too long by any standard. The alumni, among others, were recommending a practitioner and academic after the historian and theorist who had been in place. It was also clear that more practitioners from diverse backgrounds were needed as visitors. Opening up the department to a wider international world would be refreshing. I launched an international search, visited shortlisted candidates in person, and ultimately recommended Yung Ho Chang from China, who was considered a rising star. He was educated in the United States and a professor at Peking University. This was a good time for him to transition to MIT, and together we brought in two more faculty members: Nader Tehrani, who has been on the Harvard GSD faculty, and Rahul Mehrotra from Mumbai, who

was at the University of Michigan at the time. I knew from experience that it could take very few new voices to change the academic context. New faculty came with new connections and guests, and with new international studios and workshops. Two Urban Laboratories, research and teaching, were started—one in China and one in India. The China connection was very fruitful academically and also broadened my professional horizon.

Over the ten years of my tenure, we were able to fund and build the new Media Lab building, designed by Fumihiko Maki; add a mezzanine floor for undergraduate architecture students in the main building; and bring the departments into two buildings. Planning retained its status as the top program in the country; the Media Lab remained a formidable asset; and the architecture program was declared the best program in the world. The administration and the department were thrilled. My key mission over these years had been to get the Architecture Department the status it deserved.

My role as a teacher was limited during the academic year so I sought opportunities in the summer and the independent activity period (IAP). My best forms of teaching were workshops conducted with partner schools such as Southeast University (SEU) in Nanjing, China, and Shi Chien University in Taipei, Taiwan. China was the best option to bring MIT students for summer housing workshops, using real sites and programs. Later, I helped organize design-build workshops with China Art Academy in collaboration with Wang Shu and faculty from SEU and MIT. With Shi Chien University, during IAP, we spent less time but these workshops were more experimental. MIT students came from all departments, and engaged with local students from the industrial design, architecture, media studies and fashion programs to confront urban issues in that context.

During my tenure as dean I received two important international awards for contributions to architectural education. The first was the Topaz Medallion for Excellence in Architectural Education in 2009, awarded to one person annually by the American Institute of Architecture and the Association of Collegiate Schools of Architecture (ACSA). In the announcement, the jury commended my "holistic approach to architecture." Their statement said:

> Her belief that architecture transcends accommodation of programmatic requirements to also satisfy the human spirit has resulted in buildings that are characterized by abundant natural light, connections to nature, and innovative spatial arrangements. She pays close attention to the people affected by her design, whether it be community groups on the development of housing, faculty or administrative committees on institutional projects, or collaborations with artists and administrators on arts-related spaces.

The second recognition for my academic work was the Freedom Award given by the President of China to about thirty-five individuals globally for contributions to Chinese culture, mine being to graduate education. This came with a high-level visit, a banquet, handshakes with the premier, and gifts!

After my deanship at MIT, I continued to create workshops on affordable housing in Colombia, Brazil, and Guiana, which culminated in Housing+, an international conference I curated. We organized an exhibition of workshops, led by myself, faculty, and graduate students.

A summary of four workshops were shown in the European Cultural Council annual exhibition in Venice in 2021 as "Housing as Community."

My theme of "building community" started while at the University of Pennsylvania, when I was chair of Architecture. During my time in San Diego, this concept became more public, as the evolving school created opportunities for a community of professionals to meet, interact, and learn from visiting speakers almost each week.

As always, I had an open-door policy. At the beginning of each year I hosted three faculty gatherings at my house and courtyard to which all faculty were invited. Fortunately, there was a mix of faculty from different backgrounds and people enjoyed meeting new colleagues. I certainly engaged individually with faculty, their promotions, research opportunities, and career choices. I also regularly met with student groups as a way to understand issues that were evolving. To my surprise, the part that I missed most after I stepped down from deanship was being part of the MIT community, meeting each Tuesday morning with exceptional colleagues, stimulating discussions and debates on complex issues to be solved.

One day in Spring 2004, the forgotten fax machine in our office in Beijing made a sudden crack then started printing. It was a letter from Adèle Naudé, then the dean of the MIT School of Architecture and Urban Planning, inviting me to apply for the headship of the Architecture Department. In case I would agree, she was planning to come to Beijing right away to pay me a visit. I was so surprised but said yes anyway. The purpose of Adèle's trip to Beijing was primarily to check out my "natural habitat," as she put it. As soon as she landed, I took her to see our well-weathered, traditional one-story studio behind a vegetable garden we cultivated in the ruined Old Summer Palace on the outskirts of the city as well as the flat we renovated for ourselves in a 1950s walk-up apartment block in one of the back corners of the Peking University campus, where I was teaching. What did she see in these places? I wondered.

In July of the following year, I was sitting in a meeting in the dean's office of MIT School of Architecture and Planning and watching Adèle stirring her coffee with a felt-tip pen, the same pen she used to letter, not write, notes down in her sketchbook as if on a set of working drawings. That soon became a rather familiar scene with increasing number of meetings I attended.

Adèle's felt-tip pen and lettering, as well as the wide-rimmed glasses she wears, are constant reminders that she is someone who is, first and foremost, an architect, an architect who touches the world via the tools and utensils in her hands, then an educator, a dean. However, I am perhaps among the few people who do not need those reminders since I have had the opportunities to see her work in Cape Town, San Francisco, Shanghai (where we worked side by side), Somerville, and Gloucester.

After visiting her buildings on three continents, I could sense that her architectural work is her way to engage and embrace the tangible world with love, a lot of it. Adèle treats a piece of brick, a wooden beam, a plant, or a cat (she has quite a few) all with tenderness. Her burned-down foundry-theater turned home on Village Street in Somerville is a beautiful testimony of such approach to interventions to reality: Wild, lush garden juxtaposed with freestanding, darkened-by-fire brick wall fragments; everyday, at certain hour in the evening, a train roars by behind the back wall, the house full of folk-art trembles merrily along with the trees outside. It seems that Adèle designed that too. I guess that might be what she saw in Beijing, her own urban oasis, a miniature summer palace.

I believe that Adèle led the MIT School of Architecture and Planning with a sensibility that is not dissimilar to her practice as an architect: She revived design at the school with a renewed passion for using hands and brain simultaneously, true to the MIT motto "Mens et Manus." Design is about making, with technology both high and low. She pushed and grounded ideas, concepts, and theories and put architecture, planning, visual art, and the Media Lab all on the same page. During her time as the dean, everything from brick domes and rammed earth to artificial muscles and 4D printing flourished. As a leader, Adèle defines open-mindedness and sharpness. For the latter, like a seasoned detective, she senses a lead and goes after it with her instinct. Perhaps, hiring someone from as far as Beijing to head the Department of Architecture could serve as proof for both of her virtues?

As an architect myself, I share Adèle's commitment to the betterment of the living environment of humanity as well as to build. In my role as an educator, under her leadership and with her full support at MIT, I reconfigured the theory-practice relationship in architectural programs: The top-down model of theory to practice, which reduces practice to the explanation of theory, was replaced by the one of a horizontal loop for practice, which is both the departure point and the outcome of the ring, with theory injected along the way. As a practitioner, I take an ontological position and focus on the fundamental issues of architecture: material, structure, construction, space, form, and content.

This volume on Adèle Naudé's work is not only the portfolio of one architect but also a manifestation of a generation of architects, who may not voice their opinions as much while caring about the smallest details of their design and living every minute of their life devoted to architecture and who deserve our salutes.

Yung Ho Chang

Essential Kitchen

I could always count on the wooden stool in Adèle Naudé's transformed foundry kitchen as the place I could unburden, decompress, ask for advice, or work through a challenging Gordian knot. Somehow, there, in Adèle's "essential" kitchen, there would always appear all the right ingredients to nourish the body, mind, and soul. As far as I could tell, she never followed or used a recipe when cooking, she would create and plate on the spot... all the while building up those around her.

She has a special gift for building something remarkable from what others find limiting. She did this with the derelict brick foundry in Somerville. She rescued and restored it by reinventing it. She saw the raw potential in the double-height gantry space, the open but protected courtyard, and knew just which added elements were critical to reimagining the foundry as a place to live, work, and build a school. Adèle literally built the most essential foundations of the faculty in that courtyard. She hosted three evenings each fall where one third of the faculty from Architecture, Planning, and the Media Lab would come together. And as the faculty—junior and senior, techy and design-y, scholarly and applied research-y—mingled and mixed in her courtyard, fellowship flowed, mutual respect formed, and collaborations emerged. She enabled trust and nurtured potential through sharing her "home" and her ethos. Like the foundry, she could see the potential in MIT and the School of Architecture and Planning—what made it special and unique, and just the right areas that needed a nudge and a push. Adèle's leadership at MIT was bold and generous but never heavy-handed or undiscerning. Like the context of the foundry, or the ingredients on hand in the kitchen, her special form of leadership came from her ability to see potential and announce that potential with the confidence of conviction.

When Adèle arrived at MIT, I was a junior faculty member (probably the most junior of the litter). Her presence felt like a gust of warm air (with a hint of coriander, cumin, and paprika all mixed together) had blown in from one end of the "infinite corridor" to the other.

While Adèle was dean, I found myself reinstalling *White Noise White Light* (an installation I made for the Athens Olympics) outside Kresge Hall for the then new MIT President Susan Hockfield's inauguration. I also found myself co-curating the Festival for Art Science and Technology for MIT's 150th Anniversary a few years later, where we installed works by faculty across MIT (including in the Charles River). By "found myself," of course I mean it was all masterminded by Adèle. She often found ways to give junior faculty unprecedented opportunities. Because of Adèle, I not only found direction and momentum at MIT, I also found mentorship, encouragement, and honesty. She created not only opportunities but helped build in others the ability to take on those opportunities.

Without Adèle, I would also not have had found myself the head of the Department of Architecture at MIT. It was through her encouragement, support, trust, and generosity that I found academic leadership impactful. And it was also through her "nudge" that I found myself taking on a deanship at the College of Architecture, Art, and Planning at Cornell.

And even now, when I find myself with a Gordian knot, I channel all the things I learned in her "essential" kitchen.

J. Meejin Yoon

An International Collaboration

During her tenure as dean of MIT's School of Architecture and Planning, professor Adèle Naudé and her students collaborated with Southeast University's School of Architecture in a number of ways. At the time, I served as the dean of SEU's School of Architecture, and we became great friends.

She regularly visited our school over the course of this ten-year partnership, at moments several times year, which benefited both our faculty and students. Housing research served as the foundation for the partnership between the two institutions, which later developed into urban studies and contemporary rural research. We jointly founded the cooperative Advanced Urban and Rural Center at SEU in 2017, and professor Naudé and I currently serve as its co-directors. MIT, SEU, and the Chinese Academy of Art collaborated on a summer workshop under the direction of professors Wang Shu and Lu Wenyu as the center's study expanded to cover rural building and new institutions. Professor Naudé was asked to join SEU as an honorary professor in particular recognition of her long-term exceptional contributions to our university. She has garnered widespread attention for her tenacious advocacy of architectural education in China, as a result of which, in 2017, she received the highest honor given by the Chinese government to foreign specialists who have made remarkable contributions to the nation's economic and social development, the Friendship Award. I believe the honor results from genuine distinction.

I initially spoke with Professor Naudé during the two schools' inaugural collaborative workshop. In a practical project sponsored by Nanjing Suning Universal Cooperation, the objective was to investigate the novel potential of low-rise, high-density residential prototypes. As a member of the generation of urban designers who saw how China's rapid urbanization resulted in "thousands of cities with one face" and "thousands of buildings with one appearance" due to a straightforward urban regulation requiring a minimum amount of natural daylight illumination, I'm constantly looking for new typologies to address the issue. The goal of the collaborative workshop was to further this study by focusing on the architectural principles of the traditional Chinese prototype of a "家"("home residential") morphology. My first impression of her was a well-mannered, well-dressed, well-educated architect with a clear and determined mind. On the basis of mutual trust, SEU and MIT have since strengthened ties in research and teaching collaboration, academic exchanges, and practice cooperation, with the help of professor Chang Yungho and many young talents including Ge Wenjun and Zhang Yao among others.

The first time that I visited MIT was in 2009 when I made an academic presentation on the digital control method of building height of Nanjing. I went to MIT for the second time the winter of 2016. The Great Lakes region's cold current caused the temperature to plunge to close to zero Fahrenheit. However, it did not put an end to the animated conversation that followed my speech. Professor Naudé also set up a visit to her most recent timber structure house project, which was still being built at the time, for myself and my colleagues, professors Han Dongqing and Ge Ming. For those of us who understood nothing about the modern engineering, glulam system's creation, it was a great learning experience. After returning from Boston, I had the chance to participate in a state project where I was able to clarify my doubts and uncertainties regarding the building process that results in the use of contemporary timber technology in the main exhibition hall of the Jiangsu Province Horticulture Expo. In order to finish numerous important structures for the expo park, I also invited professor Naudé's team to work on the same project. The project's execution was made possible with the assistance of professor Ge Ming and several others, and it just won the Jiangsu Province first prize for the year's best architectural project. The *Architectural Journal*, one of China's premier academic publications, used a photo of our building on the cover of an article on the entire project.

Professor Naudé has a wide perspective and an excellent eye for both academic research and practice. She has devoted a lot of time, as far as I know, to studying various living conditions and lifestyles across the world. Even while residential projects make up the majority of her finished works, each one demonstrates her excellent design abilities and the results of extensive study. I appreciate her contribution to housing by creating multiple interpretations of the traditional definition of home and the conceptual evolution of the home caused by the constantly changing way of living, as well as her exploration of the dynamic relationship between the private and public in housing through the lens of micro-urbanism, and last but not least, her interest in the expansion of the power of light and shadow in architecture to increase the interaction between the built and the natural environment.

She and I worked closely together for more than 10 years, during which time she led the international assessment team at the School of Architecture at SEU. I'm extremely appreciative of the many insightful contributions she made to the advancement of the architecture field. Her advice to retain an open mind, broaden one's perspective on all types of design, enhance international collaboration, and do comparative research with other countries continues to ring true to me and serve as a reminder.

The legacy of the exchanges between the two schools has, in short, become a treasured part of the history of the School of Architecture at SEU, with plenty of inspirational tales to tell, thanks to Professor Naudé's sustained support. I have benefited from working with her as a "mentor and friend" throughout the years, and I have a great deal of admiration for her charm and brilliance, as well as how she uses both to advance the discipline of architecture.

Professor Jianguo Wang

I arrived to MIT in the fall of 2016, leaving behind my girlfriend Alessandra, a parrot called Cesarino, and a small apartment, which the three of us shared in Rotterdam. Along with my cohort, I met Adèle in December, when she joined as a guest critic for the final reviews of our design studio. Three weeks later, along with ten other students, we were flying to Cartagena for a workshop on low-income housing. I understood only later how Adèle had composed the team for that workshop, and the reason behind her peregrination to practically all the design studio reviews that fall. Not following grades but empathy, we had been invited to join in the same way in which one would choose their guests, making sure that mutual interests would be developed, skills would complement each other, and conversations would never be dull. The workshop in Colombia was to be the first of many, all inspired by the belief that the relation between practice and academia can be a gradient, and that applied research, within the design disciplines, gives dignity and meaning to the work produced. While many in academic circles were discussing the "agency" of design disciplines, the immediate implications of that first workshop in Cartagena made space for more optimistic thought—that speculative, future-oriented work becomes more radical when applied, that projects don't just respond to a context like an answer to a question, but produce contexts, and, in turn, open up possibilities for design and life.

Back in Boston, Adèle invited us all to her home in Somerville. I remember ringing the bell at the yellow door in Village Street in the snow, slipping a few times on the icy road, and being welcomed in the kind of house one would never want to leave. Adèle was cooking, some early arrivals were sharing drinks and stories, while Mio, her parrot, was doing his best to make his preferences clear, bowing to his favorite humans and shamelessly snubbing the others. Zeus and Devi, Adèle's cats, spent the evening seducing every student, a strategic move which paid off in the form of culinary bribes for purrs. The house was a collection of stories, where fragments of life and work were tied by a passion for projects, by the possibility of designing not just spaces, but relations between people, countries, animals, and objects. Her home in Somerville, and as I would later learn, most of her work, was more than the quality of its design, but a commitment to places and people, an understanding of design which encompassed the possibility of proposing not just a house, but a way to live. The sense of adventure in her home and her work still speak to me of the joy of imagining one's life through changes, chances, commitments, always through projects, through ideas and hopes for the future.

That same evening, after a few glasses of wine, I asked Adèle if she was looking for a tenant for her guest room, trying not to show how desperate I was to leave the hyper-controlled world of MIT's student housing, while promising I'd take care of her birds, cats, and plants. I felt that my experience with Cesarino would lend the necessary credibility to my proposal. Adèle laughed, and some months later, when I had moved to the studio above her office, told me just how cheeky she thought my question had been. It turned out that the little ecosystem of Village Street was one to become part of, and not just to maintain, and that the people, animals, and plants who lived, worked with, or visited her world, would also be taking care of me.

Over the next few years, along with many of the students from that first workshop in Colombia I traveled with Adèle to Brazil and then Guyana, as a borderless project focusing on low-income housing was unfolding. Along with colleagues, we were lucky enough to follow these projects beyond the time constraints of the workshop and took part in their development into long-lasting relations with institutions and associations, blurring the line between the shelter of our academic environment and the urgencies of the ground. Perched above Adèle's office, the occasional gardening and medical treatment of the cats went along with my commitment to befriend Mio the parrot, and the incredible fortune of having Adèle's feedback, criticism, and support throughout my studies. Today I'm back in Rotterdam, Alessandra and I survived the long-distance relationship, and the sense of adventure and love for projects inspired us to open our studio, which we share with our bird.

Giovanni Bellotti

Village Street
Somerville, Massachusetts
2004

278

Village Street

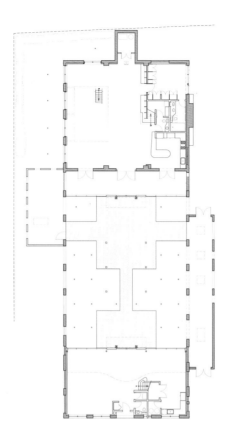

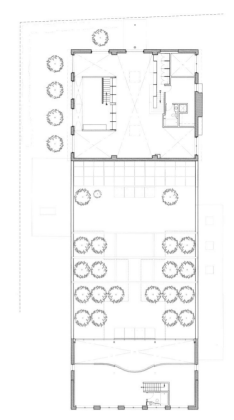

280

Upon taking on the deanship at MIT, an important task personally was to replace the live-work space I had in San Francisco with another similar environment. I knew that I would need space for entertaining as I had in San Diego and San Francisco—this was to be expressive of my architectural sensibility.

The former bronze foundry, McCann Bronze Incorporated, was built around 1860. It was known for exceptional workmanship. A devastating fire in the mid-twentieth century demolished most of the interior space, with the exception of the foundry. An artist purchased the ruin and made minimal renovations using the habitable space as her studio. In the interior garden, left by the fire, she built the Children's Circus, an outdoor performance space where children learned to become amateur performers.

The outer brick walls of the complex survived the fire and enclosed this very secret garden,

The foundry still had gantry beams and tracks, and the original timber roof was intact. When I bought the building, I stripped it down to the original 1860 conditions. All mechanical, electrical, and plumbing systems were renewed, and all windows and doors were replaced. Hydronic heating was included in a new concrete floor. I suspended a mezzanine study from the gantry beams. Two bedrooms, bathrooms, a utility area, and kitchen were built on the east side where some service lines still existed. A greenhouse was added to the south wall at the garden to insulate the building and allowed the brick walls to be exposed on both sides.

In the second phase, I added a new studio into the brick walls on the street. The workspace is double height on the north with a glass wall facing the garden. A mezzanine is suspended from glulam beams, to allow unobstructed space below. Two bedrooms and baths and a study were planned for this

level. The curved vault of the roof brings the structure down to sixteen feet on the garden side for reasons of scale. The window wall is approximately forty-eight feet long and full height. The garden is planted with flowering trees, with a large brick-paved courtyard with a shade canopy. The office was housed here, and my practice could resume.

The foundry occupied two large properties. There was also a public right of way that had been partially built on and was attached to the house. The city gave this to me plus half of the road. The second property had a storage facility that was condemned early after I bought the land. I kept this fenced until I could develop it.

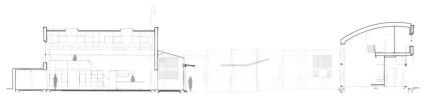

282

Village Street

23 Village Street
Somerville, Massachusetts
2013

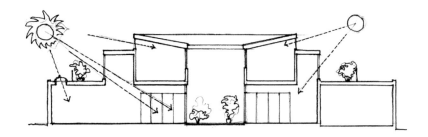

On a property adjacent to the foundry, there was a storage building on the street. This building location was allowed historically in what were setbacks, on the property line, and fifteen feet from the street. We kept the foundations and party wall and built a residence. There was space for another house at the rear, and we made a lane to serve the garage for the residency at number 23, and access to a future house at 25 Village Street.

The footprint of the house is twenty feet wide and ninety feet long. Windows are limited to the east wall. This building length allowed us to cut double-height spaces into the volume, bringing south light into the

living and dining room, and north light into the study. On the second level, the house is split into two identical bedroom suites at the center, with bridges over the voids to the lower level, which lead to roof decks at the front and back of the house. In the center, a courtyard connects an outdoor seating area to the living room and study inside. The lower level of the house can be viewed contiguously from the kitchen at the front to the garage at the back of the house, emphasizing the long spatial dimension.

Massachusetts Institute of Technology

The site adjacent to the live-work loft was part of the property occupied by another ruin. Taking advantage of old codes, we could build to the street and side property line. Two houses were possible with a driveway to the rear serving a future house and a two-car garage.

We created a central courtyard and two projections to the property edge for bedrooms on the second level. Each bedroom has a deck. Voids bring light from the decks to the ground floor, south for dining, north for the study. The projections shade west facing windows.

23 Village Street

286

23 Village Street

25 Village Street
Somerville, Massachusetts
2015

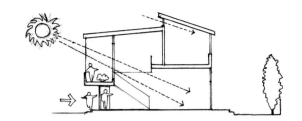

288

This house was prefabricated for ease of building. It takes advantage of the long southern view down the driveway where the studio has a high window, and the entry is covered by a balcony. On entry, the view is to the garden, enhanced by south light from the window to the balcony. The added height of the living dining space opens to the garden, protected from the railway by trees planted earlier.

The house at 25 Village Street was built after its neighbor at number 23 was completed. We decided to have this house factory-built, which was strategic: it not only saved time but allowed us to bring the building components to the site in bundles that could be lifted by a crane into the property. We worked with Bensonwood, a prefabrication company. We visited the factory several times to check on the product. Once delivered, it took four days to assemble and enclose the house. The foundation had been built in advance.

The spatial strategy at number 25 is completely different from the adjacent property. We carved out space for a real garden which is the visual focus for the 12.5-foot-high living room. The dining space has a view to the side garden but is contiguous. We upgraded the finishes of the standard kitchen because it is open to the living spaces. The house has an integrated parking garage with the second space outdoors. The garage is 8 feet high, giving the study above extra height.

The study and living room are open to each other with a spatial overlap, more than twenty feet high. This coincides with the entry to the house and view through to the garden. The study features a balcony and bay window looking south down the driveway. South light floods the living area.

Two bedroom suites are located a half flight above the study. The primary suite looks south and west, while the second bedroom overlooks the northern garden.

Massachusetts Institute of Technology

Working Artists Ventura (WAV)
Ventura, California
2005

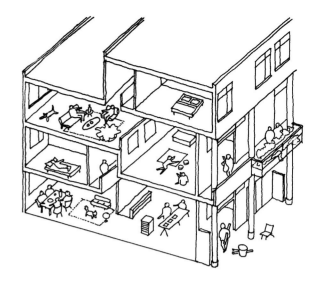

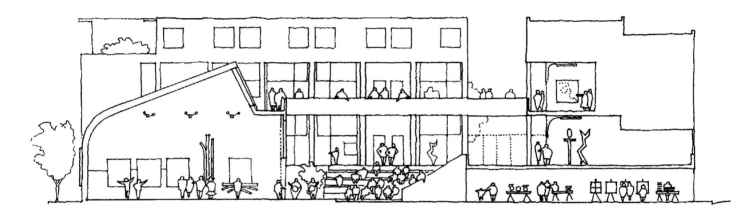

Before I left California, I began work on a mixed-income creative community project for a non-profit called Projects Linking Arts Communities and Environment (PLACE) in Ventura, California. Once I moved to Cambridge, this project became a joint focus of both our offices—on the east and west coasts.

The selected site was located on the main-street of Ventura in a semi-industrial area, close to a beach but separated by a noisy freeway. As a development with sixty-nine affordable live-work units for artists and

thirteen market-rate units, the first decision was to break down the scale of the project, as we had done in Franklin LaBrea, by creating smaller unit groupings. These would be defined by south-facing courtyards with different characteristics.

The easternmost courtyard is treated as a public plaza with an amphitheater and direct connection to the two main streets surrounding the project. The community gallery and performance space has a large roll-up door facing the plaza so that it can be converted into a stage. The middle courtyard is

developed as a residential garden for children to play. The laundry and lounge faces this space. Each unit around this courtyard is designed for separation of living and working. The living rooms and family front doors face here. The third courtyard is designed as a work space. Studios have roll-up doors allowing work to spill outdoors.

In order to provide each artist's studio with a 13.5-foot-high workspace, the floors are offset, creating two distinct choices. Most workspaces have direct access from a walkway. The family space is located on the

The courtyards all get good sunlight and are zoned to be lower in height to the west. Parking is reduced because public transportation is easy to use. All inhabitants are artists but using different media, with distinct choices of units by access. Courtyard units have roll-up doors where work can extend outdoors. The important issue was higher work spaces and easy access to family living.

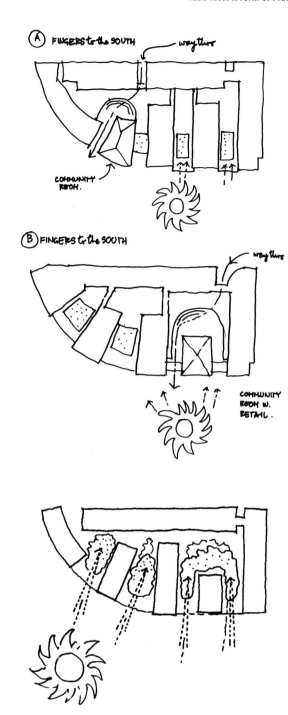

same level as the workspace or half a floor higher or lower. In all cases living rooms and bedrooms can be separated for family living. The spatial module is 20 feet wide allowing for clear spans using wood joists.

The market-rate units are located on the top floors of the development, where they have ocean views over the highway. A porch on the roof makes these units especially attractive for artists who can afford them. The purpose was to lower the financial burden of affordable units, and the developer was able to support the homeless communities by offering transitional housing units in the third courtyard.

The currently amended zoning asked for a "Spanish" styled aesthetic which the potential users strongly opposed. We were able to convince the authorities that a more industrial aesthetic was appropriately contextual. The corrugated metal panels and translucent polycarbonate walls, glass doors to balconies with metal handrails were closer to the prevailing aesthetic.

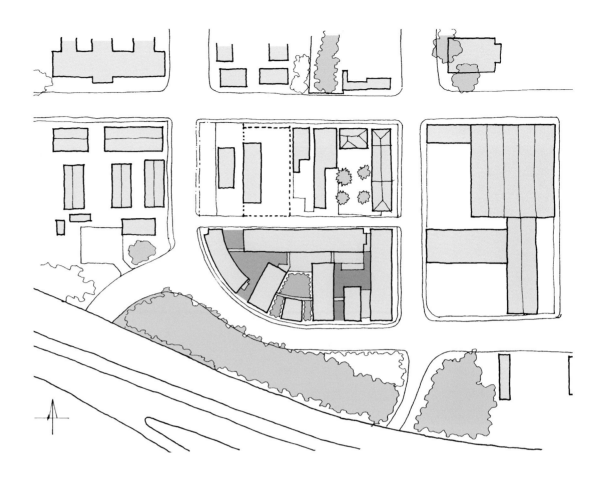

294

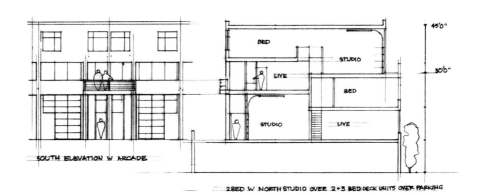

WEST FACADE SHADED BY ARCADE/COLLONADE   3 BR CONDO W. ROOF PATIO, OVER 1 BED, OVER RETAIL

SOUTH ELEVATION W ARCADE

2 BED W NORTH STUDIO OVER 2+3 BED DECK UNITS OVER PARKING

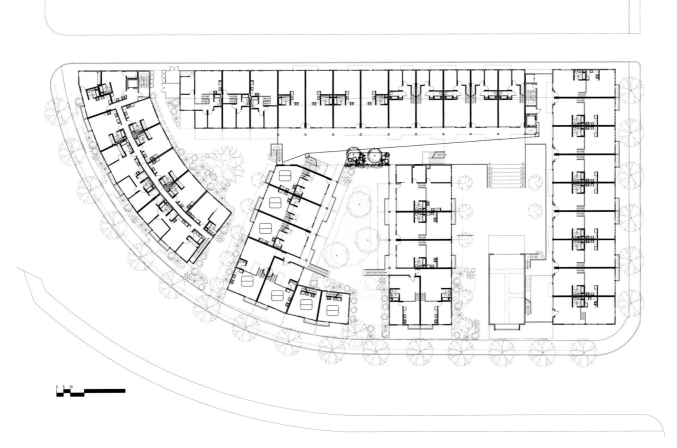

296

Massachusetts Institute of Technology

Muxbal Community Center
Guatemala City, Guatemala
2010

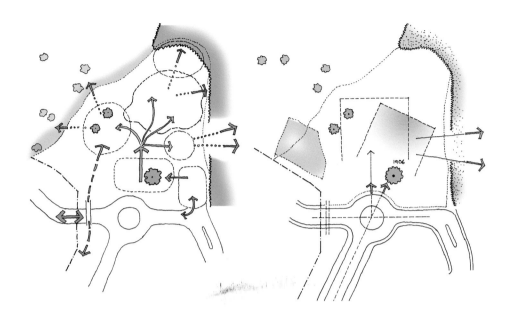

In 2010, when we were invited to design the Muxbal Community Center, Guatemala City had become quite unsafe. Driving was considered hazardous, and petty theft was rampant. Bodyguards were evident not only for the wealthy. New developments such as ours had very strictly controlled access.

Our client, Mundo Verde, aimed to have a very safe context particularly for children to have access to sports, after-school classes, as well as activities for their parents. As part of a larger community master plan, the site chosen for the Muxbal Community Center was close to the prominent entry, but spatially unique, backed by a thick forest at the top of a steep ravine. From this location, views to the city were also possible.

Designing the program, we first looked at sports facilities that could be built close to the site such as tennis courts and soccer fields. Swimming pools for adults and children were a high priority, as well as changing rooms, toilets for all activities, a

dance performance studio, a gymnasium, and a racquet-ball court. Additionally, the program included classrooms for boys and girls—both separated and together—as well as a hair salon, a convenience grocery store, a cafe, possibly a restaurant, a space for lounges and dining, and play areas that could be supervised for small kids. This added up to 29,000 square feet, and flexibility for changing uses was assumed.

The program suggested two different architectural responses: one featuring high volumes and airy spaces, and the other featuring more modest structures to secure the site boundaries.

The concept was to cover most of this program with a translucent polycarbonate roof for rain protection and enclose smaller spaces with lightweight walls. Glass was used judiciously because of cost. Where privacy was needed, walls are solid but translucent above. Even for the swimming pools, the enclosure is only made with glass up to three

meters. The effect of these translucent materials is luminous and airy, barely separating indoors from outdoors.

The site is at the end of the dominant road in the master plan, where a turning circle was established. A large forecourt, where festivals and farmers markets can take place, fronts the community center. On the axis of the main road, a very old tree was saved to anchor this space. Several functions operate independently from this plaza, like the convenience market, the hair salon, and some retail. The rectilinear buildings are modestly scaled with a covered walkway. The translucent roofed main building overlaps with this edge structure, which houses the management office and allows for a controlled entry to the property.

The lounge and dining spaces greet visitors at the entry with a cafe. The main circulation continues through to a courtyard and the forest beyond. Half of the covered volume is occupied by the swimming pools and

Safety for the inhabitants was a very important issue. The location of the center near the main entrance was recommended. This placed the complex in a wooded area surrounded by steep ravines that were not accessible. The main road started from the turning circle at the community plaza making this facility very visible.

dressing areas. The other half is used by the gym, ball court, and dance studio. The circulation continues until the roof opens to create a courtyard with flowering plants. Beyond this garden, an amphitheater is created by steps down to grade. Creating a stage, backed by trees, was a romantic idea but became well used.

The children's classrooms and play areas are separated from the recreational program for aural reasons. A courtyard with trees and a change in level suggested a ramp to the classroom roof for a playground with views down the valley. The rear of the plaza building provides covered access to these classrooms which are located to secure the boundary on this side of the property. The classrooms are actively used for changing programs, including ballet, cooking, wrestling, dancing, and language lessons.

We built this facility at a remarkably low cost, given that it required neither heating or cooling. This was built in a very short time frame by the Mundo Verde construction team. It is very well used and carefully managed. After school education has experienced teachers, and the cafe has a gifted cook and is a frequent lunchtime meeting place. The plaza has hosted many community events as well as weddings. It has served as the flexible central focus for the community of Muxbal.

300

Muxbal Community Center

302

Massachusetts Institute of Technology

Muxbal Community Center

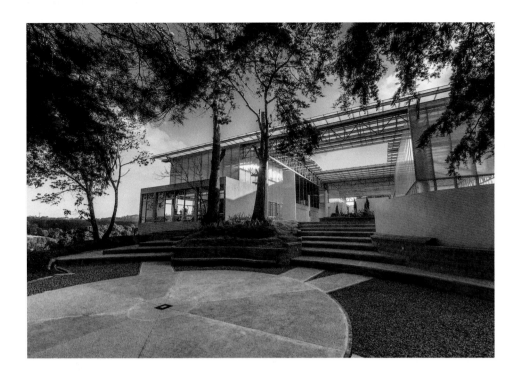

304

Foshou Lake Club House
Nanjing, China
2010

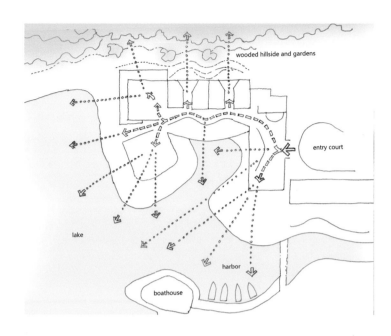

After moving to MIT, where we had academic relationships with China, we were invited to engage in architectural and urban design work there. Only a few projects were built, and several others may be built in time.

In Nanjing, we designed a clubhouse, as part of a luxury housing community developed by Suning Universal. Located on the tip of Foshou Lake, the site has two distinct edges: the sloping land of the adjacent forested hill and the water's edge overlooking the lake. The building addresses both of these, considering the forest edge for quieter and more private portions of the program—like the spa and meeting rooms—while the water edge is public, and offers an expansive view over the water for spaces such as the entry lobbies, lounges, restaurants, and swimming pools.

The building has a roof that is visible to surrounding buildings on higher land. The roof was therefore proposed to be undulating, covered with flat tiles, and constructed in concrete.

The program is distributed over two levels and entered from the upper story. The entry to the lobby and lounge opens dramatically to lake views. A wide corridor leads to grouped club rooms oriented toward the forest, while a more formal space, used for special functions, has both forest and lake views. From the terrace, a wide-splayed stair leads to the edge of the lake.

The ground level contains the larger program. The shape of the lake edge is retained for environmental and economic reasons but also offers a separation of uses. The swimming pools form a distinct edge, joined at the lower level but separated as a pavilion from above. This location gives the best platforms for sunbathing. The dining rooms are placed on the main lakefront but

have been given separate identities; one is a Chinese family- style room with many tables, while the other is an international-style bar at the upper level. A continuous terrace around the water joins the lower activities together. A rock rises out of the lake and is used as a musical performance space.

Separated from the main building, the boat docks and Seamen's Club House are the final elements that define the project and claim this part of the lake.

As with many Chinese projects, politics and circumstances can change the outcomes. Unfortunately, in this case a zoning revision for the whole lake finally prevented this land from development.

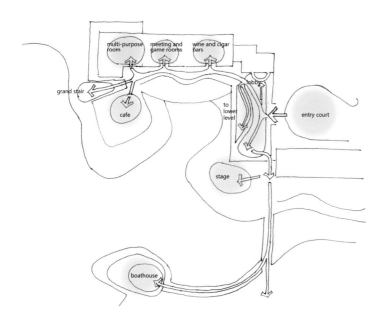

The Club House was located in an attractive zone with a long frontage on the lake and backed by a steep, densely wooded forest. The program was a combination of sociable noisy activities and more reflective ones. We used these contrasts to locate the program.

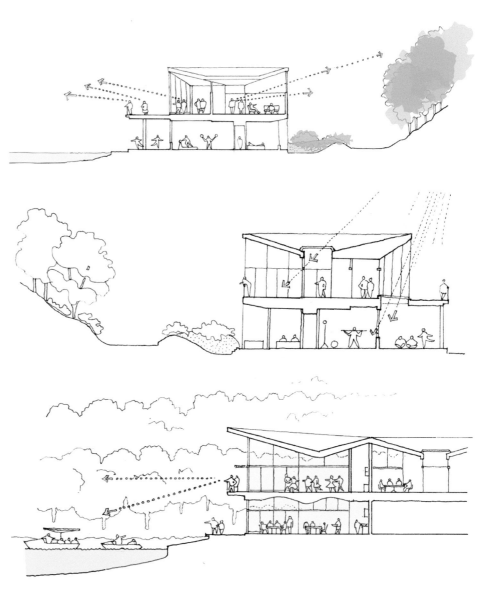

Foshou Lake Club House

308

Foshou Lake Club House

Suning Information Technology Headquarters Park
Nanjing, China
2011

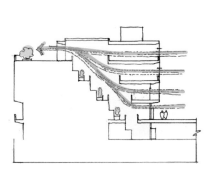
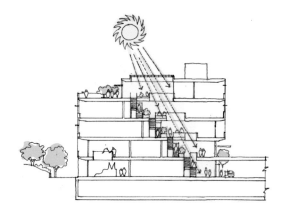

After a long debate of design alternatives, we decided on a strategy of five groupings of buildings creating hills where parking could be hidden. We designed two building types: one five-floor atrium office building and three-story workstations. The atrium buildings had a stepped interior space to allow for light penetration and good cross ventilation. Workstations had a more flexible series of spaces and included pedestrian paths.

For this company, located in Nanjing with several development sites, we designed a headquarters complex as an extension of a recent development. This was considered a focal location and included a public park.

The "Five Hills" concept for the Suning Information Technology Headquarters Park required visual impact. We decided to manipulate the landscape to create a series of small hills that complemented the surrounding dramatic landscapes. The integration of the project's vehicular circulation system with a radical topographical proposal sets the foundation for articulating two office typologies: the headquarters and the workstation building types.

The headquarters are atrium buildings organized in clusters of three around "hilltop" plazas, with two shared lower levels for parking and drop-off carved out of the sculpted landscape. The grandeur of the hilltop clusters frames the park from the north and south, while formalizing the main entry to the park and providing expansive views for the occupants.

The workstations are articulated as a series of modified low-rise spines, stretching diagonally across the site in order to take advantage of natural ventilation and daylighting. Automobile access and parking facilities are buried, enabling direct access from parking into each unit, while preserving pedestrian use above. These were envisioned as workspaces but also housing for visitors. The workstation buildings are punctuated with intimate gardens, sunken courtyards, and ground-level access paths. A central park was required by zoning, size unspecified, but designed to represent the best features and flora of this fertile region.

Headquarters are conceived as compact technologically sophisticated buildings with good natural ventilation, excellent daylight conditions. The atria include spaces for informal conversation, coffee breaks and socializing in a long day schedule. The workstations are conceived to take on more variations in size, levels, and work formations and are modular and changeable.

After construction documents had begun, the client decided to move the site but keep the conceptual ideas. The new site configuration was completely different. The parking ratios were increased substantially. Essentially this was a new project in a volatile market condition.

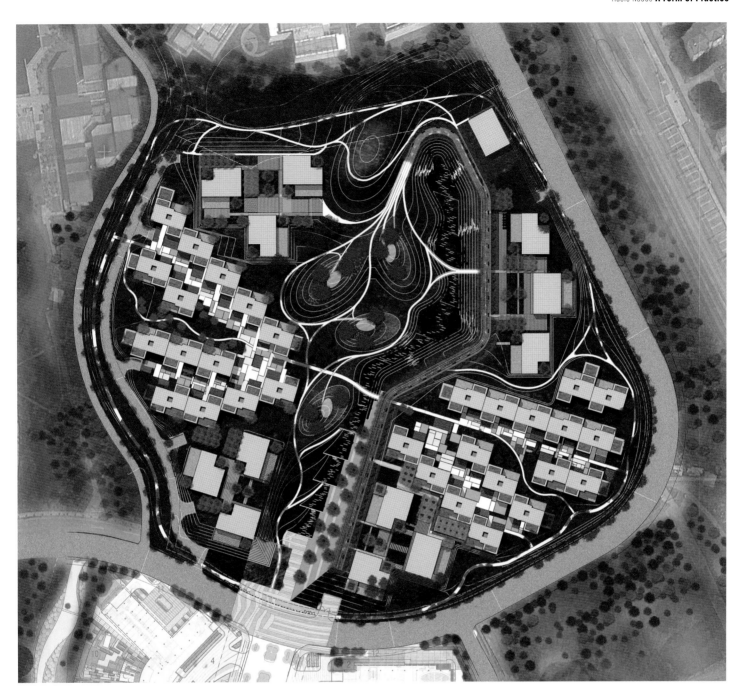

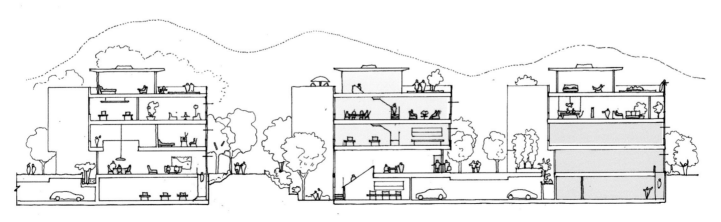

Suning Information Technology Headquarters Park

Massachusetts Institute of Technology

Suning Information Technology Headquarters Park

314

10th Jiangsu Horticultural Expo
Yizheng, Yangzhou, China
2018

The Horticultural Expo was sited in Yangzhou, an area known for beautiful gardens. The team selected to be the primary planners were from Southeast University, where I had been teaching for several summers. The dean asked us to participate in the planning and design.

We were asked to create a conceptual entry to the north end of the expo site, which served people arriving by bus. A short street led to the site and required a separate welcoming building for information, service facilities and childcare drop-off prior to the formal expo entry. This was given a large covered porch, a restful courtyard, and a souvenir shop for visitors.

The site was on the edge of the lake that joined all the facilities together. There is a significant change in level from entry to the edge of the water, which gave us the opportunity to create a dramatic surprise. The concept was to reveal the lake only after an entry process through the "Flower Hill." On the axis of the entry street, a wide aperture leads through the oval hill to the lake. Ramps around the edge of this hill arrive at a viewing platform ten meters above the entry with views of the larger gardens. This route also showcases the native flowering plants that grow taller with the rise of the hill.

The passage through the hill includes some retail, access to services, and information. Emerging from this route, the lake appears magically. A ramped garden planted with showcase flowers and waterfalls leads gently to a path around the water and to boats for passage on the lake. The hill contains two floors, with offices of administration on the upper level, and exhibition spaces and classrooms below. The program also calls for a waiting room for boat rides, a restaurant/cafe and catering kitchen, exhibition spaces for flower arrangements, and classrooms for younger children. We created separate pavilions for these programs with glass walls, sliding wooden screens on two levels, and with a porch facing the water. The green roofs are planted for energy preservation but have decks for use by the office workers on the second floor with bridges over the route around the hill. Gardens between the pavilions become part of the exhibition. We planned a stone garden, a water and willow tree garden, and a playground for children.

We also designed several other small buildings that were changed in use. The most successful pavilion, housing facilities for the upper level administration, was completed as designed. This had three formations similar in concept: a rectangle with a diagonal line affecting a change in angle for the roof. These were to be built in three sizes and grouped around a common space. The smallest pavilion housed an information center, the middle size was an exhibition space facing the entry and a classroom to the rear, and the largest was a space for celebration with dining and relaxing. The development of these floor plans had surprising results, with dramatic roof profiles that interacted together and belied the simple early diagrams. Built in wood structurally exposed from below, the roofs were covered in metal tiles. The variety of spaces, their cross sections, shared vistas, interaction with the larger landscape all give the final uses engaging choices for programmatic development.

This expo was not completed as planned but a second, larger contiguous site was added to make a more prestigious expo a few years later.

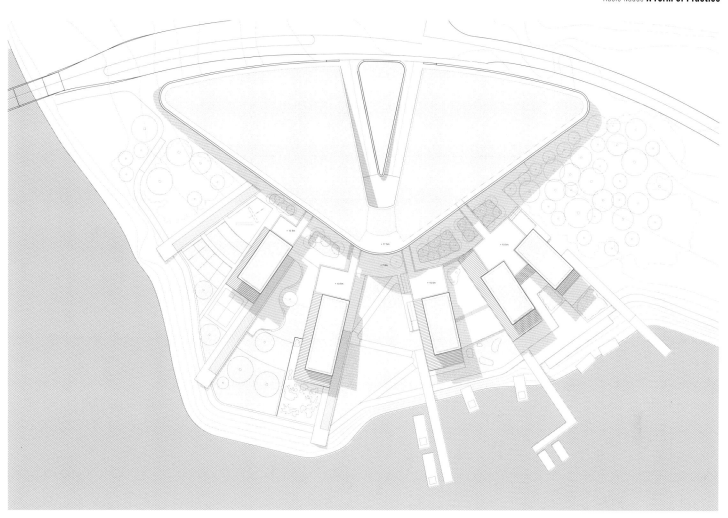

Cross section of the
passage through the
hill with the viewing
platform above.

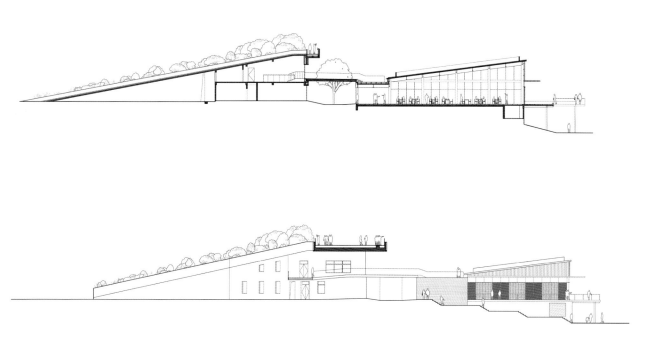

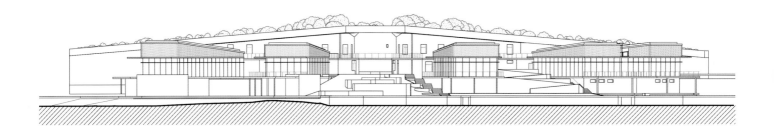

Massachusetts Institute of Technology

320

10th Jiangsu Horticultural Expo

Massachusetts Institute of Technology

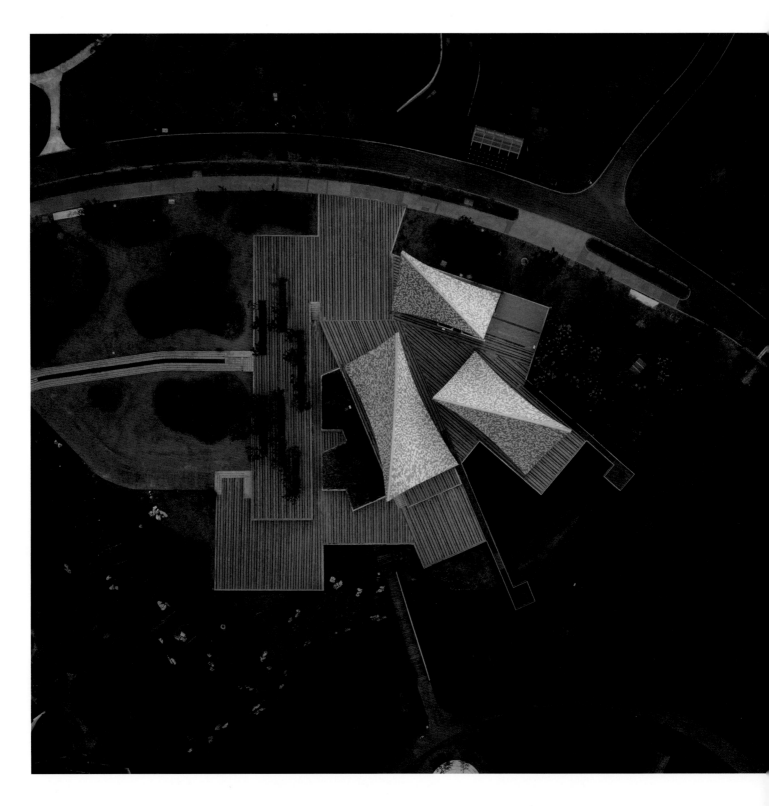

10th Jiangsu Horticultural Expo

Sifang Parkland Condominium
Nanjing, China
2018

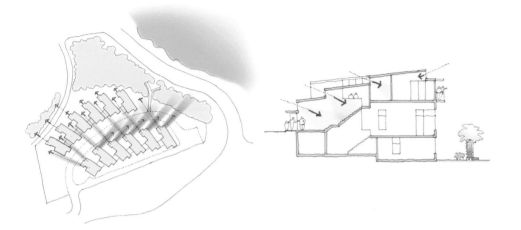
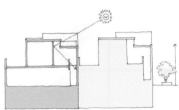

I had visited the famous Sifang architecture and art development several times to view important houses and facilities designed by international architects, including Steven Holl's Sifang Art Museum. After several meetings with Mr. Lu, the owner of the development company, I was asked to develop a housing cluster that could be sold—a change in strategy from the original concept of offering the site for short-term rentals. The site for this project was originally planned for another display house. On the edge of the first phase of the overall development, the site has sloping topography, fronting a small river. With views of the mountains and lush vegetation, it made for a pleasant context.

By regulation, single-family detached units were no longer allowed, and twin houses were becoming the norm. After years in Britain, where twin houses were a cheaper concept because of shared walls, I thought that this was not a promising idea. My assumption was that houses should be viewed as single units but connected in ways that met the legal requirements. This was an exciting approach since density was more of an issue than cost. Over the course of a few days, I created several options, two of which were especially interesting, and one seemed promising for the site. There would be two rows of houses—one adjacent to the water's edge and one up the slope. The lower houses had a single floor and a three-floor main house as viewed from the street. The upper houses were aligned to have long views through these gaps using a similar typology. These were zero-lot-line houses with a blank wall defining the courtyard of the adjacent dwelling.

We developed this concept further with three bedrooms, including a view-oriented primary suite with a balcony and two bedrooms with roof patios. The entry level consisted of a large living room with an adjacent dining room and kitchen, and a separate study. On the lower level, a room for service was typical with street entry, and an additional room for multiple uses.

The work continued with construction documents. Several of the river houses were reserved for clients. However, political change in districting occurred. The development and construction permit issued years before was revoked. The whole development site was then included by Laoshan Mountain Ecological preservation zone which does not allow any new building construction. This needed a new review process, putting this project on hold indefinitely.

Twelve condominium units are laid out in two rows with a one-way parking loop. The houses are connected at the lowest level but from the entry, they read as separate houses of one and two floors. The stepped property lines allow views of the mountains from the windows of the primary bedrooms. Different roof heights create opportunities for extra windows to light interiors.

Sifang Parkland Condominium

Sifang Parkland Condominium

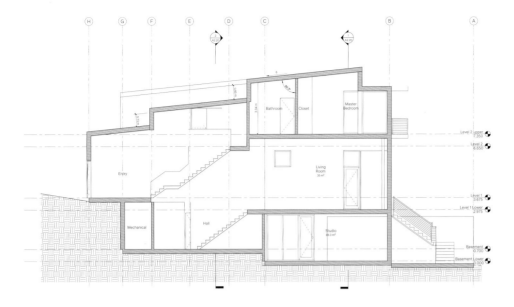

Massachusetts Institute of Technology

Sifang Parkland Condominium

Shenzhen Mangrove Museum and Urban Shenzhen
Shenzhen, China
2019

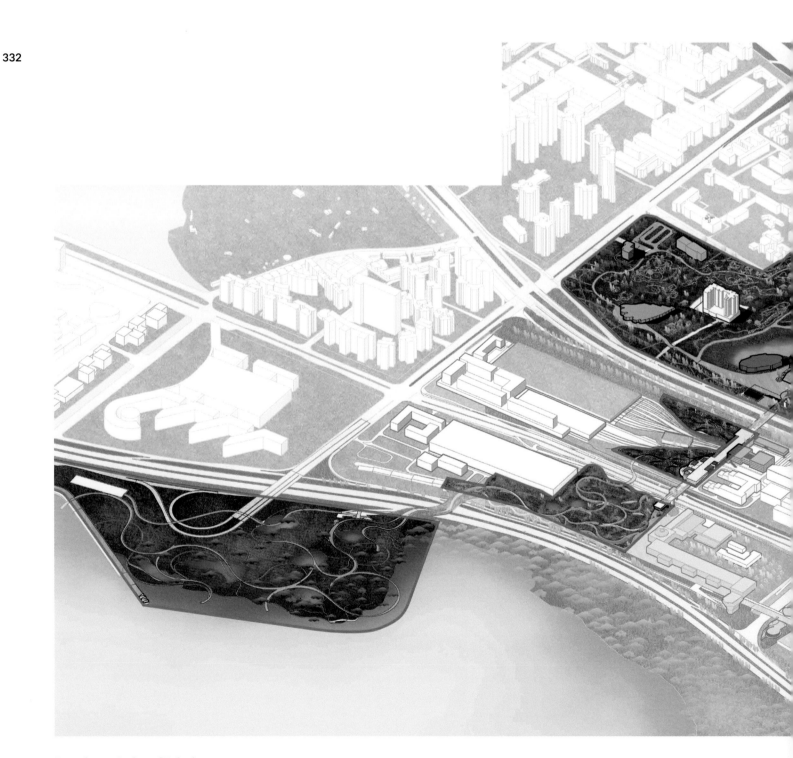

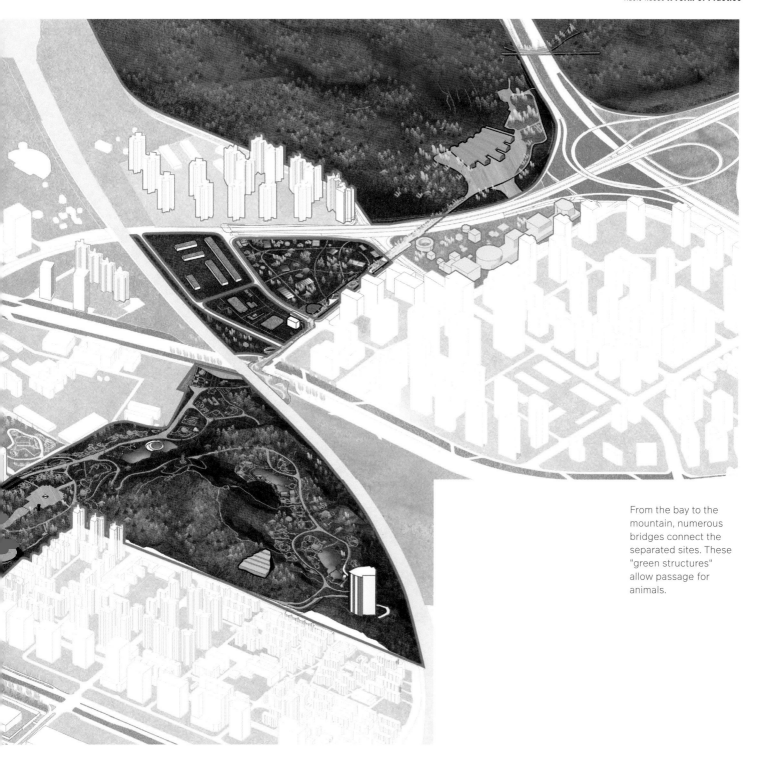

From the bay to the mountain, numerous bridges connect the separated sites. These "green structures" allow passage for animals.

The commission for the Shenzhen Mangrove Museum and surrounding urban renewal started with the need to study the urban context of the proposed museum site. The selected site was on the roof of a maintenance facility for Metro line 11, a vast concrete platform of over twenty-seven hectares. This site needed master planning because it lacked pedestrian access and visibility from surrounding streets. The temporary building on the deck was to be demolished,

and the structure of the deck had not been fully verified. Modifications later caused significant delays.

The Mangrove Museum's platform is adjacent to the national coastal reserve with mangroves, a habitat for migratory birds, plus trails for jogging and cycling. It's also a part of the city's plan for an urban ecological corridor stretching from Tanglang Mountain to Antuo Mountain to Shenzhen Bay, which is

among the city's five-year (2022–2026) action plan for the construction of eight ecological corridors that will link preexisting patches of natural green space throughout the city to form an unbroken linear park. Our study area was expanded vastly to five main zones, each of which contributed to this linear concept and covered one hundred meters of grade change.

This study defined the concept of sustainability and the restoration of poor-quality open space, of which there was a large quantity. Tree cover was needed for shade in this hot climate, for the protection of habitat for wild animals, and to modulate water flow. Continuity of pedestrian access was essential, bikeways needed to be reframed, and access to transportation was improved, as was restructuring traffic routes. Many bridges had to be designed to link sites together over roads, railroad tracks, and under highways. Each was made with continuity of landscape and separate access for animals as defined by our ecological criteria. The main focus was continuity and space-making in the north-south direction, but pedestrian linkages in the east direction to new public facilities on roof decks added to a superior pedestrian environment. Site boundaries were extended several times.

Over the course of two years, teams in Boston and Shenzhen identified and studied these five zones: the Shenzhen Bay Park, Sea of Flowers, Metro Yard Urban Crossing, the Shenzhen International Garden and Flower Expo Park, and the Agricultural Park.

334

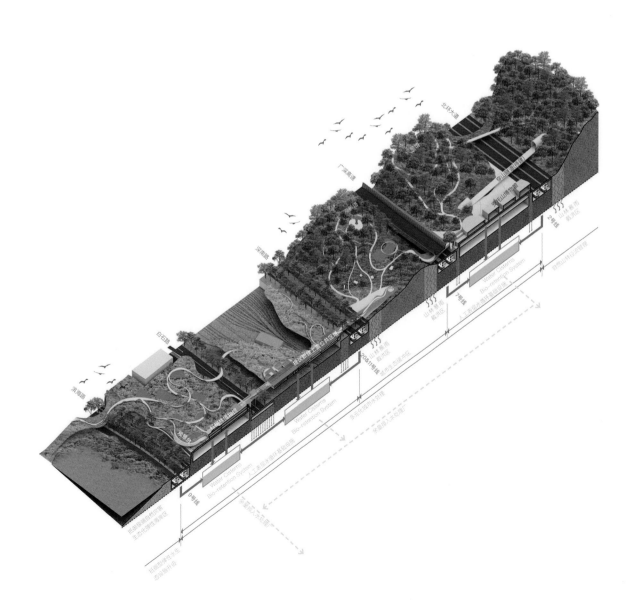

Beihuan Avenue/
Guangshen Express-
way Cycling and Ur-
ban Vitality
北环大道/广深高速
骑行与城市活力

The grade change from the bay to the mountain site for an Art Museum was one hundred meters of elevation that had to be navigated by pedestrians. The separated sites required numerous bridges that would be "green structures" many of which allowed separate passage for animals. Some of these are shown here

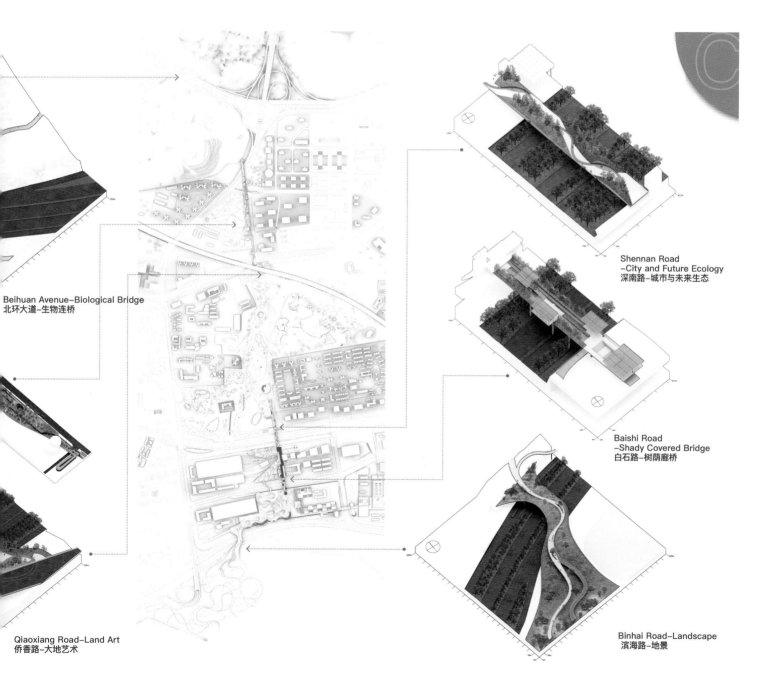

Beihuan Avenue–Biological Bridge
北环大道–生物连桥

Qiaoxiang Road–Land Art
侨香路–大地艺术

Shennan Road
–City and Future Ecology
深南路–城市与未来生态

Baishi Road
–Shady Covered Bridge
白石路–树荫廊桥

Binhai Road–Landscape
滨海路–地景

Shenzhen Mangrove Museum and Urban Shenzhen

The <u>Shenzhen Bay</u> waterfront park was extensive and culminated in the under-developed area adjacent to the mangrove reserve. Landworks Studio Inc. developed places for greater viewing of these amazing tree formations, different routes, direct and meandering qualities that led to a land bridge over Binhai Road to the deck of the potential museum. From here spectacular views were revealed across the mangrove formations to the Hong Kong mangrove edge.

Massachusetts Institute of Technology

<u>The Sea of Flowers</u> was the park fronting the future museum and occupied the area of the platform that is structurally too weak to hold any new buildings. The existing deck was flat with a replaceable two-meter ground cover, but there were no views or pedestrian access from the pedestrian level. We were able to mold the levels to create a gentle topography that forms the natural habitat for small animals and domestic plants. In contrast to the green landscape of Shenzhen Bay Park, this area showcased the best flowering plants for visitors to study. Elevated meandering paths on hilly terrain with places to sit allowed unique views of Shenzhen Bay, Hong Kong, and overseeing the national mangrove preserve that has a very low limit of daily visitor access. This garden created intimate spaces and ponds for completely different visitor experiences. From here, two bridges gave access to the next park.

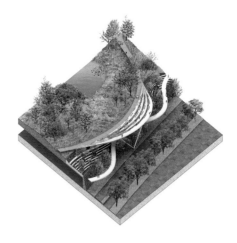

Shenzhen Mangrove Museum and Urban Shenzhen

338

The Metro Yard Urban Crossing was the most difficult zone because most of the metro maintenance area remained uncovered. For pedestrians, there were two routes: one a garden route through a forested space, the other a direct route across this long bridge directly to Shannan Road, a major east-west thoroughfare in the city. The straight route was on two levels with cafes, souvenir shopping, places to relax and dine, and views of trains crossing. The edges of the track were heavily landscaped. From here, a wide bridge crossed Shannon to arrive at the older Expo.

Shenzhen Mangrove Museum and Urban Shenzhen

The Shenzhen International Garden and
Flower Expo Park was built in the 1990s and
first opened in 2004. It was neglected by the
city's development after the flower expo. It
had now become a somewhat faded experience needing upgrading of structures and
better routes through this complex organization. To achieve the ambition of a route
through to the mountain the current terminus
needed reinvention, a difficult task under and
over a freeway. We created opportunities for
new structures to give views over the gardens,
links to places in the gardens that could be
actively used, upgraded the ecology to give
more shading of routes, and noted sites for
more sculptures.

Shenzhen Mangrove Museum and Urban Shenzhen

342

The Agricultural Park was suggested to resolve the zone along the route towards Antuo Mountain. This was speculative given unknown plans which would include a new Museum of Art on the mountain in contrast to the Mangrove Museum at the Bay. But the area faces the challenges of dramatic and complex topographical level changes intertwined with the chaos of tunnel ramps and the on-the-ground and in-the-air piping system of existing industrial sites to the south of Antuo Mountain. A new bridge system and the agricultural park could make use of the height changes to resolve the

conflict between pedestrian connection and the heavy traffic systems and meanwhile capitalize on the verdant edible plants grown on these slopes.

The process was complicated by administrative changes. Every person in a leadership position was changed more than once. Finally, the mayor who viewed this work as a high priority for implementation during his tenure was replaced as Hong Kong politics heated up. His replacement was focused on the new tensions at the border. Our thorough reports were turned in to

the National Development and Reform Commission, finalized and approved by the central government, and helped the establishment of the "International Mangrove Center" in Shenzhen as part of outcomes of the 14th Meeting of the Conference of the Contracting Parties to the Ramsar Convention on Wetlands attended by President Xi Jinping via video on November 15, 2022.

343

Below right The project was given the Grand Award for Urban Design in 2022 by the Hong Kong Institute of Urban Design.

Reflections
Working in China

During this time, many Chinese competitions for large-scale buildings and prominent urban projects opened up for an international audience of architects. As we had seen in our work in Japan, such competitions offered great opportunities to build experimental works that were not possible elsewhere. Unfortunately, however, many of these potential projects had poor outcomes with fundamental changes in programming, changing management, and non-payment of fees. Often projects go through several design competitive phases or parts that have been outlined are put out for bidding. This is time consuming and debilitating. We were to experience this later in our public work in Shenzhen.

My first opportunity to build in Shanghai was the result of an introduction to a friend of a colleague who had his financial base in Hong Kong, which was easier for financial flexibility. This was a good learning curve. Even as the design process was going well, the construction documents had to be made by a government-endorsed design office. We had little choice on which office to pick. Ongoing firms build relationships over time and anticipate how to make a smooth, controlled process. We found that it was not easy to supervise the documentation despite having a local team member. The design outcome was flawed and, more seriously, the detailing of the buildings was not to our standard. This first work is not in this publication. In this case the client paid us well and on time, which we were to discover was exceptional.

Later design opportunities came from academic relationships we had with colleagues who solved the construction complexities for us. Very few of our designs were built because regulations for sites changed, programs were altered substantially, and in public contexts leadership change was inevitable. Large international firms have a better ability to survive the obstacles we encountered by creating their own local design offices and building professional teams that include local professionals. They also have greater financial stability and flexibility.

I truly believe that Professor Naudé is the kind of scholar who approaches teaching not just as a profession, but as a means of sparking the flame of ideals that burns inside the hearts of those around her.

Due to the global pandemic, we haven't been able to meet in person for more than three years, but I still think of her and the courtyard outside of her Somerville studio quite frequently. The last time Wenyu Lu and I were invited to that small courtyard it was spring, and the entire courtyard was awash in full flower blooms. Most of them, if I remember correctly, were cherry blossoms. The cherry blossoms in that courtyard and throughout the United States seem to me to have more vigor and exuberance than the timidity and frailty of those in Asian nations. With Professor Naudé's personality, it goes quite nicely.

The courtyard, the spatial sequence, and the configuration of the working and living space of her studio are an ideal example of a scholar's place in my heart. It is a building that was once a bronze foundry from the nineteenth century, completely enclosed by brick walls with just an entrance gate leading to the street. Time has taken its toll on this unadorned warehouse-like building. The brickwork shows indications of wear and weathering as well as signs of many restorations. A completely different world, though, can be found when opening the gate and facing the flower garden, an open-air space embraced by two parallel double-story buildings in a sophisticated simplicity of division, with one side dedicated to work and the other side being where life begins. The living area displays Professor Naudé's collection of handmade objects. Some are native to South America, while others are from her hometown, Cape Town. All have either detailed carvings or vibrant colors, like a certain kind of totem from the wildest parts of nature. On the opposite side of the courtyard, where the work is done, there is a large open area with only a few scattered sketching desks that face the natural landscape of the garden through massive pieces of crystal-clear glass. I'm reminded of an ancient Chinese proverb "文质彬彬，然后君子" by the interior tranquility and the exterior vibrant spring scenery.

(The character "文" suggests someone who is so well-versed in literature and the arts that they are able to express themselves in a sophisticated and eloquent way. The character "质" denotes someone who is distinguished by their refinement, cultivation, and virtue. The phrase "君子" signifies someone who has the two characters reaching a beautiful equilibrium in one soul. "文质彬彬，然后君子" can be understood in this context as "refined in both word and deed, a noble soul indeed.")

My last visit to Cambridge was to take part in and speak at a global social housing summit that Professor Naudé was hosting. She also invited some MIT professors and the primary attendees to her studio for a celebration following the one-day meeting. Cast in the warm glow of the setting sun, gathered under the blooming cherry trees, with falling flowers on the shoulder, people were chatting, laughing, and deep in conversation. The courtyard evokes my mental images of Chinese scholar's gardens, especially those in Suzhou, which likewise open to the public street by a little gate on a tall whitewashed wall. However, once inside, it feels as though you are meandering through a completely new realm—a serene natural setting with mountains, trees, and bodies of water.

Undoubtedly, Professor Naudé resembles a spirited noblewoman more than the classic Chinese literati. I frequently ponder how she, a woman in the once male-dominated world of architecture, manages to triumph through adversity from South Africa to the United States, achieving academic excellence in numerous universities, and leading the MIT School of Architecture to be the top school.

in the world as dean for more than ten years, not to mention being one of the first few female deans at US top architectural schools. She must possess a strong spiritual strength; otherwise, it would be difficult to fathom how projects as demanding in every way as the buildings of Media Lab or Stata Center could be completed without the dedication of highly motivated people like her.

On the other hand, her provocative views on architecture also reveal her incredibly contemplative nature. When I visited her studio, one of her works that particularly struck me was a house in Cape Town with a long corridor leading further inside the structure. The mindset and approach she uses in her work always fascinate me. Although in China there is no opportunity to design a single house in a community due to the land ownership system, I have continued to be interested in small house design over the years. A little apartment building that was finished not long after my previous trip to Boston is another such endeavor that grabs my attention. It is situated outside the city in a charming, tiny bay. In contrast to the majority of architect assignments, she began the design by land searching and in-person communication with the neighbors to understand the everyday life of the neighborhood. The steeply sloped plot of land she finally purchased for this project turned out to be empty for a considerable amount of time and was obviously difficult for most people to do anything on. Her ability to make wise decisions is evident in the site she chose. She was aware that the height of the slope might naturally result in two entries—an upper slope entry and a lower slope entry—giving her two different stacked units, each with its own private access. On the other hand, due to the slope, the building occupies a space that bothered nobody, casts no shadow on others, and obstructs no neighbor's view. As a result, the community could easily accept the entire project. The project demonstrates the very rare situation of an architect who can ride the wave when their design ability matches a unique perspective without trying so hard to stand out. The materials used in the house are no more than those that can be seen in the surrounding neighborhood, but with a closer look at her design, the concise and exquisite language makes it somehow outstanding. The lower unit was sold to cover the construction costs, and the upper unit was kept as her weekend getaway. It wasn't until Wenyu Lu and I were once invited to the apartment for a dinner that I realized the rooms were actually modest, but the tall and large sliding doors of the main living space brought the best view of the cove within the room, capturing the sense of the Chinese expression "小中见大" (seeing a bigger picture from small matters).

Since 2016, Wenyu Lu and I have organized a summer on-site design-build workshop for graduates of three schools in villages outside of the city of Quzhou in south Zhejiang Province, with the assistance of Professor Ming Ge from Southeast University's School of Architecture and Professor Naudé. The villages that Wenyu Lu and I chose for students to stay in and work for were mostly in the less developed areas of the isolated mountainous region, with the goal of giving students real-life experience through an arduous journey and allowing them to make a genuine contribution to the local people. The idea is for students to spend five weeks a year living in the houses of the villagers while also constructing some useful infrastructure for the community. We all agreed, after talking with Professor Naudé, that the best way for students to leave behind the conceptual and abstract methodology learned in the city is for them to spend enough time in the village. This will allow them to truly understand the domesticity, local materials, and traditions of local construction craftsmanship. According to our plan, the five-week workshop was divided into three sections: a week of local research, site selection, and program definition for their project; two weeks of designing in groups; and two weeks of creating 1:1 real-material mock-ups to test the viability of the construction with the paired craftsmen from the village. The professors from three universities, along with the village representatives, select the project that is most likely to be put into action during the final review weekend. Based on the trust that Wenyu Lu and I developed over the years of practice with local authorities in the same broader rural region, the village government will implement the chosen scheme following the workshop.

I wasn't expecting Professor Naudé to spend time with students in the isolated areas, but she insisted on it from the workshop's first year on. The excitement among the students was obvious. The students' performance that year was extremely exceptional. Although the designs of the three groups were all excellent, we had to select the most useful one to implement in accordance with the workshop's specified rules. The final design was for a multipurpose rural public restroom. It was a bamboo building that significantly improved the lives of the nearby villagers. Following its completion, it quickly created quite a stir online and attracted many visitors to the area. Shortly after the workshop, the villagers got in touch with us and expressed interest in having another one of the students' projects constructed. As a result, we promptly recommended another project that was constructed in another hamlet soon after.

The workshop had continued for four years until the outbreak of the COVID-19 pandemic. The range of project types gradually expanded from public toilets to gazebos and farmers markets. In the second year of the workshop, two out of three student group projects were built. With Professor Naudé's constant encouragement, an increasing number of MIT faculty members visited and stayed in the village with students each year. This traveling course, which is primarily concerned with social relevance, necessitates actual construction and a protracted annual trip to the countryside year after year, is challenging to keep up with. One or two years alone could be viewed as a significant success. It is hard to imagine that students from the US would have had such travel and building opportunities overseas for so many years if it weren't for Professor Naudé's perseverance.

In my mind, this is the contribution a professor with ideals can make.

Wang Shu

Rock Houses
and Gardens
Gloucester, Massachusetts
2017

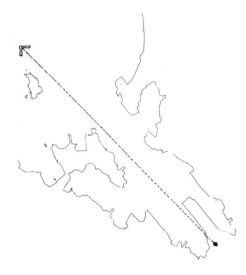

I had never owned a weekend house as a retreat from my live-work daily functions. After stepping down as dean at MIT this became an essential idea. The criteria for the land were simply time of travel—one hour from my Village Street home—a big view, and a garden for indoor/outdoor living. This would become the opposite proposition to the spatially defined urban compound in Somerville. In addition, I've always enjoyed topographic complexity and difficult spatial limits—a site with characteristics could also reduce the

price! Surprisingly the perfect solution was found the first week of exploration: a granite rock that had never been built on, with a big view of the harbor in Gloucester, a one-hour drive from Somerville.

Key questions were buildability, legal issues that had consumed a decade of conflict with neighbors, and an approval process that might be time consuming and difficult. I proceeded with these conditions anyway, which took several years. The site boundaries

were consolidated, the neighbors finally accepted that this would be built on, and after several public meetings we got approval to build two stacked houses on the site. I had built rock houses before in San Francisco and was confident that this would not be conceptually difficult.

Access for vehicles was the first issue solved by extending an unbuilt road to the top of the site. Each house would have independent parking. A public staircase was constructed

Massachusetts Institute of Technology

Rock Houses and Gardens

joining levels together, needed for service and fire safety. The site faced southwest with views across the harbor to the open sea. Each unit was planned with large decks off the living areas. Wall Street was essentially one-sided, allowing views across neighboring properties. A large open space at the top of the rock at thirty feet was left open to give the neighbors an ocean view. Later, land was added to the rear to create a special garden shared with neighbors.

A family from Venezuela bought the lower house, which has two levels, one at grade with the garage and separate entry. The front door on the second level has easy access to the upper open space. This floor comprises generous living dining spaces with partially covered decks and two bedroom suites. The living room has a taller ceiling created by a split level in the unit above.

I designed the upper house for myself. It has the same ocean view decks, a large living room, and dining area and kitchen opening to a garden at the rear. The roof slopes up to fourteen feet to the boundary with high windows bringing in southwest and east light. Tall sliding glass doors open the southwest diagonal view to the deck and dramatic view to the sea passage from the harbor. Off the living room steps lead to an upper TV room and primary bedroom suite, giving extra height to rooms below. A second bedroom suite is located near the kitchen. The setback from the neighbor below increases in width giving them privacy, allowing windows to face the rear garden and provide blank walls between the houses. The contrasting green and blue views are important conceptually.

The building was designed to be energy-efficient, using triple glazing and solar panels on the roofs, The rainscreen siding made from durable tropical wood gives an additional level of resilience.

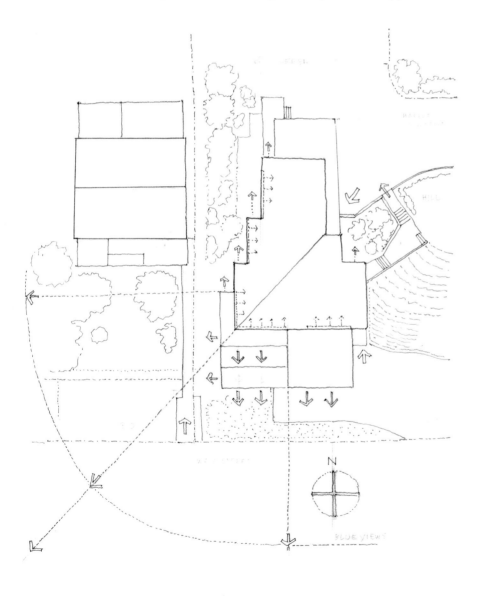

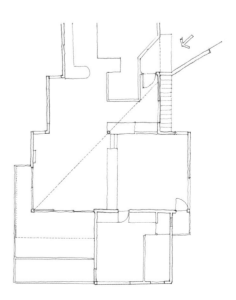

Land to the rear of the property had no access and was inexpensive. My neighbor and I decided to buy this. This site had never been built on and was covered with vegetation. Most of the trees were in poor condition because the soil was too shallow. The ground was mostly rock and trees needed to be located where they could survive. Most of the trees were removed with one mature group of three that we preserved. This could not become a formally contrived garden, but we made an unusual series of spaces between rock outcroppings, and two stone patios with harbor views. This needed to be a year-round garden space as well. The program was a sauna and an outdoor but covered kitchen with a dining deck under the existing trees. The roof deck was designed to be a "tree house" for the children and also had great views. Conceptually, the shape of the building took its influence from the rock formations, and the roof was sculpted to bring light into the sauna and the kitchen. This compact unusual building was covered with wood siding referring to the main house. Most of the new trees planted were flowering. An expert in native plants, especially ones that grow in rocky landscapes, created a vibrant, seasonal landscape that included many species. The houses and playful garden made an exceptional place for retreat.

352

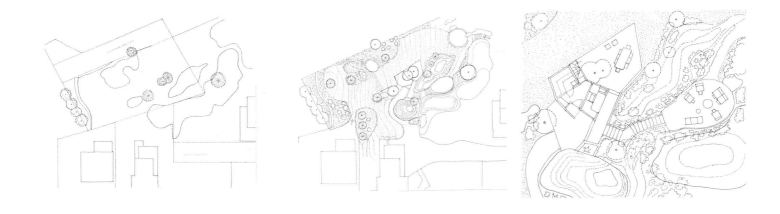

354

Massachusetts Institute of Technology

356

Rock Houses and Gardens

358

"This time, perhaps, she has gone too far, bitten off too much," I said to myself during my first site visit to Adèle's property in Gloucester. A dilapidated house was tenuously wedged into (and not perched above) a crevasse of a thirty-five-foot-high granite outcropping adjacent to an industrial-scale fish processing plant on the harbor.

Adèle has a well-documented history of delightfully occupying forlorn, post-industrial buildings in San Francisco and Somerville, MA, and elsewhere. In all cases, she has utilized simple, thoughtful, and insightful tweaks to create warm and unique live/work environments for her family, friends, and co-workers, where a key ingredient of a contemporary, art-filled lifestyle is a celebration of context, history, and authenticity. However, despite this, I still just could not quite see the allure of this Gloucester house and site. Nor could I understand her enthusiasm as we continued to climb the crumbling stairs and as we meandered through the warren of dimly lit rooms with tiny windows. The entire experience was underscored by the musty smell of abandonment.

However, as we made our way vertically through the building, there came a moment (three or four stories up) where the floor under our feet became coplanar with the grade at a mid-landing spot in the surrounding bedrock hillside. From that spot, we emerged from the house into a magical world of granite outcroppings, glacial erratics, and a mixed deciduous forest. As we turned our gaze to the east and north, the industrial harbor below and the breakwater at the mouth of the harbor beyond, revealed themselves. And then I got it!

Regardless of the project or the project type that have defined my numerous collaborations (adventures, really) with Adèle—whether the Xiantang Village Rejuvenation Study in Nanjing, the Taichung Library Competition in Taichung, Taiwan, or the Mountain to Bay Ecological Framework Plan and Mangrove Museum Study in Shenzhen (the list goes on)—I have been struck that Adèle's typical point of entry to design has been to utilize the cross section.

In her work it seems to me that the figure of the plan and necessary program adjacencies, while not subordinated to, are instead evolved in the awareness of sectional connectivity and flow, and simultaneously calibrated to the scale of the human body or bodies. Accordingly, as I have come to learn, Adèle's work is far less predicated upon architecture as object, but more so on the study of the possibilities of the interconnection of space and program; a more systems or "fabric"-based notion of architecture. Adèle seems inscrutably interested in the power of threshold, transition, and overlap in pursuit of achieving continuity of experience, seamless relationships between inside and out, and between the site and the larger context, urban or otherwise.

Ultimately, I feel this is one of the reasons it's been such an honor and pleasure learning from and working with my friend Adèle. Her method applies fluently across ranging project types whether architecture or landscape/site and it nicely scales upward or downward from the scale of urban design to the local design of a single structure, or to the very intimately detailed moment of garden architecture.

Which ultimately brings me back to Gloucester Harbor and her project there. Of course, from the beginning, Adèle saw the power of the topography of the site as the primary generator of a new structure, one in which each level of the new building would engage the site in unique and highly local ways of optimizing the exchanges between architecture and landscape, solar orientation, and both long and contained views. Her work there creates a symbiotic relationship between the structure of the building and the morphology of the site, where each are allowed to inform the other and which results in multi-scalar experiences for people moving through both the building and site. The project also rifts on the play between the machined perfection of prefabricated building systems and the idiosyncratic realities of the big rock on which the house/building sits.

Not stopping there, and true to form, Adèle continued up the section of the slope, establishing a lovely garden, including bends in the pathway which conform with and reveal particular characteristics of the rocky terrain: when to pause to take a breath, when to frame a view, and how to make appropriate cross connections through the site. I suspect Adèle made only a few, if any, drawings for the series of gardens that were created. Instead, I believe she relied upon her innate understanding of materiality of place and intuited the resolution of the role of the garden in the context of the existing hillside.

Ultimately, the program for the garden thoughtfully evolved as part of Adèle's incredibly generous spirit of communing with those close to her and as a part of her extended community of friends and colleagues.

Michael Blier

Workshops

Since my first teaching position at the University of Cape Town decades ago, housing has been a focus—particularly looking at issues involved in building subsidized housing units but also building spatial communities. It was clear that housing was a large part of urban development. Habitat is also a concept that is always current. Later, I saw housing development as essential to building satisfying communities and titled this "Housing as Community."

In academic contexts affordable community development was a research focus for me, but in practice, building housing for both public and private clients was inevitable. I developed Housing Theory courses at Rice University which were modified over time to confront different cultural economic and political contexts. From my chairmanship of architecture at the University of Pennsylvania onward, I started creating design workshops that could respond to critical international events such as the volcanic disaster that smothered the Colombian town of Amero in mudslides. Over the course of two years, we sent teams of students and faculty to help design responses to this tragedy. Needless to say there were also multiple unresolved issues not prompted by disasters, and summer workshops became productive opportunities for cross-cultural exchange. I began with housing workshops in collaboration with Balkrishna Doshi at CEPT in Ahmedabad, India.

As I spent more time in academic leadership, two recurring summer workshops took place at Southeast University (SEU) in Nanjing. These were also housing-focused and sponsored by Suning Universal, a housing developer. A workshop with more of an interdisciplinary focus in IAP was sponsored by Shih Chien University College of Design in Taipei. We recorded these creative efforts with booklets that describe some remarkable work. The two different educational experiences proved to me that intense hands-on experiences in real contexts produced remarkable learning curves. These were scheduled for six days a week, full-time for about three weeks. Students commented enthusiastically on how much they learned.

Starting from these housing workshops at SEU, MIT Architecture collaborated to create another form of summer workshops that looked at improving the lives of rural villagers with new housing and needed community buildings. This was done with faculty and students from the Chinese Art Academy (CAA), headed by Wang Shu with strong participation of his partner Lu Wenyu. Faculty and students from MIT and SEU were invited to collaborate, while living and working in the selected villages. The intention was to design and propose construction drawings for the relatively simple buildings. We did this for several years in adjacent villages known to faculty in the CAA. The villages were clustered outside Quzhou, near Hangzhou. The best of these proposals would be constructed after the documents were refined during the next spring semester. Several of these proposals were built.

From an academic perspective these short, intense, real-life experiences were exciting and productive for the students. These were also very much in the spirit of the MIT philosophical ethos of "Hand and Mind." Later workshops by invitation to work on recurring issues in housing engaged both faculty and students. These were conducted in situ and were a perfect way to bring productive practice and academia together. Sponsored by non-profits, international banks, individuals, and academic research labs, these were more complex enterprises to plan for. In the 2018 MIT Housing+ Conference, six of these workshops were exhibited with models, videos, and booklets. In the Venice Biennale of 2021, in the European Cultural Center exhibition Time Space Existence, four were shown under the title "Housing as Community" with analytical drawings, video clips and conceptual designs.

Affordability was an important factor and implementation would be a big challenge later in a politically changing context. All of the sites were visited ahead of the workshops to meet local team members, to be sure the issues were viable, and that we could make significant design contributions to the identified problems.

To bring my academic life full circle I proposed a final workshop with the University of Cape Town, which looked at a new housing policy that proposed building affordable units on public land with market rate housing to increase the financial viability. Mixed-income housing has had limited success globally and none of these typologies have been built to date in South Africa, where past obstacles to this concept still exist.

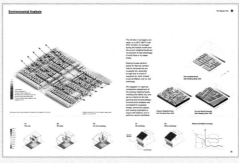

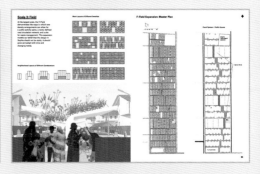
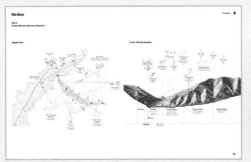
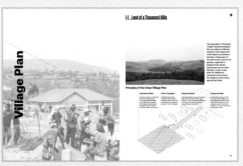
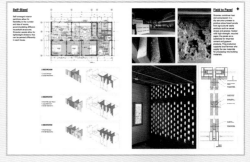

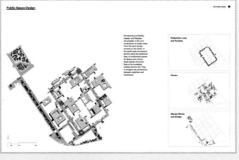

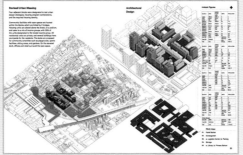

Acknowledgments

There are many people to thank who inspired the production of this monograph. From early advice from colleagues who knew about such publications, Roi Salgueiro Barrio, to faculty who had been urging me to publish a monograph, such as Anna Miljacki. Michael Meister, my husband, spent years discussing my work as this idea progressed, and friend and architect Andrea Leers and I were early women pioneers as principals of our firms, sharing experiences together.

To everyone who contributed to the production of this book I must start by thanking ORO editions Gordon Goff who was the first to respond within hours of my enquiry. We followed up with wonderful conversations and useful suggestions! Julia Van Den Hout of Original Copy for her work as editor who has been a creative partner from the beginning. Chris Grimley of SIGNALS excelled in his role as graphic designer and visual editor. Jake Anderson oversaw the production from ORO and gave everyone confidence in the process.

From Santos Prescott and Associates, my partner Bruce Prescott of over twenty years fortunately has an amazing memory, and a good filing system. Essential records were uncovered and poured over. Ethan Lacy, who worked with me in Somerville for eight years, found important images to be used, and Yao Zhang was an essential collaborator in all things in China, including translation of letters from colleagues there.

This book is a testament to a life filled with adventure and explorations of the built world, and wouldn't be possible without them.

Adèle Naudé, 2023.

Cape Town

House Naudé
Client The Naudé Family | Orpen Lane Kenilworth | **Architect** Hugo Naudé, designer Adèle Marie Naudé

Rowan Lane Houses
Client Margaret Molteno | **Designers** Adèle Naudé and Antonio de Souza Santos | **Engineer** ARUP & Partners | **Quantity Surveyor** Walker Mare

House Stekhoven
Client & Builder M. Stekhoven | **Designers** Adèle Naudé and Antonio de Souza Santos | **Quantity Surveyor** Walker Mare

House Shear
Client Shear Family | **Designers** Adèle Naudé and Antonio de Souza Santos | **Quantity Surveyor** Walker Mare

Scott Road
Client Damian Properties | **Designers** Adèle Naudé and Antonio de Souza Santos | **Engineer** ARUP & Partners | **Quantity Surveyor** Walker Mare

IONA Apartments Rondebosch
Client Oscar Wollheim | **Designers** Adèle Naudé and Antonio de Souza Santos | **Quantity Surveyor** Walker Mare

Ormonde New Town
Client Rand Mines Property Ltd. | **Urban Design Consultants** (Principals Roelof Uytenbogaardt, L. Anthony Barac, Antonio de Souza Santos, Adèle Naudé) | **Engineer** Ove Arup & Partners | **Landscape Planning and Design** Richard K. Unterman | **Ecologist** RT Schnadelbach | **Cost Consultants** Walker & Walker | **Liaison** Real estate development and research company

Santiago Redevelopment
Designers Adèle Naudé and Antonio de Souza Santos

Early Years in the USA

The Invisible City Documentary Film Series
Based on design studio work by Professor Adèle Naudé with Professor James Blue of the Rice Media Lab | **Documentary Film Director** Prof. James Blue | **Co-director** Adèle Naudé Santos | **Camera and sound** Lynn Corcoran | **Camera** Tom Simms | **Producer** Southwest Alternate Media Project (SWAMP) | Funding provided by an award from the Texas Committee for the Humanities | SECA award winning project

Plants for Passive Cooling A preliminary presentation for the Oak Ridge National Laboratory
Landscape Architecture Professor Anne Whiston Spirn | **Architecture and Urban Design** Professor Adèle Naudé | **Research Assistant** Mark Rios

134 Beach St. Loft
Loft master plan with Andrea Leers | **Design** Adèle Naudé | **Owner** Adèle Naudé

2009 Naudain St.
Design Adèle Naudé | **Owner** Adèle Naudé

Honda Settlement Field Workshops
Workshop at the Graduate School of Fine Arts University of Pennsylvania | **Faculty** Professor Adèle Naudé | **PhD Student** David Glasser | **Teaching Assistant** Luis Longhi

Housing Workshops
Center for Environmental Planning and Technology with Balkrisha Doshi | **Faculty** Adèle Naudé, Jon Lang, and Dean Lee Copeland

Maison Matsuda House
Client Taeko Matsuda | **Designers** Andrea Leers and Adèle Naudé | **Contractors** Takanaka

SDC Headquarters
Client SDC Corporation | **Design Architect** Adèle Naudé and David Glasser | **Registered Architect** Yazuo Ohdera | **TIS Engineers** Norihidei Imagawa

SDC Guest House
Registered Architect T&T | **Design Architect** Adèle Naudé Santos and Associates Robert deJager | **TIS Engineers** Norihidei Imagawa

Tokyo Fantasia Office Building
Design Architect Adèle Naudé Santos and Associates, Bruce Prescott | **Registered Architect** Yazuo Ohdera | **TIS Engineer** Norihidei Imagawa

Pacific Center for the Media Arts
Design Architects Adèle Naudé Santos and Associates with Kinya Maruyama for the first phase

Albright College Center for the Arts
Executive Architects Jacobs Wyper | **Design Architects** Adèle Naudé Santos | **Artist Collaborator** Mary Miss | **TIS Engineer** Norihidei Imagawa

Institute of Contemporary Art
Executive Architects Jacobs Wyper | **Design Architects** Adèle Naudé and Bruce Prescott | **Contractors** Barclay White, partners for Design Build Project

Franklin Labrea Family Housing Competition
Client Redevelopment Agency of Los Angeles with the Los Angeles Contemporary Art Museum | **Executive Architects** Carde Ten | **Design Architects** Adèle Naudé Santos and Associates, Bruce Prescott | **Developers** Thomas Safran & Associates

California

New School of Architecture @ UCSD
Founding Faculty | Craig Hodgetts architect, design, tech | Dana Cuff, scholar, theory of practice | Susan Ubbelohde, tech focused architecture | William Curtis, historian | Edward Allen, construction

Center City East UCSD Final class in Urban Futures, done with local collaborators including the planners from the city, colleagues from UC campuses, and professionals, visitors from other academic institutions; **UC San Diego faculty and staff** Dana Cuff, Craig Hodgetts, George Loisos, Susan Ubbelohde, Fran Hegeler | **Colleagues from the UC system** Peter Bosselmann UCB and Mark Mack UCLA | WRT Planning + **Design** Ignacio Bunster-Ossa, Laura Burnett, and Kathy Garcia | **Taft Architects** John Casbarian, Danny Samuels, and Robert Timme | **Collaborators** Teddy Cruz, Renee Davids, Julian Beinart, Prof. Architecture & Dir. Environmental Design, MIT | John Casbarian, Prof. Architecture, Rice University | Miriam Gusevich, Planning & Development Manager, Chicago Park District | John Kaliski, Architect & Urban Designer Alex Istanbullu John Kaliski Architecture | Alex Krieger, Dir. Urban Design Program, Graduate School of Design, Harvard | David Lee, Architect & Urban Designer, Stull and Lee, Boston | Mario Noriega, Urban Designer, Noriega Restrepo & Asociados Bogota | Spurlock Poirier Landscape Architects, Andrew Spurlock, Martin Poirier | Rob Wellington Quigley, Architect & Principal, Rob Wellington Quigley Architects | Ricardo Rabines, Architect & Associate, Adèle Naudé Santos & Assoc., San Diego | Peter Rowe, Dean, Graduate School of Design, Harvard University | Danny Samuels, Prof. Architecture Rice University Houston | Mario Schjetnan, Landscape Architect & Urban Designer Grupo de Diseno Urban Mexico | Harry Teague, Harry Teague Architects, Aspen | Robert Timme, Dean, University of Southern California | Max Schmidt, Vice President of Planning & Engineering, Centre City Development Corporation, San Diego | Michael J. Stepner, Special Projects, City Manager's Office, San Diego |

Arts Park
Architects Hodgetts + Fung, Adèle Naudé Santos and Associates, Adam Glaser | **Landscape Architects** Rios Pearson | **Artist** Mary Miss

Perris Civic Center
Design Architects Adèle Naudé Santos and Associates, Ricardo Rabines | **Landscape Architects** WRT San Diego | **Artist** Mathieu Gregoire

Rokko Island Town
Developers Misawa Homes | **Program Organizer** Taiko Matsuda | **Architects** Adèle Naudé Santos and Associates, Bruce Prescott | **Landscape Architect** WRT | **Environmental Engineers** Loisos & Ubbelhode

Kadota Housing
Client Kitakyushu City | **Executive Architects** SAM | **Design Architects** Adèle Naudé Santos and Associates, Tsutoma Sato | **Engineers** TIS Engineering

Dairi Nishi Apartments
Client Fukuoka Prefecture | **Executive Architects** SAM | **Design Architect** Adèle Naudé Santos and Associates, Tsutoma Sato | **Engineers** TIS Engineering

Yerba Buena Gardens Children's Center
Winner of the Rudy Bruner Award Gold Medal for Urban Excellence | **Executive Architect** Jerry Lee, LDA | **Design Architect** Adèle Naudé Santos and Associates, Ricardo Rabines | **Landscape Architect** Paul Friedberg | Artists Chico McMurtty, Douglas Hollis

John O'Connell High School
Executive Architect Marshall & Lee Architects | **Design Architect** Adèle Naudé Santos and Associates

5 Units Ritch/Zoe Street Studios
Client Adèle Naudé | **Developer** Adèle Naudé Santos and Associates

Bryant Street Lofts
Client Adèle Naudé | **Design** Adèle Naudé Santos and Associates

Mission Creek Senior Community
Winner of the Gold Nugget Award in mixed use category 2006 | **Client** San Francisco Redevelopment Agency | **Community Executive Architect** HKIT Architects | **Community Design Architect** Adèle Naudé Santos and Associates Bruce Prescott | **Library Executive Architect** Bruce Prescott

Rock Houses
Client Adèle Naudé | **Design Architect** Adèle Naudé Santos & Associates | **Engineer** Raj Sahai from SDE

Massachusetts
Village Street Studio
Client Adèle Naudé | **Developer** Adèle Naudé Santos and Associates

23 Village Street
Client Adèle Naudé | **Developer** Adèle Naudé Santos and Associates, Morgan Pinney

25 Village Street
Client Adèle Naudé | **Developer** Adèle Naudé Santos and Associates, Ethan Lacey

Ventura WAV
Executive Architect Carde Ten | **Design Architect** Santos Prescott Architects | **Developers** PLACE (Project Linking Art Community and Environment)

Muxbal Community Center
Client & Developer Federico Ariano of Mundo Verde | **Planner** Mario Noriega of Noriego Restreppa, Bogota | **Design Architect** Santos Prescott Architects | **Builder** Mundo Verde

Foshou Lake Clubhouse
Client Suning Universal Group, Ltd. | **Design Architect** Santos Prescott and Associates, Wengun Ge | **Local Design Institute** Architecture Design and Research Institute of Southeast University

Suning IT HQ Park,

Client Suning Universal Group, Ltd. | **Design Architect** Santos Prescott and Associates, Wengun Ge | **Landscape Architect** Landworks Studio

The 10th Jiangsu Horticultural Exposition Main Office Pavilion
Client Ministry of Agriculture and Rural Affairs, Jiangsu Housing and Urban-Rural Development Group Co., Ltd. | **Collaborator** Design and Research Studio of Jianguo Wang, Academician of Chinese Academy of Engineering | **Local Design Institute** Architecture Design and Research Institute of Southeast University | **Design Architect** Adèle Naudé Santos and Associates, Yao Zhang

Sifang Parkland #6 Site Luxury Condominium,
Client Ministry of Agriculture and Rural Affairs, Jiangsu Housing and Urban-Rural Development Group Co., Ltd. | **Collaborator** Design and Research Studio of Jianguo Wang, Academician of Chinese Academy of Engineering | **Local Design Institute** Architecture Design and Research Institute of Southeast University | **Design Architect** Adèle Naudé Santos and Associates, Yao Zhang

Shenzhen Mangrove Museum and Surrounding Urban Renewal
Client Shenzhen Government, Shenzhen Land Resources Bureau, Shenzhen City Planning Bureau, Bureau of Public Works of Shenzhen Municipality, Futian National Nature Reserve, Shenzhen Mangrove Museum | **Design Architect** Santos Prescott and Associates, Yao Zhang | **Landscape Architect** Landwork Studios | **Rendering Credit** Jingu Visualization Studio | **Technical Director** Huang Weidong | **Local Executive Design Institute** Urban Planning & Design Institute of Shenzhen

Rock Houses
Client Adèle Naudé | **Design** Adèle Naudé Santos and Associates, Ethan Lacy | **Builder** Geoffrey Richon

Gardens, Gloucester
Client Adèle Naudé and Jose Vicente Aguerrevere | **Garden and Landscape Design** Adèle Naudé with Jose Vicente Aguerrevere | **Garden and Plants** MK Gardens & Landscape, Tara Connelly | **Masonry** Coastal Tree Works, Scott Prentiss

Partners
Antonio de Souza Santos
Alan Levy
Bruce Prescott

Associates and Staff
Philadelphia Lesley Bain | Robert de Jager |
Matt Elliot | Adam Glaser | Fran Hegeler | Felix
Heidgen | Joe Iano | Frances Leone | Alan Levy |
Libby Marsh | Shannon Russell | John Murphy

San Diego Ricardo Rabines | Tsutomu Sato

San Francisco Nicholas Anderson | Sarina
Kennerly | Jennifer Brodie | Jason Brody | J.
Jarrell Conner | Alexandre da Silva Souto

Boston Wenjun Ge | Jae Kim | Ethan Lacy |
Kanda Song | Jongwan Kwong | Yao Zhang

**Collaborating Architects and Landscape
Architects** Jacobs/Wyper Architects ICA, CFA |
Carde Ten Architects FLB, WAV | LDA Architects
YBG | T&T Architects Ninomiya, Illuminacion,
Tsukasa-Cho | TIS and Partners CFA sculpture,
Kachofugetsu-kan, Misawa | David Evan Glasser
Kachofugetsu-kan | SAM Kadota, Dairi | Andrea
Leers House Matsuda, | Charles Bloszies Ritch/
Zoe Studios | James Robbins 2947 First Ave
| Yasuo Ohdera Kachofugetsu-kan, | Kinya
Maruyama Pacific Center for the Media Arts |
WRT Perris, Rokko | Lois Sherr Hillside Housing
| HKIT Architects Mission Creek | Loisos-
Ubbbelohde Rokko, Futureplex

Letters
I would like to extend most gracious thanks to all
of my friends and colleagues who contributed
letters to this catalog of my life and work.

Lucien le Grange—Director of the School of
Architecture at University of Cape Town 2005-
2010; founder Lucien le Grange Architects and
Urban Planners.

Marco Chiendetti—Sculptor and Ceramicist who
purchased and renovated House Naudé.

Ann Yu-Chien—Dean of the College of Design at
Shih Chien University; graduate of University of
Pennsylvania.

Craig Hodgetts—Hodgetts + Fung; founding
member of UCSD, School of Architecture; long
time faculty member of UCLA; co-founder
hplusf design lab.

Andrea Leers—Founding Principal of Leers
Weinzapfel Associates; Harvard GSD Adjunct
Professor in Architecture and Urban Design.

Balkrishna Doshi—Pritzker Prize winning
Architect (2018); founder of Vastu-Shilpa
Consultants; founding Director of School of
Planning and founding Dean of the Centre
for Environmental Planning and Technology in
Ahmedabad.

Giovanni Bellotti—Co-founder Studio Ossidiana;
graduate of MIT School of Architecture and
Planning.

Wang Shu—Pritzker Prize- winning Architect
(2012); Dean of the School of Architecture of the
China Academy of Art; co-founder of Amateur
Architecture Studio.

Dana Cuff—Professor at UCLA Architecture and
Urban Design, founder of cityLAB.

Wang Jianguo—Director of the Ministry
of Education's Steering Committee on the
Teaching of Architecture; Vice President of the
Architectural Society and the Urban Planning
Society of China.

Yung Ho Chang—Former head of the
Architecture Department at MIT; founding
Partner and Principal Architect of Atelier
Feichang Jianzhu (FCJZ).

Bruce Prescott—Partner at Santos Prescott
Architects; Principal at Adèle Naudé Santos and
Associates for many years. Has taught graduate
level design at UPenn and UC Berkeley.

Fran Hegeler—Director of External Relations,
UCSD School of Architecture. Currently
Marketing Director DES Architects + Engineers.

Meejin Yoon—Dean of the School of
Architecture, Art, and Planning at Cornell
University; former head of the Department of
Architecture at MIT; co-founder and managing
partner of Höweler + Yoon.

Mike Blier—Founder and Principal of Landworks
Studio.

Photography

Marco Chiandetti
14 (bottom, mid), 17

Rahul Mehrotra
27-9

Pierre Mare
24-5

Lewis Tanner
99-102

Nikkei Architecture
155

Kenhciku Bunka
115

Hiroyasu Sakaguchi
122-25

Barry Halkin
135-149

Mary Miss
138 (bottom)

Constance Mensh
150

Squidds and Nuns
157

David Hewitt and Anne Garrison
158-161

Tom Bonner
188-190, 296-97

Shinkenchiku
214-215

Antonio Garbasso
221, 227-28, 229, 230-39, 245

Richard Barnes
226, 228, 229 (top)

JD Peterson
244,246-47

Sharon Risedorph
262, 263 (top)

Thomas Heinser
263 (bottom)

Eric Oxendorf
281-283

Ethan Lacey
284, 290, 352-357

Sangsuri Chun
350, 357 (bottom)

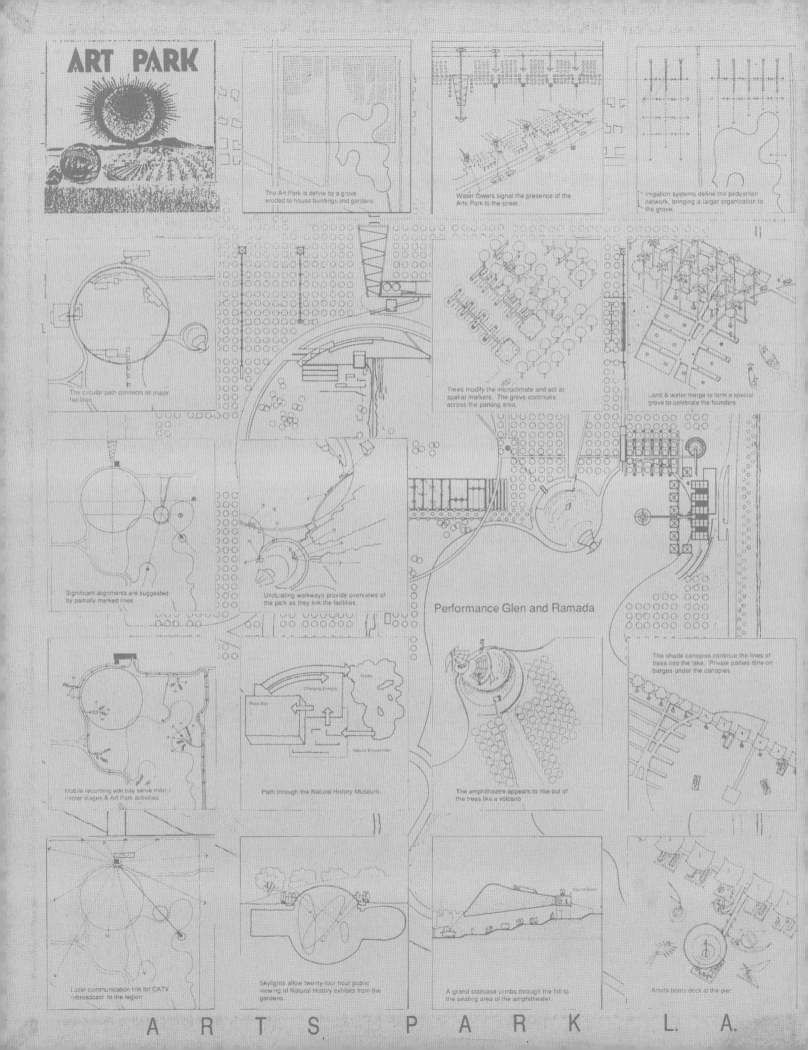

ART PARK

The Art Park is define by a grove eroded to house buildings and gardens.

Water fowers signal the presence of the Arts Park to the street.

Irrigation systems define the pedestrian network, bringing a larger organization to the grove.

The circular path connects all major facilities.

Trees modify the microclimate and act as spatial markers. The grove continues across the parking area.

Land & water merge to form a special grove to celebrate the founders.

Significant alignments are suggested by partially marked lines.

Undulating walkways provide overviews of the park as they link the facilities.

Performance Glen and Ramada

The shade canopies continue the lines of trees into the lake. Private parties dine on barges under the canopies.

Mobile recording edit bay serve medical center stages & Art Park activities.

Path through the Natural History Museum.

Black Box · Changing Exhibits · Grotto · Natural Enrichment

The amphitheatre appears to rise out of the trees like a volcano.

Lazer communication link for CATV rebroadcast to the region.

Skylights allow twenty-four hour public viewing of Natural History exhibits from the gardens.

A grand staircase climbs through the hill to the seating area of the amphitheater.

Artists boats dock at the pier.

A R T S   P A R K   L.A.